Sybex's Quick Tour of Wi... S0-BMG-888

THE DESKTOP

The Desktop is where your applications, folders, and shortcuts are located. You can choose between the classic Windows Desktop, which is familiar from previous versions of Windows, or you can use the new Active Desktop, which brings the Web directly to you.

My Computer lets you browse the contents of your computer, open folders, open documents, and run your favorite applications.

My Documents is a desktop folder you can use to store documents, graphics, and other files that you want to access quickly.

Internet Explorer starts up the Internet Explorer Web browser.

Network Neighborhood opens a viewer that presents system information about your computer's place in a network.

Recycle Bin makes it easy to delete and undelete files and folders.

The Microsoft Network opens a connection to Microsoft's online service.

My Briefcase lets you synchronize files between two computers.

Online Services allows you to access one of the popular commercial service providers, such as AOL.

Outlook Express opens the Outlook Express e-mail program.

The **Start button** pops up the Start menu, from which you can run almost all of your applications.

The **Quick Launch toolbar** provides an easy way to start frequently used applications.

The **Taskbar** displays a button for every program running on your computer.

The **Channel bar** lets you open your favorite Web site without first opening your Web browser.

Every **Window** has a **Minimize**, **Maximize** (alternating with **Restore**), and **Close** button.

The **Standard toolbar** provides fast access to common functions.

The **Address toolbar** shows the location of the page currently displayed in the main window; this may be an Internet address or a file or folder stored on your hard disk.

The **Links toolbar** lets you access different parts of Microsoft's Web site.

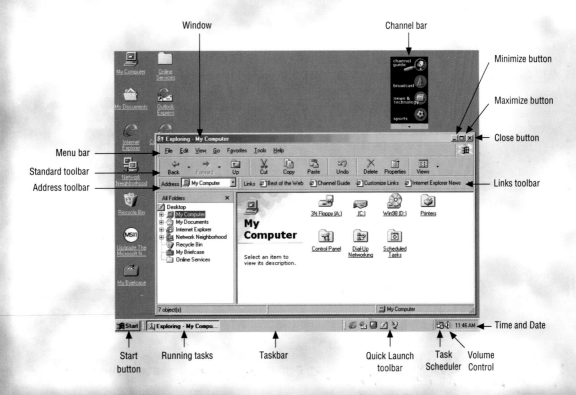

START MENU

Click the Start button to do almost anything on your computer, from running an application to configuring your printer.

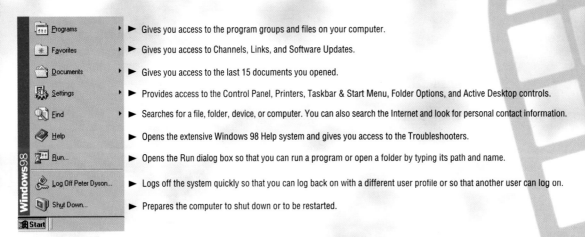

Programs ► Gives you access to the program groups and files on your computer.

Favorites ► Gives you access to Channels, Links, and Software Updates.

Documents ► Gives you access to the last 15 documents you opened.

Settings ► Provides access to the Control Panel, Printers, Taskbar & Start Menu, Folder Options, and Active Desktop controls.

Find ► Searches for a file, folder, device, or computer. You can also search the Internet and look for personal contact information.

Help ► Opens the extensive Windows 98 Help system and gives you access to the Troubleshooters.

Run... ► Opens the Run dialog box so that you can run a program or open a folder by typing its path and name.

Log Off Peter Dyson... ► Logs off the system quickly so that you can log back on with a different user profile or so that another user can log on.

Shut Down... ► Prepares the computer to shut down or to be restarted.

RUNNING A PROGRAM

To start an application, click Start ➢ Programs, choose a program folder to open the next menu (if required), and then click the name of the program you want to run.

ADDING AN APPLICATION TO THE START MENU

The quickest way to add a program to the top of the Start menu is to open the folder that contains the program, and then drag the program's icon onto the Start button.

FINDING THINGS QUICKLY

Windows 98 adds several powerful items to the Find menu, which in

addition to finding files and folders, now includes options for finding a computer, information on the Internet, or information about people.

To locate a file, click Start ➢ Find ➢ Files or Folders. Type the name (or part of the name) into the Named field, enter any text you think the

file might contain into the Containing text field, and click Find Now. A window opens displaying the files that match as Windows finds them.

To locate a computer, click Start ➢ Find ➢ Computer, enter the name of the computer into the Named field, and click Find Now. To track down information on the Internet, use Start ➢ Find ➢ On the Internet. This option connects you to a single Web site giving you access to some of the most powerful and popular search engines on the Internet, including Infoseek, AOL NetFind, Lycos, Excite, and Yahoo. To find information such as a person's e-mail address, click

Start ➢ Find ➢ People. In the Look In list, select the name of the directory service you want to use, type in the information on the person you are looking for (usually just the first name followed by the last name), and click Find Now.

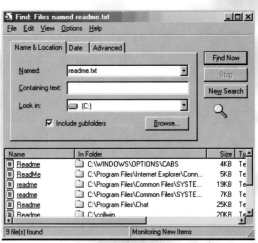

Upgrading to
Windows 98

Upgrading to
Windows® 98

Charlie Russel and
Sharon Crawford

SYBEX®

San Francisco - Paris - Düsseldorf - Soest

Associate Publisher: Gary Masters
Contracts and Licensing Manager: Kristine Plachy
Acquisitions & Developmental Editor: Sherry Bonelli
Editors: Ben Miller, Davina Baum
Technical Editor: Maryann Brown
Book Designer: Catalin Dulfu
Electronic Publishing Specialist: Kate Kaminski
Production Coordinator: Charles Mathews
Production Assistant: Beth Moynihan
Indexer: Ted Laux
Cover Designer: Caryl Gorska
Cover Illustrator/Photographer: Caryl Gorska

Screen reproductions produced with Collage Complete.

Collage Complete is a trademark of Inner Media Inc.

SYBEX is a registered trademark of SYBEX Inc.

TRADEMARKS: SYBEX has attempted throughout this book to distinguish proprietary trademarks from descriptive terms by following the capitalization style used by the manufacturer.

The author and publisher have made their best efforts to prepare this book, and the content is based upon final release software whenever possible. Portions of the manuscript may be based upon pre-release versions supplied by software manufacturer(s). The author and the publisher make no representation or warranties of any kind with regard to the completeness or accuracy of the contents herein and accept no liability of any kind including but not limited to performance, merchantability, fitness for any particular purpose, or any losses or damages of any kind caused or alleged to be caused directly or indirectly from this book.

Photographs and illustrations used in this book have been downloaded from publicly accessible file archives and are used in this book for news reportage purposes only to demonstrate the variety of graphics resources available via electronic access. Text and images available over the Internet may be subject to copyright and other rights owned by third parties. Online availability of text and images does not imply that they may be reused without the permission of rights holders, although the Copyright Act does permit certain unauthorized reuse as fair use under 17 U.S.C. Section 107.

Library of Congress Card Number: 98-84007
ISBN: 0-7821-2190-X

Manufactured in the United States of America

10 9 8 7 6 5 4 3 2 1

Acknowledgments

Mere thanks aren't enough for Dean Denno, who deserves the Hero of Publishing Labor medal for his work investigating every detail of Windows 98. This book would not have been possible without him. In truth, he did all the heavy lifting and we're immensely grateful. The many changes and shifts in the pre-release versions of the software were a challenge he met with aplomb and unfailing good nature.

When Windows 98 reached the point in pre-release testing that we could write with some degree of confidence, editor Ben Miller kept us and the book on track at an almost breakneck pace. His attitude was supportive, helpful, and relentless. He could give lessons to a sheep dog on how to move the flock forward without sacrificing anything—or anyone—in the process. Thanks, Ben.

We very much appreciate the contributions of the technical editor, Maryann Brown. She dedicated her time and her computers to finding and fixing errors in the manuscript—saving our readers much aggravation and making us look much smarter. Needless to say, any errors that might remain are our responsibility and ours alone. We also thank production manager Scott McDonald, production coordinator Charles Mathews, production assistant Beth Moynihan, and electronic publishing specialist Kate Kaminski, who were able to combine speed and flexibility with the high production standards that characterize Sybex books.

Thanks to Tom Cavanaugh of TC Solutions who generously offered the use of his Croom, Maryland, Web page to post the sample material we created in Chapter 7.

Finally, special thanks to Dianne King and the late Rudolph S. Langer who first started us down this road. It's been great.

Contents at a Glance

Table of Contents

Introduction

Windows 98 is another step forward in desktop computing. While not perfect (it was made by human beings, after all), it integrates more of the things most users do with their computers, and provides smoother transitions from one function to another. It also makes further progress in the direction of computers that spend the majority of time serving you—as opposed to *you* spending time serving and servicing them.

What This Book's About

This book gets you started with Windows 98 and shows you how to make the most of its features. Though we don't pretend to cover every single aspect of Windows 98 (it's a system you discover as you use it), this book points out many valuable tips and shortcuts you'd probably take a long time to learn on your own.

Who This Book Is For

The emphasis is on folks coming from Windows 95 or 3.1, but if you're a hard-core DOS user or even an OS/2 or Mac convert, this book will quickly get you rolling with Windows 98. Those of you who don't possess a lot of technical knowledge needn't fret over hardware, networking, or connecting to the Internet. Windows 98 makes things so simple in these formerly "difficult'" areas, we can easily talk about them in a book for ordinary computer users.

What's in This Book

You don't need to read the book in sequence; in fact, if you need to install Windows 98 yourself, you'll want to look at the appropriate Appendix before you get too deep into the rest of the book. After that, if you want, you can putter around Windows 98 (and this book) addressing the areas that interest you most.

Windows 98 has many improvements that aren't apparent at first, so you might want to consult the Table of Contents for those not-immediately-obvious topics.

Chapter 1 is a summary of the features that are new in Windows 98; many of these are related to the Internet and World Wide Web.

Chapters 2, 3, and 4 go into more detail about Windows 98 and its desktop. Some of this will be review for Windows 95 users, but this is also where many improvements have been made.

Chapter 5 describes the Windows Explorer. This will be of use mainly to those upgrading from Windows 3.1.

Chapters 6, 7, and 8 discuss Internet services that were not part of Windows 95. Even if you have been using Internet Explorer, most of Chapters 7 and 8 will be new to you.

Chapters 9 and 10 cover online services and other features related to staying connected and taking your work with you.

Chapters 11 and 12 discuss how to set things up. The Control Panel has some new elements, and if you need to run fussy DOS programs, you may need the information in Chapter 12.

Chapters 13 and 14 tell you how to make use of Windows 98's sizable collection of small applications, system tools, games, and multimedia applets. Most of them are quite useful (even the games, if you want to stretch the point).

Chapters 15 and 16 are about protecting your system from problems and solving those problems you can't avoid.

The Appendices are your guide to a smooth and problem-free installation. There's one for those using Windows 95 and another if you are coming from Windows 3.1.

NOTE **Microsoft and the Department of Justice: Many of the features we describe in this book as being part of Windows 98 are intimately tied to version 4 of Microsoft's Internet Explorer. The U.S. Department of Justice has sued Microsoft to end the company's practice of requiring computer manufacturers to include Internet Explorer with Windows. Although a temporary agreement was reached in January 1998, with regard to Windows 95 it isn't clear how this issue will ultimately be resolved. It does seem likely that at least most users of Windows 98 will have access to those features that depend on Internet Explorer. This doesn't in any way inhibit your ability to install and use Netscape Navigator if you prefer.**

How the Book Looks

We try to spend as little time as possible in irrelevant blather. Every entry is as succinct and to the point as we could make it. A couple of explanations are in order. This arrow ➤ is used to separate the steps of a menu selection. For example, the sequence View ➤ Toolbars ➤ Text Labels means "Click View in the menu bar, slide down the menu to Toolbars, then slide to the flyout menu and down to Text Labels, and click." We use a + to indicate keys that should be pressed together. Ctrl+C means hold the Ctrl (Control) key down while pressing C.

For simplicity and readability, we have used Windows 3.1 to refer also to Windows 3.11 and Windows for Workgroups.

TIP You'll see lots of these. Each is a helpful bit of inside information on specific tasks or functions.

For Windows 3.1 Users

A sidebar box like this contains additional information for readers who are upgrading from Windows 3.1 or Windows for Workgroups. It's usually important information that should already be familiar to Windows 95 users.

NOTE You'll see a number of notes. Sometimes these notes point toward additional information elsewhere in the book, and sometimes they contain interesting facts relating to the subject at hand.

WARNING A warning means Watch Out! Failure to heed the advice in this box could get you into trouble.

What's Next

Now that you've cracked the cover, it's time to switch on your computer, turn the page, and get started. As you read through this book and discover what works best for you, address any complaints, corrections, or compliments (especially compliments!) to our e-mail address at **upgrade98@scribes.com** and we'll try to fix any errors in future printings.

We sincerely hope you enjoy the book. We *know* you'll enjoy Windows 98.

THE FUTURE, AGAIN

Although the advance publicity for the release of Windows 98 may not have been quite up to the standard set by Windows 95, this newest version of the Windows operating system is indeed another big step forward.

Windows 98 offers substantial improvements in the user interface. Recognizing that the Internet and related technologies have become a vital part of what people do with desktop computers, Microsoft has designed Windows 98 to integrate seamlessly with the new version of its Internet Explorer browser. Windows 98 itself works more like Internet browsing, so that there is greater consistency between the online and offline worlds.

Windows 98 includes better multimedia and gaming support than its predecessor. In addition, it builds in support for lots of new hardware, such as Digital Versatile Disk (DVD) drives, multiple monitors, and Universal Serial Bus devices.

We aim to cut through the hype and hoopla about Windows 98 and explain what's really there. This book is a reliable guide to getting Windows 98 installed and working in the way that best suits you—whether you are upgrading from Windows 95 or making the big leap from Windows 3.1.

Must Be the Season of the Web

Some of the most important changes in Windows 98 are right up front, on the desktop and in the folders. They include simplified basic operations such as point-to-select and single-click-to-open, along with corresponding visual clues: underlined icon titles and a mouse pointer that changes to a pointing hand.

NOTE **You may not see these changes the first time you start Windows 98. The Windows 98 setup program attempts to keep options that you may have set under Windows 95, so the initial view is variable. For that reason, we will generally avoid talking about "default" conditions of the desktop and folders; they are too variable. What we will do, within the first few chapters, is tell you how to achieve whatever look-and-feel you want.**

Why the change? One of the main concepts pioneered by graphical user interfaces such as Apple's Macintosh is the consistent user interface. Microsoft has pushed the same idea in relation to Windows and programs written for Windows—as far as possible, they should all work the same way. Windows users have come to take it for granted that menus appear at the top, with File on the left and Help on the right. Toolbars have also become standard, and there is even a bit of consistency with regard to the images used on them.

But why do away with the venerable double-click as the way to open a document or launch a program? Because some of the most important resources and programs now used on Windows computers are the Internet and World Wide Web browsers, and they work in a different way. If you've ever browsed the Net, you know that when you point to a link with your mouse, the link is automatically highlighted. One click and the browser takes you there. Windows 98 can work the same way.

Notice that we say *can*. You don't *have* to use the new method. But Windows 98's setup process recommends it, and we agree: it only takes a bit of getting used to, and it really is easier. We expect that even users who don't spend much time online will see this and other changes as improvements.

The Big Difference

Even though millions more people now use computers than when Windows 95 was released, many are still intimidated when faced with using the Internet. Windows 95 helped make PCs easier to use, but the Internet remained a whole different world. The Internet's most popular features are those on the World Wide Web, accessible with browser software. The most popular browser over the last several years has been Netscape Navigator, although recently Microsoft Internet Explorer has gained in popularity. All browsers work with objects and links in ways that are different from the Windows 95 desktop.

Windows 98, which includes Microsoft's latest version of Internet Explorer, aims to simplify Internet use in several ways. Some basic functions of the Windows 98 interface work like a Web browser, to simplify the transition between locally based and Internet-based work. These features can be easily configured to each user's preferences and level of comfort with the Internet. Figure 1.1 illustrates the seamlessness possible between the desktop and the Internet.

One of the basic design objectives for Windows 95 was visual and functional consistency throughout the system. Windows 98 and Internet Explorer 4.0 extend this consistency of look-and-feel to the World Wide Web, while maintaining full compatibility with older software.

For example, in Windows 95 the desktop windows in which folders are viewed are closely tied to Windows Explorer. It is no accident that folders and Windows Explorer offer similar options; they are simply different views of the same interface. Windows 98 extends this concept to the Internet. Type an Internet address (URL, for Uniform Resource Locator) in the address bar of any open folder or of Windows Explorer, and the window turns into Internet Explorer to take you where you want to go. Likewise, you can enter the path to a folder (on your hard drive or local area network) in the address bar of Internet Explorer, and it will open the folder.

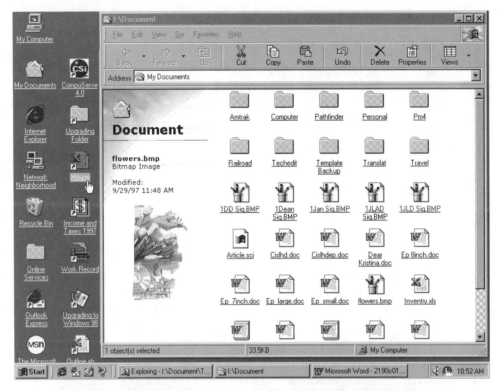

FIGURE 1.1: The new desktop can work like the Web: point to select, and click to open.

Growing a New Shell

The change from Windows 3.1 to Windows 95 was a radical one. It wasn't just the exterior that changed; the plumbing and wiring were completely redone to give the system important new capabilities such as true multi-tasking.

The step up from Windows 95 to Windows 98 is less drastic. While the core operating system code has been tuned for better performance, it remains the same basic plumbing and wiring. A big part of the story this time is the exterior. Although Windows 98 doesn't shed the Windows 95 shell, it stretches it in a new direction and encourages the user to follow. The new direction is toward the Internet, and the range of new options points the user that way. At one end of the spectrum is full Web immersion, in which the user "lives" in Internet Explorer and never sees the desktop. The suggested option is less radical: a desktop that integrates smoothly with Web browsing. And it's even possible to stick with Windows 95–style behavior.

Windows 98 may have a greater impact on how people use computers than did Windows 95. If you have used Windows 95, you can think of Windows 98 as a former caterpillar emerging from its cocoon; genetically, it's the same creature, but now it has brilliant colors, and it can explore a whole new world, because it can fly. Follow it, and you may find that you see with new eyes.

For Windows 3.1 Users

If you were one of the many who chose to stick with Windows 3.1 but now want to upgrade to Windows 98, you can take heart from two facts. Many millions of people have made the change to Windows 95, and you can benefit from their experience. In addition, you will get even more immediate benefits than did those who migrated to Windows 95 a couple of years ago.

Find What You Need

Windows 95 introduced the concepts of folders and shortcuts. "Folder" is really just a new name for what used to be called a "directory"—a division of a hard drive or other storage device in which files and other folders can be stored. Though it took a while, the new name is catching on. Earlier versions of Windows, as well as other operating systems, have long used a file folder icon to represent a directory. Referring to directories as folders makes the name consistent with the image, and more accessible to users with little technical knowledge.

Shortcuts

Shortcuts were genuinely new with Windows 95, and they are unchanged in Windows 98. Many users, however, are still learning how to make the best use of them. Windows 98 makes a significant improvement in one of the shortcuts set up during installation. Microsoft's Office 95 and Office 97 suites attempt to force users to keep their work in a folder called My Documents, an approach that might not suit everyone. Windows 98 rescues the idea of a standard location for documents, without attempting to force the user to give it a particular name. The My Documents icon on the Windows 98 desktop is a system icon, but you can modify it to point to any folder you wish.

For Windows 3.1 Users

Shortcuts are similar in some ways to the icons in a Program Manager group, but they are so much more flexible that the comparison could be misleading. Shortcuts are small files that serve as pointers. "Opening" a shortcut actually opens the object that the shortcut points to. That can be a program, as in Windows 3.1, but it can also be a document, a folder, or another resource available to your computer, such as a printer.

In addition, shortcuts can be placed anywhere you want them: on your desktop, on the Start menu, or in any folder. Shortcuts are a big part of Windows 98's efficiency and ease of use. Details about shortcuts are in Chapter 3.

Seamless Web Connections

Windows 98 doesn't merely improve access to documents in folders on your hard drive or local area network. Where it really shines is with Internet or intranet access, which is quicker and more direct than in the past. You don't need to start your browser and make a connection before you open your Favorites list or type in an Internet address. Instead, you have two direct paths to the Internet available from any open folder or Windows Explorer. You can enter an Internet address (URL) in the address bar, or you can go to the View menu and open one of four Explorer bars shown in Figure 1.2.

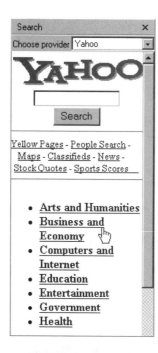
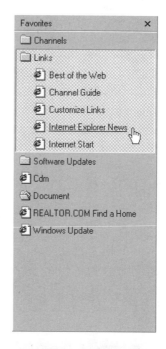

FIGURE 1.2:   These Explorer bars give you direct access to Web sites and services.

The Explorer bars offer direct access to your favorite Web sites and to any site you have recently visited (as shown in the History bar). The new Internet channel technology has its own bar, explained in detail in Chapter 7. You also have a direct connection to a variety of Internet search engines.

Additionally, Windows 98 contains a completely new help system that integrates the built-in help files with online resources. System help files have been rewritten and are displayed in a window that looks like a simple browser. For more about your help options, see Chapter 2.

What about My Mail?

Windows 98 includes a new program for handling Internet e-mail, called *Outlook Express* (see Figure 1.3). It's much less complex and easier to use than the Exchange/Windows Messaging system that was part of Windows 95. This is mostly good news for home users and those with small offices that don't have their own e-mail systems. Offices and companies that do have their own e-mail systems based on either a local area network or an intranet can, of course, continue to use it.

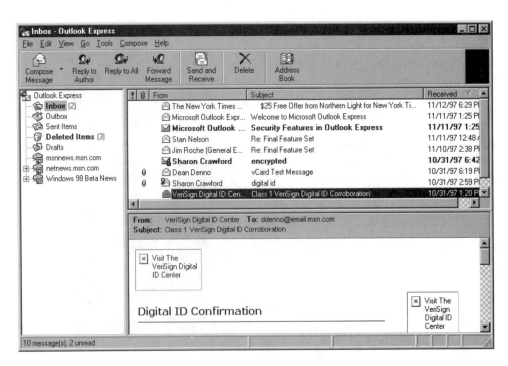

FIGURE 1.3: Outlook Express is excellent for handling Internet mail.

Besides handling Internet e-mail, Outlook Express allows you to make use of Internet newsgroups. This is a big advance, as Windows 95 had no built-in access to newsgroups. Now you can sign on to an Internet news server and participate in discussions on any imaginable topic. The Internet has tens of thousands of newsgroups, with topics ranging from assassination conspiracies to software support. The uses of Outlook Express are described in detail in Chapter 8.

WARNING **The switch from Exchange to Outlook Express has one big drawback: Windows 98 has no built-in fax capability. If that's important to you, you might want to continue using Exchange. We discuss this and other options in Appendix A on installing for Windows 95 users.**

You're Not Connected Yet?

Windows 98 can help you correct that lamentable situation! After installing Windows 98 you will find an Online services folder on your desktop. Opening it will reveal shortcuts to setup programs for several major online services and Internet service providers. These include America Online, AT&T WorldNet, CompuServe, the Microsoft Network, and Prodigy Internet.

As long as your machine includes a modem, all you have to do is choose a service and Windows 98 will install the software and allow you to connect and set up an account. The details are in Chapter 9, along with information on the various services to help you choose.

Getting It Delivered

Some of the most important new features of Windows 98 and Internet Explorer 4.0 are the ones that automatically download Web sites so you can view them offline. These include channels, which are designed to provide easy access, and Active Desktop subscriptions, which download ordinary Web sites on a schedule, to be displayed on your desktop. There is also an automated system for updating Windows 98 components over the Internet.

Channels

Windows 98 includes a mechanism for subscribing to channels. An Internet channel is a connection to a particular Web site. When you *subscribe* to a channel, content that you specify is delivered to your computer on a schedule that you can also specify. A wide variety of content providers such as PointCast, Disney, The New York Times, and National Geographic are designing channels. Many less well-known companies and organizations are also setting up channels. The Windows 98 desktop includes a channel bar for quick access to the channels you choose, and Microsoft's Web site even provides an online Channel Guide (Figure 1.4) to keep you aware of new channels.

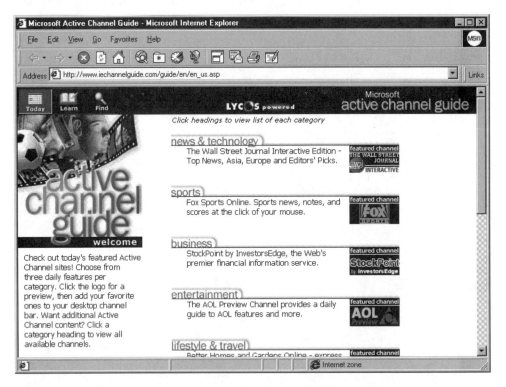

FIGURE 1.4: The Channel Guide tells you who is ready to push their material your way.

Part of the design of a channel is a recommended update schedule. This allows your computer to update the channel's content based on the provider's plans to update the site. Then you can view the channel content when you are ready, without having to go online. The channel content can be presented in several ways: in Internet Explorer, in a special full-screen window, on your desktop, or as a screen saver. The full details on channels are in Chapter 7.

Active Desktop

The Windows 95 desktop has a single layer to display all open windows, and the window in which you are working always comes to the foreground. The Windows 98 Active Desktop has two layers. Behind the windows where you work with your applications is an HTML layer that can display images of the Web sites of your choice. This HTML layer can also contain windows that display information from continuous-feed sources, such as a newswire or stock ticker, if you have a full-time Internet connection.

TIP   HTML stands for Hypertext Markup Language, the computer language in which Web pages are written. Windows 98 includes an HTML editor called FrontPage Express, which you can use to create documents for your Active Desktop or to create your own Web page. There's more about FrontPage Express in Chapter 7.

You can put any Web site you like on your Windows 98 desktop, but to keep it current it has to be updated. Windows 98 does this with subscriptions, which allow you to tell your computer when to go online and connect to a Web site to update it. Subscriptions and the Active Desktop are explained in detail in Chapter 4.

Windows Update

One of the big problems faced by many computer users is keeping their system up-to-date. You may be one of the millions who have installed a new game or other video-intensive program, only to find it won't run because your system doesn't have the latest driver for the video display. Drivers for video, sound, and many other types of hardware are constantly being updated, but few companies send these updates out routinely, even if you have registered your hardware.

Microsoft has set the very ambitious goal of solving this problem with Windows 98. The Windows Update program is designed to compare the drivers and other system software you are using with a master database stored on Microsoft's Web site. When it finds that a newer version is available, it will offer you the option of upgrading. Using Windows Update is covered in Chapter 15.

Other Cool Stuff

The Windows 98 package has lots more new goodies, from system tools, to new hardware support, to a new file system that makes better use of large hard drives. Here are some of the most important ones:

Windows Tune-Up and System File Checker   Windows 98 includes several new system tools to keep your computer running at its best and to help avoid problems. These are discussed in Chapter 15.

New busses for connecting peripheral devices   Some Universal Serial Bus (USB) devices and Accelerated Graphics Port (AGP) graphics cards are already available. IEEE 1394 devices are still in the future, but Windows 98 includes support for all of these connections.

New types of input and output devices   Details on such treats as digital cameras and force-feedback joysticks, among others, are in Chapter 11.

Power management functions   Newer computers can go on standby, with greatly reduced power consumption, and still carry out scheduled tasks such as hard disk maintenance and downloading of Web pages. The computer can restart quickly, with programs running just as you left them.

FAT32   This is a new method of storing information on hard drives that uses larger drives more efficiently. It is an important upgrade to the hard drive file system that came pre-installed on some Windows 95 computers, but it was "not available in stores" until Windows 98. Chapter 15 and the appendices have more on FAT32.

DirectX   This feature provides improved playback of 3-D graphics and other multimedia.

Desktop Themes   These fun add-ons, some from the Windows 95 Plus Pack, are included in Windows 98.

For Windows 3.1 Users

The introduction of Windows 95 brought some major improvements over Windows 3.1. Here's a rundown of some of these features, which haven't changed in Windows 98.

One of the most crucial improvements is the change from a 16-bit operating system to one using 32-bits. You don't really have to know anything about the jump to 32-bits other than the fact that it makes lots of good things possible.

Because this is a 32-bit system and built with today's computers in mind, other features and refinements are possible. One of the biggest is the switch to what's called 32-bit memory addressing, which is a way of identifying bits of memory.

Intel introduced a microprocessor that allowed 32-bit addressing back in 1988, but DOS and Windows 3.1 are limited by a very peculiar system that manages to encompass a sort of 20-bit addressing. One result of this poor construct is the 640 kilobytes available for DOS programs. Another is the 64 kilobytes available for Windows 3.1 resources. This explains how you can have multi-megabytes of RAM and still run out of Windows resources.

With Windows 95, we finally have full 32-bit addressing. This means, among other things, that a 32-bit application running in Windows 95 has access to essentially unlimited amounts of memory—in fact, up to 2 gigabytes.

Although Windows 3.1 could multitask—sort of—Windows 95 really can. This means the system makes decisions about priorities and doesn't depend on an application to release its hold on the CPU before taking care of other business.

In actual practice, it means that even if the hourglass is showing for one of your programs, you can usually switch to another program and do something useful. You can copy or format disks while printing a document. Or you can be downloading your e-mail from the Internet while writing letters or entering information into a database.

You will also notice that multitasking works lots better than it ever did in Windows 3.1. For one thing it's faster, and most importantly, a disagreement between programs is much less likely to bring your whole system to a halt.

Another improvement is the introduction of long file names. Everyone coming from the world of DOS and Windows 3.1 has had to deal with the burden of the MS-DOS 8.3 file-naming restrictions. With only eight characters (often the extension was used by the program itself), your files ended up with names that were cryptic at best. What are you to make of a file called SSCRANRL.DOC?

Six months down the road, were you likely to remember what it stood for?

Windows 95 brought relief in the form of long file names. Now instead of SSCRANRL.DOC, you can call the file Susan Stamberg's Cranberry Relish Recipe. File names can be up to 255 characters long, can include spaces, and lowercase letters are preserved.

What's Next

Now that we've given you an overview of Windows 98, we'll start digging into just what you can do with it. The next chapter shows you what's new in the Windows 98 interface, as well as reviewing some of the things that haven't changed from Windows 95 but will be news if you're upgrading from version 3.1.

BRAVE NEW WINDOWS

In this chapter, we'll take a tour of the Windows 98 interface and get you acquainted with the new looks in Windows 98. And *looks* is indeed the correct word. There's no longer just *one* look, there are many looks, and pieces of the interface can be mixed and matched as much as you like.

At each point, we'll refer you to the chapters where specific features are described in detail.

New Possibilities

If you go back as far as Windows 3.0, you may remember the transition to 3.1 as fairly seamless. Windows 3.1 was a big improvement over 3.0, but the learning curve wasn't difficult because the system still looked and acted pretty much the same. For the experienced user of Windows 95, the situation will be similar when moving to Windows 98. Although there are many new features, Windows 95 users will find that they can jump right in. We'll point out the changes and improvements, but you can learn the new features at your own speed.

Windows 3.1 users will find the jump to Windows 98 more challenging. However, in exchange for a few hours of fumbling about, you get a system that's faster, easier to use, and far more stable and powerful than Windows 3.1. Applications can still crash, but they won't necessarily take the whole system down. Like Windows 95, Windows 98 lets you close applications that are misbehaving (and usually reopen them as well) and get on with your business.

In true evolutionary fashion, Windows 98 is faster and much more powerful than Windows 95. No matter what version of Windows you were using, you'll find that Windows 98 opens a world of new possibilities.

Have It Your Way

The Windows 95 desktop offered a workspace with quick access to the documents, applications, and other computer resources you used most, including those located on an office network or the Internet. Double-clicking a desktop shortcut could immediately open any folder or document, wherever it was located. In addition, folders, documents, and scraps could actually be stored on the desktop for easy manipulation.

Windows 98 offers all these familiar capabilities, and most of them work just like they did in Windows 95. But double-clicking on the desktop is a thing of the past (unless you feel you can't do without it), and a number of other changes make Windows 98 look and behave more like the World Wide Web.

The full Web style in Windows 98 includes the Active Desktop, a new view in open folders, and icon titles and file names underlined the way links are on a Web page (see Figure 2.1). In addition, the mouse works the way it does in a Web browser—pointing to an item selects it and a single click opens it. We'll introduce these features in the course of this chapter, and tell you where in the book to find more details. All these new features are under your control, and it's possible to set the Windows 98 desktop to look and behave just like Windows 95.

For Windows 3.1 Users

Windows 98 greatly expands the ability to open a document directly, without first opening the program that created it. Windows 3.1 allowed you to do this by double-clicking the document file in File Manager, but in Windows 98 you can put a shortcut to the document (or even the document itself) on your desktop. You can open it without having to search for it first. In fact, Windows 98 is another step toward true point and click operation.

An inventory report, for example, exists as a document (inside a folder). You can open and update the report by simply clicking it or by clicking a desktop shortcut to it. (The details on shortcuts are in Chapter 3.) You don't have to know what application created the report, and you don't have to open the application first. Likewise, to print the report, you can just drag it to a printer shortcut.

You can still use applications in the old Windows 3.1 way: open the application and then open the file (document). The newer way, explained in the next chapter, is to organize your work in folders and open your documents directly from there. If you love the new approach, jump right in, but you'll probably develop folders gradually (as we have) as the system starts to make more sense to you.

In many ways, the Windows 98 desktop continues to function pretty much as it did in Windows 95. You can choose what shortcuts you want and where to put them. You can still reach all your programs, recently used documents, and a variety of resources through the Start Menu. The Taskbar and System Tray also work as they did in Windows 95, with a few added features. And you can continue to navigate your computer and network either with Windows Explorer or by opening folders on the desktop.

Active Desktop...

Another important change is that the Windows 98 desktop can hold HTML-based components including ActiveX controls and scripts. This is what Microsoft calls the Active Desktop. It allows you to put an Internet Web page on your desktop as shown in Figure 2.2, and have it updated automatically. You can also place a stock ticker or news service on your desktop to give you a continuous flow of information, if you have a full-time Internet connection. The Active Desktop is covered in detail in Chapter 4.

FIGURE 2.1:   A basic Windows 98 desktop with an open folder showing the Web style

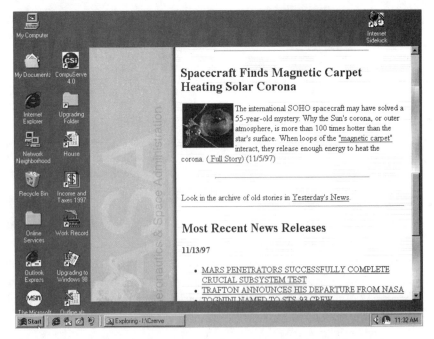

FIGURE 2.2:   The Windows 98 Active Desktop with a Web page as background

A desktop, whether active or not, is probably the easiest way to work if your documents and other resources are located mainly on your computer or a local area network (LAN). But if your work centers on the Internet or a company intranet, you may want to organize your work with Microsoft's Web browser, Internet Explorer, rather than the desktop.

...Or No Desktop

Internet Explorer 4.0 (the version included with Windows 98) can serve as your primary interface for Windows 98. It can do this because its address bar can distinguish between Internet (or intranet) addresses and local drive and folder paths. Type **www.microsoft.com** in the address bar, and Internet Explorer takes you to the Microsoft home page. But enter **c:**, and you'll see the files and folders in the root directory of your C: drive, as shown in Figure 2.3. Internet Explorer allows you to browse the resources of your computer and local network just as you browse the Internet. The Toolbar also changes to offer tools appropriate to the area you are browsing.

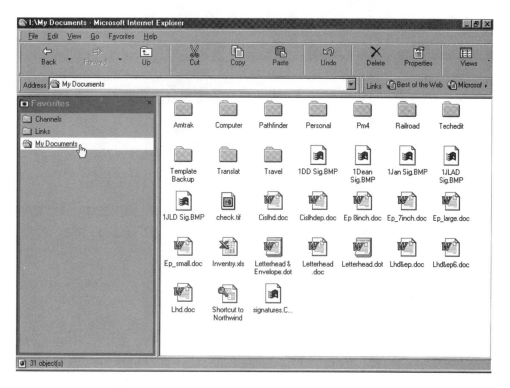

FIGURE 2.3:   Internet Explorer can serve as the gateway to your computer as well as the gateway to the Internet.

NOTE   **Full details on using Internet Explorer as your Windows interface are in Chapter 6.**

Navigating in Windows 98

Exactly what an open folder looks like when Windows 98 is first set up depends on the details of the installation. If your folders don't look like Figure 2.1 (with a title and properties area on the left), enlarge the window by dragging either side. If that doesn't work, you can go to Folder Options on the View menu to open the window shown in Figure 2.4. Choose Web Style, then click OK.

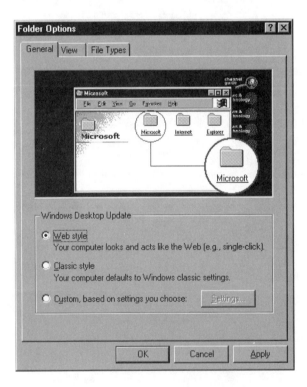

FIGURE 2.4: Choosing your view also sets your mouse clicks—unless you choose Custom.

An open folder will now resemble a Web page. In addition, the desktop itself will have something of a Web-like look. Each icon's name is underlined like a Web hyperlink. Slide the mouse pointer to an icon, and the pointer turns into a hand.

 Just pointing to an item is enough to select it and a single click will open it. Not having to double-click items any more may be disconcerting at first—particularly when you find yourself opening windows you didn't intend to open. However, if you give it a fair trial, we think you'll find it both easy and efficient. For more navigational tips and information on selecting multiple files, see Chapter 5.

If you absolutely can't bear to give up your double-click, open any Windows 98 folder and select View ➤ Folder Options. As shown in Figure 2.4, you can choose to have your desktop in the Classic style (that is, pretty much like Windows 95). This will return your mouse to its previous capability—single-click to select, double-click to open.

You can also choose Custom, then click Settings to pick exactly which features of the new desktop you'd like to use and which you want to keep as they were in Windows 95.

NOTE   Throughout this book we will assume the use of Web style. That means pointing to something on the desktop or in a folder highlights it (*selects* it) and clicking once causes some action to be taken. If it's a program, it'll run. If it's a folder or document, it'll open, and so forth. You should bear this in mind if you are using the Classic settings (where a single-click selects and a double-click is required for action).

TIP   Web style only eliminates double-clicking on the desktop and in folders. Dialog boxes and other areas where double-clicking causes an action are not affected.

The Right Mouse Button

Windows 98 continues to employ a helpful feature that started with Windows 95. Point your mouse to an object and click the right mouse button once to open a pop-up menu.

The content of the menu varies depending on the type of object. For document files, you will generally find at least Open, Print, and Send To options. Most files have Cut and Copy options; areas where you might want to put a file or folder will have an option for Paste and also New, where a sub-menu allows you to create a folder, shortcut, or various types of files.

Nearly every pop-up menu includes an item called Properties, which opens the property sheet for the selected object. This method of access to settings for programs, folders, or devices is consistent throughout the operating system.

NOTE   **Details about using some of these options are explained in Chapter 5. There's more on making new folders and on property sheets later in this chapter.**

Starting It Up

In the remainder of this chapter, we will discuss some basic elements of the Windows 98 desktop. We'll leave the option of ignoring the desktop and using only Internet Explorer as your Windows 98 interface for Chapter 6.

The opening screen will vary, depending on what you chose to install and whether or not you're on a network. Figure 2.5 shows a possible opening screen for Windows 98.

Variations in hardware, software, and installation choices may cause your opening screen to show different elements than ours. Don't worry, you'll soon see why the differences exist.

Desktop Icons

The default opening screen has several icons in place in the upper left corner. One of them is called My Computer.

When you open it, you'll see objects representing your computer's drives as well as folders for the Control Panel, printers, and perhaps a few other items depending on what you chose to install (see Figure 2.6). The idea is that you're looking inside your computer to see what you have to work with.

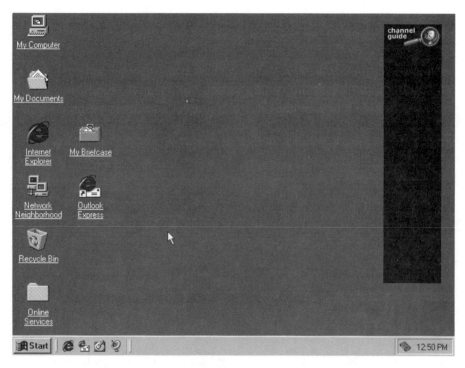

FIGURE 2.5:   An opening screen for Windows 98

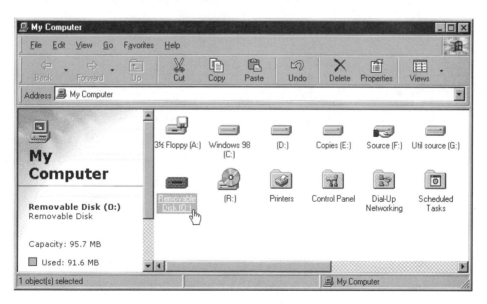

FIGURE 2.6:   You can use the My Computer icon to get to your drives as well as to other control functions. The hand holding an icon indicates that the drive (or folder) is shared over a network.

By default, individual windows display large icons. If you want more information or a more efficient use of space, pull down the View menu in the My Computer window, and select List or Details. Figure 2.7 shows the same My Computer window using the Details option from the View menu.

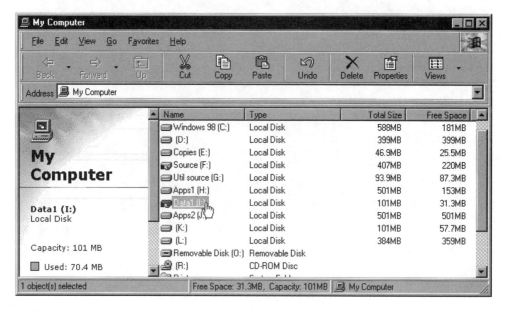

FIGURE 2.7:   Select Details from the View menu, and the window will show additional information about your files.

For helpful hints about menu items, make sure that the Status Bar on the View menu has a check mark next to it. Then, when you rest the mouse pointer on a menu item, information about that item will appear at the bottom of the window. Other options on the View menu are covered in Chapters 3 and 5.

The other icons you may see on your desktop are:

My Documents   Windows 98 creates a folder called My Documents as the default location for keeping documents created by most applications. The My Documents icon is a shortcut to this folder, even though it lacks the arrow in the lower left corner that normally indicates a shortcut. If you prefer, you can change the properties of this icon to point to any folder you wish.

Internet Explorer   Starts Internet Explorer, the Web browser included with Windows 98.

Network Neighborhood   You'll have this icon if you're on a local area network. Like My Computer, it opens a window showing the other computers on the network and the resources they make available to you.

Recycle Bin   All your deleted files are dumped here—in case you have second thoughts later and decide to retrieve one or more. Chapter 3 includes details on the Recycle Bin.

Online Services   Contains software for connecting to companies that provide Internet access. See Chapter 9 for information on making that connection.

Outlook Express   Starts the Internet mail and newsgroup client that comes with Windows 98.

Set Up The Microsoft Network   Microsoft gives its own online service a prominent position on the desktop; it's also covered in Chapter 9.

And the Button

Like Windows 95, Windows 98 suggests where to start—namely with the Start button. All you have to do is click this button once to get a menu that's somewhat familiar. Run the mouse pointer up to Programs, and another menu opens (see Figure 2.8) containing a list of installed programs plus a few other items we'll discuss later.

FIGURE 2.8:
Clicking the Start button gives you somewhere to go.

For Windows 3.1 Users

In Windows 3.1, you had to click a menu item and hold down the left mouse button to open any cascading menus under the original item. Windows 98 has a different approach. After you click the Start button, you don't need to hold down the mouse button to open the various cascading menus. In fact, holding the button often gets you results you hadn't anticipated. It'll probably take a little practice before you stop opening things inadvertently. The correct technique is to click an item once, slide the pointer around the menus to the item you want, then click once again.

A Deeper Desktop

An experienced user of any version of Windows will be able to do a lot in Windows 98 without any instruction at all. However, before you go too far, you'll find it helpful to understand the way the desktop works, how to use folders and shortcuts, and some of the tricks that your newly intelligent mouse can perform. First, we'll discuss the desktop.

TIP   **The area at the bottom of the screen is called the Taskbar. We'll talk about that a little later in this chapter.**

With Windows 98, your screen is a lot like a real desktop. It's even two-layered, like a desk with a glass top. In other words, it starts off fairly uncluttered—except for a few standard items—then you decide what goes on the desk. The degree to which you can do this is very impressive, as you'll see.

Folders

Folders aren't a difficult concept to grasp—they're just directories made graphical. In addition to the usual array of folders created by applications, or by you, Windows 98 creates a number of system folders for special purposes. We'll mention the important ones throughout this book as we discuss the various functions and applications they serve.

Creating Folders

Folders are easily made and can contain any combination of objects: documents, programs, your printer, even other folders. Using the right mouse button, you can click on the desktop and choose New ➤ Folder from the menu that opens (see Figure 2.9).

FIGURE 2.9: A right button click on the desktop opens a menu from which you can create a new folder.

TIP You can make new folders almost anywhere. Just click the right mouse button, and if the menu that opens (like the one in Figure 2.9) includes the item New, move the pointer to New and then to Folder. If the menu *doesn't* include New, then you need to move the pointer to a location where folders are permitted.

And Naming Folders

A newly created folder has the default name "New Folder." The name is already highlighted, so you can just type the name you want. Renaming an existing folder is as easy as creating one. Point to the folder (or its name) to highlight it. Then click the right mouse button and select Rename. Type in the name you want. Files and most other objects can also be renamed this way.

If you chose to keep the double-click option for opening documents, you can also rename a file by clicking the name a second time, after you have selected the file with a first click. But we agree with the designers of Windows 98, and suggest you use the single-click method. You may have to get used to the right-click method for renaming, but you probably open files much more often than you rename them.

NOTE   **Chapter 3 has more information on making folders and using them effectively.**

Shortcuts

Shortcuts are very handy tools that were introduced with Windows 95. The idea is that you can have a reference to a program or device (like your printer) anywhere you want it. For example, you may want to put a shortcut to your printer or personal calendar in every folder you work in regularly.

TIP   **A shortcut is identified by the small arrow in the lower left corner of its icon.**

A shortcut isn't a copy of the program, it's a pointer. So you can open your spreadsheet program, say, from any of a dozen different locations depending on where you're working on the desktop. Shortcuts are very smart pointers. Even if you move the original object, Windows 98 will usually find it.

Shortcuts can be created in several ways. The simplest is if you have the original 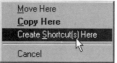 object (document or program file) in view. Use the right mouse button to drag it to where you want it. Choose Create Shortcut(s) Here from the menu that appears when you release the right mouse button.

NOTE   **There's much more on shortcuts and their many uses in Chapter 3.**

A More Advanced Taskbar

The developers of Windows 98 went to a lot of trouble to prevent lost windows and to minimize the amount of time you spend looking for stuff on the desktop. The Taskbar serves as a resting spot for all your open documents, folders, and programs. It can even return you to your desktop to find a scrap or shortcut that's buried there, or take you back and forth between the standard desktop and the browser interface.

For Windows 3.1 Users

The Taskbar is a replacement for the underused and underrated Task Manager in Windows 3.1. Because the Taskbar is usually visible, it's not as likely to be forgotten as the Task Manager often was.

Always on Top

Every active window can be found on the Taskbar. Even if your program is buried several windows deep, click a button on the Taskbar and the corresponding window pops to the top. By default, the Taskbar will appear at the bottom of your screen and is always on top of any open application. It provides a consistent home base so that no matter how messed up the screen gets, you can always return to the Taskbar to get reoriented.

Or Any Way You Want It

For more flexibility in your workspace, you can click any blank portion of the Taskbar and drag the whole thing to the top or to either side of your screen. There are lots of other ways you can reconfigure your Taskbar, too. Chapter 4 covers the details.

Exploring the System

Windows Explorer is the program you'll probably use to navigate through your system (as well as any other computers you're networked to). Click the Start button and select Programs ➤ Windows Explorer (Figure 2.10).

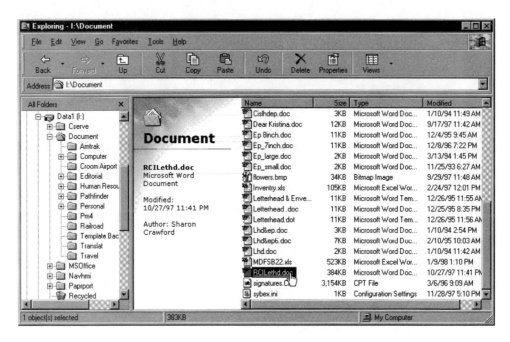

FIGURE 2.10:   This is one view of Windows Explorer, but you can also get other versions.

The left side of Windows Explorer shows the resources available to your computer. Click the + in front of a drive, folder, or other item to expand the view and show subfolders. The icons that appear to be held by a hand are folders shared over a network. When you highlight a folder in the left pane, the right pane will show the contents of that folder.

NOTE   **The uses of Windows Explorer are described in detail in Chapter 5.**

For Windows 3.1 Users

Windows Explorer looks and works a lot like the old File Manager. The main difference is that the left window shows drives and other resources, instead of showing only the directory tree of a single drive. This is a definite improvement and shouldn't be hard to get used to.

Doing Windows

The basic structure of a window is unchanged from Windows 95, and it won't present any great difficulties for a Windows 3.1 user, either. In the next sections, we describe the component parts of windows and how to manipulate them.

Title Bar Convenience

Every window has a title bar running across the top. At the left end of the title bar is an icon representing the window's contents. Windows Explorer's window has an icon like the one at left.

When you point to the icon and click once, you get a System menu. It offers the same options as in previous versions of Windows, where it was called the Control menu.

Mini, Maxi, and Gone

In the upper right corner of the window, there are three buttons representing four familiar functions.

From left to right, these buttons minimize, maximize, and close the window. If the window is already maximized, the middle button will restore it to its normal size. You can also close any window by clicking the icon in the upper left corner of the window and selecting Close.

TIP   **Another way of closing the active window is to press Alt+F4.**

Higher Property Values

A property sheet is a special kind of dialog box that is always opened the same way—by right-clicking an object and selecting Properties from the pop-up menu.

Within the property sheet is all the information about the configuration of the selected object. Figure 2.11 shows the property sheet for the desktop.

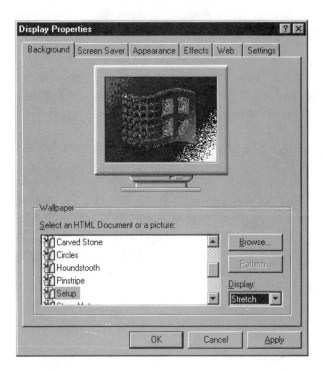

FIGURE 2.11: Every object, including programs, folders, and the desktop itself, has a property sheet.

Tabbed pages allow property sheets to contain lots of information divided into logical categories. Some property sheets provide visual cues; for example, when you're selecting display attributes, you get a picture of what your selection will look like.

TIP   **For help in configuring the properties for the desktop, see Chapter 4.**

You *Can* Get Good Help

Windows 98 offers several ways of getting help. When you come across something mystifying, particularly in a property sheet or other dialog box, place your mouse pointer on the point of confusion and click the right mouse button. If context-sensitive help is available (it generally is), a *What's This?* box appears.

Click the box and another window opens with useful information about the specific item. Click once (with your left mouse button) somewhere else on the desktop and the window goes away.

Help by Feature or Phrase

When you have a general question about a certain Windows 98 function, select Help Topics from the Help menu of an Explorer window or folder. Point to the Index tab as shown in Figure 2.12. Type in the name of the feature, and the window scrolls to the subject. Click the Display button, and the help topic appears.

The Contents and Index pages of the Help screen are familiar places to Windows users. However, if you have a problem and can't fathom how it might be listed in the Help topics, Windows 98 can assist you with another approach. You can search for specific words or phrases in the Help files, so you don't have to know what the Microsoft gremlins filed it under.

On Your Computer

Windows 98 uses a new Help system in which the help files installed on your computer are just the starting point. When you have a general question about some Windows 98 function, select Help from the Start menu to open the window shown in Figure 2.12. You can also get there by choosing Help ➤ Help Topics in any open folder or Windows Explorer.

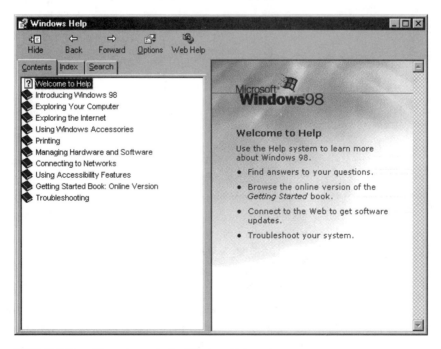

FIGURE 2.12: The entrance to the Windows Help system

Click on any closed book icon to open it and see its subcategories. When you get down to actual Help topics, the icon is a question mark. Click it, and the topic will appear in the right frame of the Help window. For example, while exploring Help categories under "Introducing Windows 98," you can find "If you're upgrading from Windows 3.1," as shown in Figure 2.13.

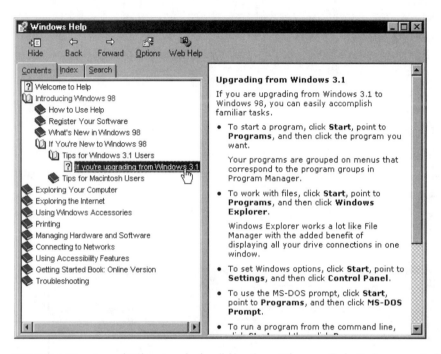

FIGURE 2.13:   Expand Help categories by clicking them. When you find a topic you want, click to see it in the right frame.

To use the Help Index, click the Index tab. Start typing a word and the window scrolls to the subject, if it's included in the index (see Figure 2.14). You can also scroll through the index and click on any entry that interests you. Click the Display button, and the help topic appears. (If there's more than one topic for the subject you've typed, you first get a dialog box to select the topic you want.)

You can also search the text of the Help system. Click the Search tab, and type in one or more keywords. Click List Topics to see topics that contain all of the words you typed, without regard to order. Double-click the topic you want, and it will be displayed. Search even finds other forms of words you enter. As Figure 2.15 shows, entering **hardware add** finds topics containing the phrase "adding new hardware" as well as those containing "add new hardware." Remember that spelling counts, and you must use complete words—those topics won't be found if you enter **hardware ad**.

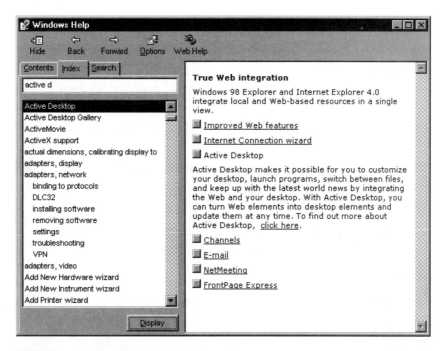

FIGURE 2.14:   The Help index is quite extensive.

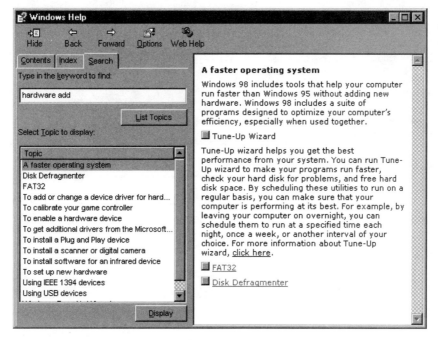

FIGURE 2.15:   Search is a powerful Help tool.

Or Online

If you can't find what you need in the local help file, click the Web Help button on the toolbar. This opens a Help topic that contains a link to Microsoft's technical support Web site. Clicking the link starts Internet Explorer and connects to the site (assuming you have Internet access and you've set it up, as discussed in Chapter 6). As Figure 2.16 shows, you can type in a question or use a variety of other tools available at the site.

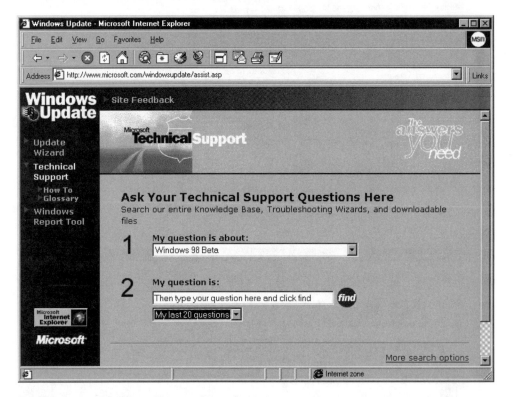

FIGURE 2.16:   The Help system can take you here.

Of course, you still have to be able to come up with words that somehow relate to what you want to know, which is one of the reasons you still need a book like this one.

What's Next

Now that you've had a brief tour of the concepts underlying your new operating system, let's move on to a more in-depth look at the desktop: what's new about it and how to set it up the way you want it.

WORKING ON YOUR DESKTOP

With Windows 95, the entire area of your monitor's screen became a useful workspace, called the desktop. Windows 98 retains all of those capabilities and adds quite a few new ones. It packs more functions into the same space with a grab-bag of improvements and new features that all add up to one thing: making every square millimeter of your screen earn its keep. You could call it desktop speedup.

In this chapter, we'll translate what you find on the desktop and provide basic information about getting around. We'll also explain how to add some of the things that can make it truly *your* desktop. Windows 98 usually has more than one route to a destination. We try to show you the easiest way, but once you have the basic navigational skills down, don't be afraid to experiment.

Opening My Computer

As you explore Windows 98, you'll find there are many ways to work, and you'll adopt the ones that seem most natural for you. One direct route to the resources on your system is to click the My Computer icon found on your desktop. The contents of the window that opens will vary based on what's on your computer—including networked drives. Figure 3.1 shows a computer with one floppy drive and two hard drives (C: is being shared over a network). The Control Panel and Printers, as well as the facilities for dial-up networking and scheduling automatic tasks, are system folders that are present in virtually all Windows 98 installations.

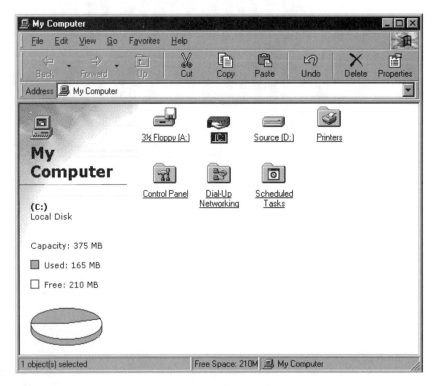

FIGURE 3.1:   Point to an icon for information, or click for access to its contents.

Figure 3.1 shows the Web page view of My Computer. It's called Web page view because it is supposed to look and act like a Web page, and because an HTML template is used in the folder to display the large title and icon at the top and the information along the left side.

For Windows 3.1 Users

If you feel more comfortable with the File Manager approach, click the Start menu, select Programs, and then Windows Explorer. Chapter 5 has more on Windows Explorer and related functions.

TIP   **Have you found My Computer (or My Documents, or Network Neighborhood) too redolent of My Little Pony or Mr. Rogers? Simply right-click the icon and select Rename. Enter a new name and then click somewhere on the desktop to save it. (Only the Recycle Bin cannot be renamed.)**

The New Look in Windows

Some new window controls were introduced in Windows 95. Windows 98 continues the trend of allowing users more control over the arrangement of their desktop and the items on it. Toolbars can now be moved and re-arranged, and their power has been expanded to give direct access to the entire range of resources available to you, from your own computer's hard drive to your local area network to the Internet or company intranet. Figure 3.2 names the basic components of a Windows 98 window.

In addition, the folder itself has become a chameleon. The change from Figure 3.1 to Figure 3.2 was made by removing the check mark from As Web Page on the View menu, returning to the classic Windows 95 look. This view lacks the instant information offered by the Web view, but it saves considerable space. Details on this and related options are in the "Working with Folders" section later in this chapter.

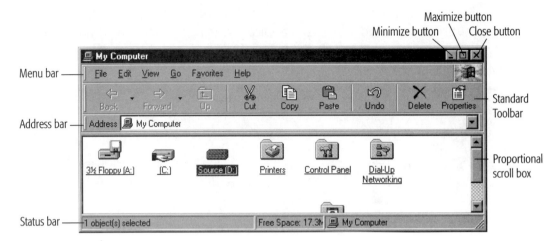

FIGURE 3.2: Windows 98 offers new toolbars and toolbar options.

Toolbar Choices

The toolbars are a standardization and extension of a visual device that's been used in a lot of Windows applications. In Windows 98, their role expands further. Though they began simply as collections of icons that provided shortcuts to the functions on the menus, toolbars can now be added, removed, and rearranged.

By default, the address bar and standard toolbar appear below the menu bar. The address bar consists of a single combination box. You can use the drop-down list to browse your computer, your network, or the Internet. Or you can type an address directly in the box. Any valid address will work, from **c:** for your computer's root directory, to a LAN address like **\\rci\data1**, to an Internet or intranet URL.

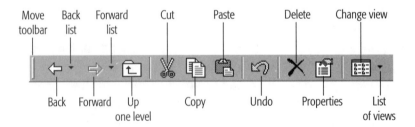

Reading from left to right, the buttons on the standard toolbar do the following:

- Move back to the previous item you viewed in this window
- Pick from a list of previously viewed items
- Move forward through the list of items you've viewed (available only after using one of the Back buttons)
- Pick from a forward list of items viewed
- Move up one level in the folder (directory) hierarchy
- Cut the highlighted item(s)
- Copy the highlighted item(s)
- Paste what you've just cut or copied
- Undo the last operation
- Delete the highlighted item(s)
- View the property sheet for the highlighted item
- Change the view by cycling through the four options: large icons, small icons, list, or list with details
- Change the view by choosing from a list

Position your mouse pointer over a toolbar button and a little window will open telling you what the button does.

On the View menu you can make several changes to the toolbars displayed in your windows. Under View ➢ Toolbar you can add a Links toolbar with buttons that will take you directly to a specific address. Configuring the links is a topic we'll discuss in Chapter 6. You can also choose to add or remove the text labels for the icons on the standard toolbar.

TIP   **The Map Network Drive buttons have been dropped from the default toolbar. To put them back, click View ➢ Folder Options. Click the View tab and check the box labeled Show Map Network Drive Button In Toolbar.**

You can also re-arrange toolbars virtually any way you like within the area below the title bar. Drag the vertical handle at the left end of any toolbar to move or size it. Notice that this also applies to the menu bar.

NOTE Each time you customize the toolbar settings and arrangement, the new setup takes effect for all new folder windows you open. After you shut down your computer, all folders you open will use the most recent arrangement. To save space and improve clarity, most illustrations in this book were created using customized toolbar arrangements.

Proportional Scroll Boxes

The scroll bars and boxes in a Windows 98 window work as they do in earlier versions of Windows. With Windows 95 the boxes became proportional. The size of the scroll box tells you how much of the window contents is being displayed. A scroll box that fills half the bar tells you that you're looking at half of what there is to see (in that particular window).

Working with Folders

Folders are the ideal way to organize work and minimize clutter. As mentioned earlier, they're really directories, but it's easier to think of them as folders. In DOS/Windows 3.1, all the files connected with a program could be—and often were—in the same directory. You can still do things this way, but we think it makes great good sense to take advantage of the folder concept in Windows 98.

Making New Folders

You can make a folder from a variety of spots, including the desktop itself. To make a folder, just follow these steps:

1. Right-click on the desktop or a blank area inside a folder.
2. Select New ➤ Folder from the menu that opens.
3. A new folder is created where you clicked, with the label already selected, so you can type in the name you want for the folder.

For example, Figure 3.3 shows a new folder being made in the right pane of Windows Explorer (the left pane is one of the few places you can't create a new folder). Figure 3.4 shows the result.

FIGURE 3.3:   Right-click, then select New ➤ Folder.

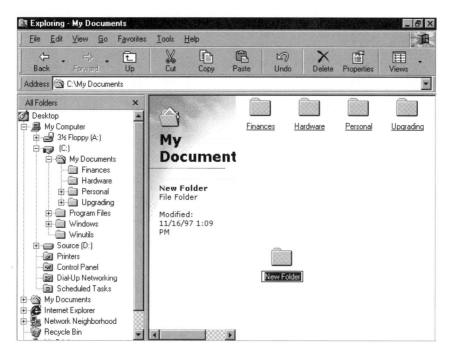

FIGURE 3.4:   A new folder appears in the selected spot. Type in the folder name and you're done.

How They Work

You can see the contents of a folder by clicking its icon: it will open in a window. Add files to a folder by dragging and dropping them on either the folder icon or in the folder window. Move the folder itself by dragging and dropping the icon to some new location, such as another folder, local drive, or network drive. The folder can contain other folders, individual documents, and shortcuts to virtually anything on your system.

Figure 3.5 shows a folder called Finances that includes shortcuts to a couple of Excel spreadsheets, a calculator, and a phone dialer (for emergency calls to the accountant, one supposes).

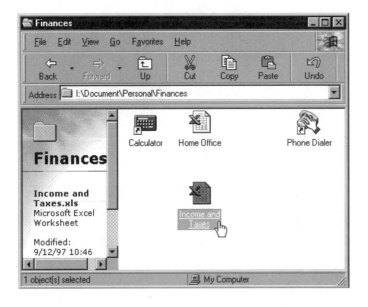

FIGURE 3.5:
You can put everything you need to meet your money needs in the Finances folder.

TIP   **You may find this handy if you keep Internet-related work together in a folder: any open folder can be instantly changed to Internet Explorer. Just go to the View menu, choose Explorer Bar and then Search, Favorites, History, or Channels. In the Explorer bar, choose the Web site you want to visit, and the window will turn into Internet Explorer and connect to the site.**

If you don't like the icon look, you can set up your folder as a list. You can also specify a lot of detail, and you can remove the Web page features along the left side of the window for a more compact folder.

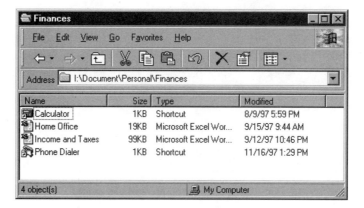

All of this can be configured from the folder's toolbar or from the View menu. Notice the changes in the toolbars in the last example.

NOTE   Setting the View option for a folder affects that window only. There's no way to set a global option for all folders to have a list view or a details view. On the other hand, toolbar arrangements are not tied to a specific folder or window and take effect globally as folders are opened.

Thumbnail View

Windows 98 offers a new way to view the contents of a folder: as thumbnail sketches of the files. The thumbnails work for file types that are commonly used on the World Wide Web, which makes the feature especially helpful in folders that contain Web page components.

Before you can use thumbnail view, you must enable it for the particular folder where you want to use it:

1. If the folder is open, close it.
2. Right-click the folder's icon and choose Properties to open the folder's property sheet, as shown in Figure 3.6.
3. Put a check in the box labeled Enable thumbnail view.
4. Click OK.

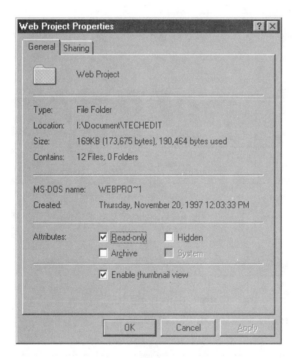

FIGURE 3.6:
Enabling the thumbnail view for a folder

Now you can open the folder and choose Thumbnails from the View menu. The thumbnails take up a lot of space, so Web page view in the folder is automatically turned off when you select Thumbnails. Figure 3.7 illustrates the new thumbnail view.

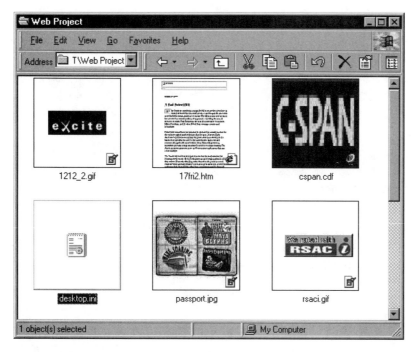

FIGURE 3.7: Thumbnail view can be very useful for reminding you of what's what in a collection of graphic and HTML files.

Folders as Web Pages

One of the options on the View menu of any folder is As Web Page. This option is a toggle: a click turns it on or off. When you view a folder as a Web page, its appearance is controlled by a hypertext template. The default template uses roughly the left one-third of the folder window to display the folder name and a variety of useful information.

When you select an object in the folder, information about the object appears in the left pane of the folder window. The type of information depends on the object. For a document file, it may include such properties as the author's name and the file date and time, as in Figure 3.5. Graphics files may display a thumbnail image. For disk drives, the information includes space used and space available, along with a pie graph, as in Figure 3.1. For system folders and other objects, there is a general description that indicates the object's function.

Customizing Folders

The View menu also has an option to Customize This Folder. Choosing it starts a wizard of the same name, which offers three choices:

- You can choose to Create or Edit an HTML Document that will control the appearance of the folder when View ➤ As Web Page is selected. This sounds good, but beware: as the next wizard dialog explains, this really involves working with a Hypertext template, not a simple HTML document. The template may be opened in Notepad. This is fine if you know how to code Hypertext templates, or want to experiment. Otherwise, don't go here. For more information, see the FrontPage Express section of Chapter 7.
- You can Choose a Background Picture. Any picture in .bmp, .jpg, or .gif format can serve as a background for the folder view.
- Or you can Remove Customization to return to a plain background. This also returns you to the default template for the Web view if you have selected View ➤ As Web Page.

Selecting Options

Every folder has a Folder Options selection on the View menu. When you select Folder Options, Windows 98 opens a dialog box much like the one shown in Figure 3.8. The settings you make here are global, unlike the View menu settings just described. In other words, you can't change the options for just one folder. Any changes you make here take effect throughout your whole system.

The General Page

This is where you get to set the basic look and behavior of your folders. You can choose the Web style, in which:

- The folders you browse will all open in the same window, rather than in a new window for each folder.
- All folders have a default Web view, as in Figure 3.9, which you can customize if you like.
- The names and icons of files and sub-folders look and behave like links: they are underlined, they are selected when you point at them, and they open with a single click.

FIGURE 3.8:
The Folder
Options dialog
box lets you set
global properties
for all your folders.

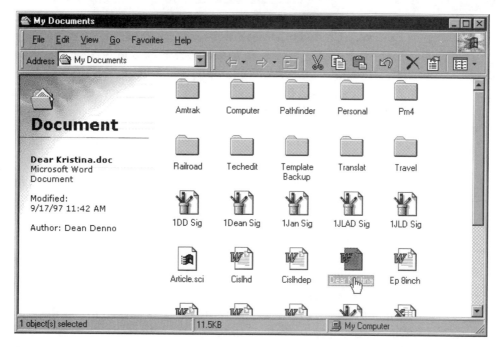

FIGURE 3.9:   The browser-style pointer selects an object when you point to it. A single click will open it.

The Classic style will give you a Windows 95 look-and-feel:
- Each folder opens in a new window.
- Folders are given a Web page view only if you choose As Web Page on the View menu.
- Click to select an item and double-click to open it.

TIP   Here's an idea for reducing clutter if you use Classic settings and browse with a new window for each folder. Open folder windows until you get to the one you want. Then move back to that folder's parent folder and click the Close button while holding down the Shift key. This will close the entire chain of parent folders.

If you prefer some combination of these options (such as Classic Windows looks with single-click file opening), choose Custom and click the Settings button to set your individual preferences.

NOTE   We suggest using the single-click-to-open setting because we think most people will find it easier once they get used to it. Except where noted otherwise, this book assumes you are using the single-click setting. However, to keep our illustrations clear and (relatively) uncluttered, we will generally avoid using the Web page view in folders. Also for clarity, we have used custom settings so that only the selected icon name is underlined.

The View Tab

The View tab includes settings for how files will display in folders. The two buttons in the Folder Views box allow you to give all your folders the same view. The Like Current Folder button sets all folders to the same view as the folder you are currently working in. Reset All Folders sets them all back to the Windows 98 default view. In either case, changes take place the next time you open a folder.

You can also toggle a variety of folder properties in the Advanced Settings list. Here are the choices you can make:

Remember each folder's view settings   This option ensures that a given folder always opens with the view (Large Icons, Small Icons, List, or Details) to which you last set it. If you uncheck this, the same view setting will be applied to all folders you open in that window.

Display the full path in title bar   Ordinarily, the title bar of a folder will show only the folder's title. Sometimes, of course, you may want to see just where on your hard drive a folder resides, or maybe you just miss the DOS command line. In that case, select this option and the full path will be displayed on the title bar of each folder.

Hide file extensions for known file types   This option is selected by default, which means that you won't see the file extensions for files that Windows 98 already knows how to use. So don't be dismayed to see that your file names look peculiar without their familiar tails—like .EXE or .DOC—because any file without an extension can just be clicked to open. With this option selected, the only files with extensions will be those that have no associated application. (See The File Types Tab for information on how to tell Windows 98 about an unrecognized file.)

Show Map Network Drive button in toolbar   Adds the button for mapping network drives to every toolbar.

Show file attributes in Detail View   If you always want to see individual file attributes (whether a file is backed up or a system file, for example), check this box.

Show pop-up description for folder and desktop items   This controls the descriptive boxes that open when you move your pointer over icons such as My Computer. Remove the checkmark when you've seen enough of them.

Allow all uppercase names   Do you want folders with NAMES ALL IN CAPITAL LETTERS? Check this box, and you've got 'em.

Hidden files   Choose one of these options:

> **Do not show hidden or system files**   Reduces clutter by not showing files with either the Hidden or System attributes. This will help make sure you do not accidentally rename or otherwise tamper with system files.

> **Do not show hidden files**   Reduce clutter and increase the security of your system a bit by not showing files whose Hidden attribute has been set.

> **Show all files**   All files will be listed, regardless of attributes.

There are also settings for a few screen options. These duplicate options are on the Effects page of the Display Properties dialog, which is discussed in the next chapter.

The File Types Tab

Click the File Types tab in the Folder Options dialog box to see a listing of all the file types that are registered with Windows 98 on your machine. If you highlight a file type, you'll see details as shown in Figure 3.10. This includes the extensions used for the file type and the name of the program that works with the files.

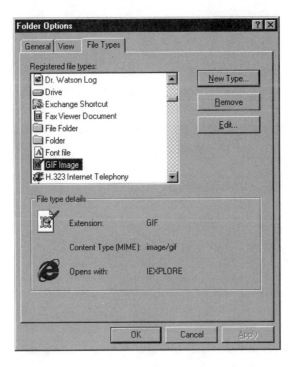

FIGURE 3.10:
This list shows the file types that are registered with Windows 98.

Normally, when you install an application, it registers all the file types it can open. You are most likely to use the File Types tab for one of two reasons:

- You want to use an application to open files that do not have one of the extensions normally used by that application.
- You have more than one application that can open files of a given type and want to change which application will actually be used by Windows.

Let's say you have a communications program that creates logs of online activity. The files are plain text and have the .log extension, and you want to open them in Notepad by clicking the file in a folder. To add a new file type, follow these steps:

  1. On the File Types tab, click New Type. In the window that opens, fill in the top two boxes:

Description of type   This is what will show up in the list of file types. In this case, we chose "Connection Log" as the description.

Associated extension   Type in the extension. More than one extension can be associated with the same application—just leave spaces between them. No periods are required.

2.   Click New. Enter the type of action to be performed (usually **Open**) and the application used to perform the action. Browse to find the application, if necessary. Click OK.

3.   Click Change Icon if the one shown is not to your liking. Click Close when you're finished.

Figure 3.11 shows the completed Add New File Type window.

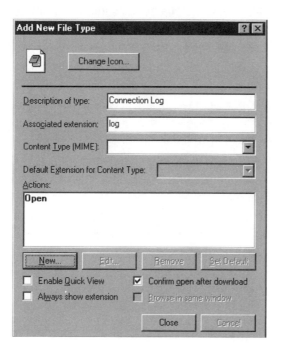

FIGURE 3.11:
With this information completed, Windows 98 knows which application to use to open a specific type of file.

There's a much easier way to do an on-the-fly association. Right-click the file and select Open With from the menu. Type a description of the file type in the top window, then highlight the program you want to use and click OK. If the program you want isn't on the list, click Other and use the Browse window to find it. Highlight the program, click Open, and then OK.

To change the application associated with a file type, go to the File Types tab and click the file type in the list. Then choose Edit. You can change the description if you like. Select the action you want to change, then choose Edit again to change the application used to perform that action.

NOTE   **Chapter 5 has more details on registering file types with Windows 98.**

How to Take Shortcuts

Shortcuts were among the really obvious benefits introduced in Windows 95, and their use is unchanged. As mentioned in the last chapter, a shortcut is a pointer to a program or file or folder. Look back at Figure 3.6. Notice that the two Excel files lack the small arrow in the lower left corner that indicates a shortcut. Those two files are actually located in the Finances folder. The Phone Dialer and Calculator are shortcuts: the programs are elsewhere, but we have instant access where we need it.

Shortcuts let you have as many "copies" of your printer as you want—one in every folder plus one on the desktop, if that's your choice. Of course, a shortcut to the printer isn't really a copy of the printer, just a pointer. With shortcuts you can have your word processor in as many locations as necessary and only use a minimal amount of hard disk space for each instance.

Shortcuts can be created in several ways. The Create Shortcut option is available on an object's pop-up menu and also on the File menu of a folder, if an object in that folder is selected. If you right-click the desktop, you can choose New, then Shortcut. The system will prompt you to create a shortcut if you try to move or copy something that can't be moved or copied.

With the Original in View

To make a shortcut when you have the original object in view, follow these steps:

1. Right-click the object (file, application, etc.) and select Create Shortcut.
2. The shortcut will appear in the same folder as the original. Right-click on it and choose Rename.
3. Type in a new name. This eliminates the long captions that result when every shortcut is identified as a Shortcut To whatever.
4. Drag the shortcut to the desktop or the folder where you want it.

NOTE   **To create a shortcut to a folder by this method, you need the folder visible as an icon, not an open window.**

Here's another method, using the Finances folder in Figure 3.6 as an example:

1. If the object to which you want to create a shortcut is an open folder, click the Up One Level button on the toolbar to see it as an icon in its parent folder. Skip this step if the object is already visible as an icon.
2. Using the right mouse button, drag the folder or other object to where you want the shortcut.
3. Release the right mouse button and choose Create Shortcut(s) Here from the menu. See Figure 3.12.

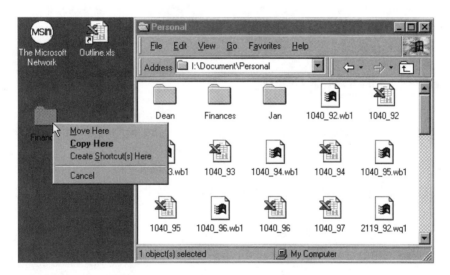

FIGURE 3.12:   Creating a desktop shortcut to the Finances folder

4. Right-click the new shortcut, choose Rename, and give it your chosen name.

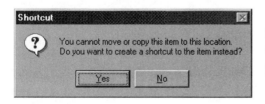

If you try to move or copy something that can't be moved or copied, the system will prompt you to create a shortcut instead.

To Absent Objects

If the original object isn't handy or you don't want to go find it, you can still create a shortcut as follows:

1. Right-click the desktop or a folder and select New ➤ Shortcut.
2. In the dialog box that opens, type the location and name of the original object. If you don't know the path (and who ever does?), click the Browse button.
3. Using the Browse window, mouse around until you find the file or object you want to link to. Highlight the file with the mouse (the name will appear in the File name box) and click Open.
4. The Command line box will now contain the name and location of the object. Click Next and accept or change the name for the shortcut.
5. Click Finish and the shortcut appears on your desktop or in the folder where you started.

To Moved or Renamed Originals

As has been mentioned, the shortcut is only a pointer to the original object—a pretty smart pointer, but with limitations. If you move the original object, the shortcut can usually find it. (It may take a few seconds the first time for the search to be made.) Even renaming the original object doesn't thwart Windows 98.

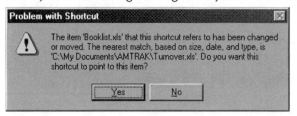

However, if you move the original across drives or both move and rename the original object, the system will search and come up with a suggestion. Admittedly, the suggestion is often wrong if you've moved the original to another drive.

If the proposed solution is correct, click Yes. If it's not, select No. Right-click the shortcut and select Properties. In the property sheet, provide the correct path for the shortcut.

WARNING **Shortcuts to DOS programs will probably not be so forgiving. So if you move your DOS-based game to another drive or rename a batch file, plan on making a new shortcut.**

Customizing Shortcuts

You can customize any shortcut you create to specify how the program should run or to change its icon. Such changes are made on the shortcut's property sheet. Right-click the shortcut, select Properties, and you will see a property sheet similar to Figure 3.13.

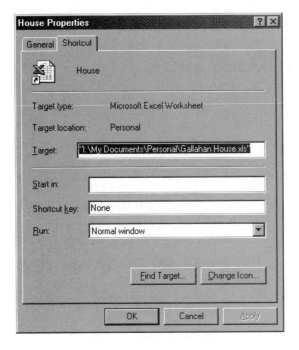

FIGURE 3.13:
The property sheet for a short-cut called House

The General page of the property sheet contains information about the shortcut file. On the Shortcut page you can set the following options:

Target contains the command line to start the program or open the document. You can add any command line parameters that the program may require. If the shortcut isn't working because the target file has been moved, click the Find Target button to browse for the file.

Start In allows you to specify a default directory for the program's data files. However, if the program has its own method for specifying such a directory, the Start In field will generally be ignored.

Shortcut Key sets up a key combination to quickly start the program from the keyboard. This only works for shortcuts on the desktop. Use Windows Help to get the details: Click the ? button in the upper right corner of the window, then click in the Shortcut Key box.

Run is a drop-down list where you can choose how the program should start: in a normal window, minimized, or maximized.

Use the Change Icon button to select a different icon for the shortcut. If you don't like the initial offerings, click Browse to look for more. When you find one you want, highlight it and click OK.

Learning to Recycle

The Recycle Bin is a permanent icon on the desktop that represents a storage place for your deleted files. It's insurance against that inevitable day when you delete an irreplaceable file (or two).

Setting It Up

To check the settings, right-click the Recycle Bin, then select Properties. You'll see a Global tab as well as tabs for each hard drive on your system. You can change any of the settings, but the default settings are probably optimal—unless:

- Your hard drive is very full and you can't spare the default ten percent that the Recycle Bin takes for deleted files.
- Your hard drive is very large and the default setting reserves more space than is necessary.

If you have more than one hard drive (or multiple partitions) and want to use different settings on each, you have to select Configure Drives Independently on the Global tab.

TIP   The Recycle Bin is a very nice safety device, but there are definitely times when you know you absolutely, positively want to delete something and you don't want those deadbeat files sitting around taking up space. In that case, you can delete a file once and for all by holding down the Shift key while you click Delete. Be cautious, because this is permanent, and there's no way to recover a file that's been deleted in this way.

Recovering Files

When you need to recover a file that's been sent to the Recycle Bin, click the Recycle Bin icon to open a window like the one shown in Figure 3.14, then follow these steps:

1. Select the View menu and click Details.

2. Click the Date Deleted button at the top of the date column. Click again to reverse the date order. That'll bring the most recently deleted files to the top of the list. (Of course, you can sort using any of the other criteria if you think that'll make finding the file easier.)

3. Find the file you want to undelete and highlight the name. To restore more than one file, press the Ctrl button and hold it down while you select the files.

4. Click the right mouse button and select Restore from the menu. The file or files will be restored to their original directories.

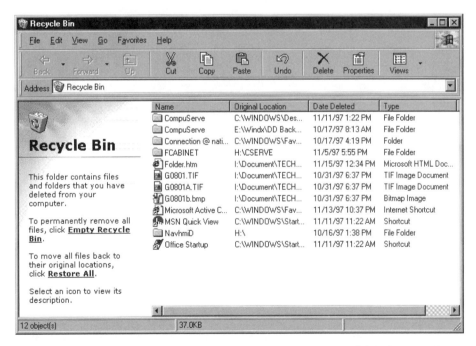

FIGURE 3.14:   The contents of the Recycle Bin in Details view. You can click the button at the top of a column to sort the list by that parameter. Click the button again to reverse the sort order.

Of course you can always click the file and simply drag it out of the Recycle Bin. It'll be restored to wherever you drag it.

WARNING Files deleted from a floppy disk will not be saved to the Recycle Bin. However, you will see a dialog box warning you of this fact before the deletion is carried out, so you won't be taken unawares.

Emptying the Bin

The easiest way to empty the Recycle Bin is to right-click the icon and select Empty Recycle Bin from the menu. To get rid of particular files, open the Recycle Bin by clicking the icon. Hold down the Ctrl key while clicking the object(s) you want to banish. Then press the Delete key or click the Delete button on the toolbar.

Running Programs

To run a program in Windows 98, just go to Programs in the Start menu, click on the correct folder, and click the program. This will certainly do for programs you use fairly infrequently. For programs you use often, you may want to create a shortcut on the desktop. As shown in Figure 3.6, you can also group shortcuts to programs in a folder, along with related documents that you use for a particular project.

There's also a StartUp folder where you can put programs that you want loaded when you start Windows 98 (more about this feature coming up). Use the property sheet to set how these programs should run.

Organizing the Start Menu

When you open the Start menu and select Programs, you'll see a list of programs you can open instantly. Many programs will automatically add themselves to this list when you install them. However, since this list is so handy to use, you'll probably want to customize it.

Adding Items

You probably have some programs that you use frequently but not often enough to have them cluttering up your desktop. The Start menu is an excellent place for such applications. To add a program to the Start menu, follow these steps:

1. Find a shortcut to the program. If you can't find one, create one as described in "How to Take Shortcuts," a few pages back. Be sure the shortcut has the name that you want in the Start menu.

2. Drag the shortcut to the Start button. If you want the shortcut to appear at the top of the Start menu, as shown in Figure 3.15, just drop it on the Start button. You're done.

FIGURE 3.15:
To add programs to the top of the Start menu, it's just a matter of drag and drop.

3. If you want the program to appear on the Programs menu off of the Start menu, hold the shortcut over the Start button until the Start menu opens.
4. While still dragging the shortcut, move to the Programs menu, and to a sub-menu if you wish. The horizontal black line shows where the shortcut will appear on the menu when you drop it (see Figure 3.16).

You can place shortcuts to any object on the Start menu along with programs. When you select any item on the menu, Windows 98 will open that item for you to use.

TIP **You can rearrange the shortcuts at the top of the main Start menu and on the Programs, Favorites, and Documents sub-menus by dragging them around to where you want them.**

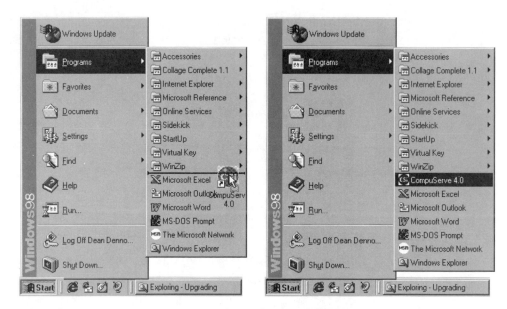

FIGURE 3.16: Positioning a shortcut on the Programs menu, and the result when you drop it

Deleting Items

When you install a new program, it will often put a shortcut on the Start menu. If you don't want it there, just right-click it and choose Delete. The same thing works for shortcuts on the Programs and Documents menus, and on the sub-menus under Programs and Favorites. Remember, this only deletes the shortcut, not the program.

NOTE
The Start menu and its tree of sub-menus starting from Programs reflect the contents of the Start menu folder in the Windows folder. The Advanced button on the Start Menu Programs page opens Windows Explorer with the Start menu folder at the top of the tree. You can easily rearrange the menu structure by dragging and dropping shortcuts and folders in Windows Explorer.

Using the StartUp Folder

If you want a particular program to start each time Windows starts, do this:

1. Find or create a shortcut to the program.
2. Drag the shortcut to the Start button and hold it there until the Start menu opens.

3. Continue dragging the shortcut. Drag it up to Programs; when the Programs menu opens, drag it to StartUp and into the StartUp group, then drop it.

4. If you want to set how the program should run, right-click the shortcut you just added and choose Properties.

Using the Document Menu

To open a document you've used recently, click Start ➢ Documents. Select the document from the list, and Windows 98 will open the document in whatever application it requires.

Windows 98 will add shortcuts to recently used documents to this menu until it becomes quite large. To clear the Documents menu, follow these steps.

1. Click the Start button and select Settings ➢ Taskbar & Start Menu.

2. Click the Start Menu Programs tab.

3. Click the Clear button and then OK.

The Documents menu will be completely cleared.

To remove a specific document from the Documents menu, right-click it and choose Delete.

| TIP | Some programs can't add files to the Documents menu. If you need to find a recently used document that isn't there, click the Start button, point to Find, then to Files and Folders, and click once. Chapter 5 has more on using the Find function. |

What's Next

In the next chapter, we turn our attention from the items on the desktop to the character of the desktop itself. We'll show you how to adjust and tweak it to your preferences, and how to use active elements to keep up with the latest from your favorite Internet sites—automatically.

AS YOU LIKE IT

In the last chapter, we discussed how the Windows 98 desktop can work like a Web browser. There is another difference between the new desktop and earlier versions. Your desktop can now include Internet-based content. You can put a Web page on your desktop and have it update automatically. You can even include active Web-based components that provide a continuous stream of information.

The taskbar has evolved, too—it now has a quick access area. You can click the Desktop icon to instantly clear the desktop by minimizing all open windows. You can also drag shortcuts to this area for easy access even when folder or application windows hide the desktop icons. In addition, Taskbar buttons now blink to tell you when a program running in the background needs attention.

Let's take a tour of the desktop.

For Appearance' Sake

The desktop includes the overall display, the Taskbar, and some fairly permanent objects such as the My Computer and Recycle Bin icons. Of course, you'll have other objects, both temporary and permanent, based on your individual installation.

To change the desktop's overall appearance, move the mouse pointer to an empty patch of desktop and click the right mouse button. Select Properties from the menu that opens. The dialog that opens is the property sheet for your display. It is headed Display Properties (see Figure 4.1), and has tabs for setting various aspects of the display. To move from one page to another, click on a tab. Click the OK button when you're done.

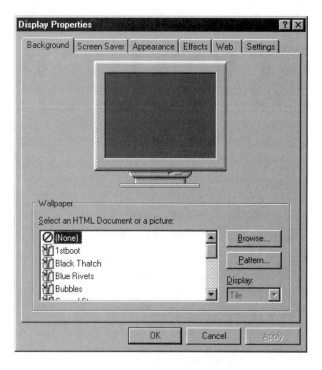

FIGURE 4.1: Most of the settings for the appearance of your desktop are available in the Display Properties dialog box.

For Windows 3.1 Users
Just What Are Property Sheets?

A Property Sheet is the dialog box that opens when you right-click an object and choose Properties from the pop-up menu. Just about everything on the desktop (and everywhere else in your Windows 98 system) has a property sheet attached to it.

What you find on the property sheet can vary from the single sheet of information attached to a typical file to the multipage extravaganza described here for the display. The role of the property sheet is to provide you with information on the object and allow you to change its settings.

If the object is a file or a folder, you'll get information about the object's size, location, dates created and modified, and attributes. If the object is a piece of hardware or the desktop (or anything on the desktop like the Taskbar or the Recycle Bin), the property sheet will have multiple pages and cover all the possible settings for the object in question.

As a rule, when you see something you don't understand or just want to know more about, try the property sheet first. You can often find as much as you need to know right there and save yourself an unnecessary trip to the Help system.

Establish a Background

You can select wallpaper from the rather limited list provided, or you can click the Browse button and select any .BMP file you happen to have lying around. The Wallpaper Display drop-down list determines how your bitmap image will be displayed: it can be centered or it can be either stretched or tiled to fill the background.

Find a neat image on the Web that you'd like to use as wallpaper? Here's one way:

1. Adjust your Internet Explorer window so the entire image you want is displayed.
2. Press the Print Screen key (or PrtSc) to save an image of your screen on the Windows clipboard.

3. Start the Windows Paint program (Start ➤ Programs ➤ Accessories ➤ Paint).
4. Paste the clipboard image into Paint by pressing Ctrl+V.
5. Select the part of the image you want to use. (See Chapter 13 for more about using Paint.)
6. Choose Copy To on the Edit menu to save the selected area as a .bmp file. Save it in the main Windows folder.
7. Close Paint. Your file will now appear on the list of available wallpaper.

TIP   **To add bitmaps to the list of wallpaper available, move .bmp files to the \Windows folder.**

You can use a background pattern either instead of wallpaper or to surround a centered wallpaper image. Set the Wallpaper to None or the Display drop-down list to Center to enable the Pattern button. Once selected, any of the patterns can be edited by selecting the Edit Pattern button.

Choose a Screen Saver

Windows 98 comes with several screen savers that are a bit better than the Windows 95 selection. You can click on the Screen Saver tab (see Figure 4.2) and select one of them. Or you can install your own amazingly cool screen saver such as Second Nature or After Dark and gain access to the settings through this page.

If you want to hide your screen from the eyes of casually prying coworkers when you take a coffee break, check the box labeled Password Protected. Then click the Change button and enter a password that will be required to restore your screen after the screen saver has been activated.

The Screen Saver page of Display Properties also gives quick access to Power Management functions. Click the Configure button near the bottom of the page to set times for monitor off and system standby functions. These are described more fully in the Power Management section of Chapter 11.

Set the Decor

Click on the Appearance tab to set the color scheme and size of window elements such as title bars. The included color schemes are generally more usable in Windows 98 than in previous versions. There are also quite a few schemes with large and/or high contrast elements to assist users with limited vision.

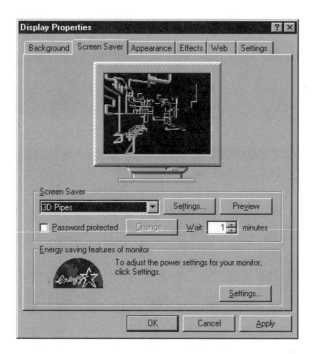

FIGURE 4.2:
Here's where you
make screen saver
settings.

Being Picky

The Appearance page also lets you adjust practically any part of a window in all
sorts of ways, no matter how ridiculous. Select a component either by clicking directly
on the sample screen or by selecting it from the Item drop-down list. Adjust the size,
colors, or font of as many windows and window elements as you like. When you're
done, you can save your whole arrangement as a new scheme by clicking the Save As
button.

Icon Spacing

Settings for the spacing of icons on the desktop are hidden away on the Appearance
page. Pull down the Item drop-down list and select one of the icon spacing choices.
You can also select Icon and change both the size of your icons and their font.
However, we strongly recommend that you make note of the original settings, because
it's fairly easy to make a hash of your desktop and not remember where you started.

TIP When available, the Apply button lets you see the outcome of your
choices without closing the property sheet. If you like what you see,
click OK to close the sheet. Otherwise, you can try different settings
and click Apply again to see the outcome.

Make a Resolution

The Settings page of Display Properties (see Figure 4.3) allows you to make resolution changes—to the extent your hardware supports them. Select an available resolution by dragging the Screen Area slider. You can also change the color depth, using the Colors drop-down list.

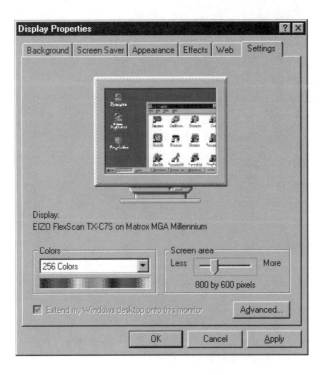

FIGURE 4.3:
Don't be afraid to experiment with the display. Windows 98 won't let you do anything you can't undo.

If you make a change and then click either OK or Apply, the system will attempt to implement the change. In fact, your screen may disappear in a welter of static for about fifteen seconds and have the appearance of being invaded by space aliens. If the change is possible (as defined by your hardware), the new screen will appear. If the change can't be done, Windows 98 will inform you of the fact and restore your previous settings.

If the desktop area or color depth you want is not available, it's possible that Windows 98 has incorrect information about your video adapter or display. Click Advanced to open the property sheet for your video hardware. Check the Adapter and Monitor tabs to see how Windows 98 has identified your display hardware. If the information shown on either page is wrong, or you suspect newer drivers might be available to improve performance, click the Change button.

If you have an Internet connection set up, Windows 98 can connect to the Windows Update Web site to check the availability of newer drivers. The Update Wizard will start and walk you through the necessary steps. The Wizard's second dialog (your first decision point) is shown in Figure 4.4.

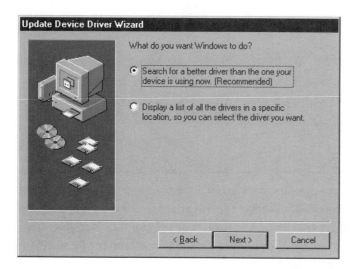

FIGURE 4.4:
The Update Wizard is a big help when dealing with driver issues.

An accurate driver search depends on correct identification of your hardware. If your hardware is correctly identified and you want to check for newer drivers, choose the option to search for a better driver and click Next. In the following dialog box, choose the place you want to search. If you have newer drivers on a diskette or CD, check the appropriate drive. The Microsoft Windows Update option will only be available if you have set up an Internet connection. Click Next again and continue through the steps of the wizard. If you chose to use Windows Update, the Web site will require you to register your copy of Windows 98, if you have not already done so.

If the Adapter or Monitor page showed incorrect or generic hardware information, cancel the Internet connection and choose the second option in the dialog shown in Figure 4.4. Click Next to proceed to the dialog box shown in Figure 4.5.

If it's the monitor you need to change, and you have an information disk that came with it, insert the disk and click Have Disk. If you don't have a disk supplied by the monitor manufacturer, try any alternate designations Windows 98 offers under Show Compatible Devices. If this doesn't work, you may need to select Show All Devices for a complete list of options.

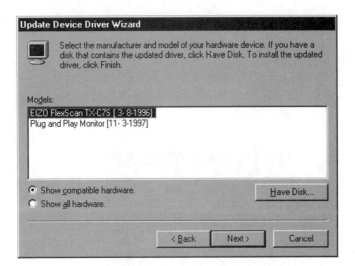

FIGURE 4.5:
Here's where you can fix a problem of mistaken identity.

WARNING   **If your monitor isn't listed, look for a monitor from the same manufacturer with similar specifications, but be careful not to select one whose maximum resolution or refresh rate is higher than those of your monitor. You could damage your monitor by sending it signals it can't handle.**

Incorrect identification of your video adapter is less likely, unless it's one that came on the market after Windows 98. In that case, you should have a driver disk from the manufacturer. For hardware that Windows 98 knows about, you might still want to use the manufacturer's driver, if it offers options not included in the Windows 98 driver. Make note of the current adapter identification (as shown in Figure 4.6), in case you want to return to it.

The Adapter page also includes a refresh rate setting. Generally, this should be set to Optimal, but remember that it will only function properly if both your video adapter and your monitor are properly identified. If the Optimal setting leaves you with a screen that seems to flicker, you can choose a refresh rate from the drop-down list, but remember: check your monitor's documentation and *never* set a refresh rate higher than the specified maximum.

There are three other tabs on the property sheet for your video hardware. On the General page is a setting labeled Font Size. You can use it to change from the default font sizes to a set of larger fonts. The change will affect all fonts, from the desktop and menus to your word processor and most other applications. It will also affect on-screen rulers and other features that relate screen image size to printed or real world size. This is because the Font Size setting determines what Windows 98 considers to be 100 percent sizing. The default assumption (using the Small Fonts setting) is that 96 dots on the screen equals one inch. Changing Font Size to Large Fonts sets Windows 98 to assume 120 dots per inch.

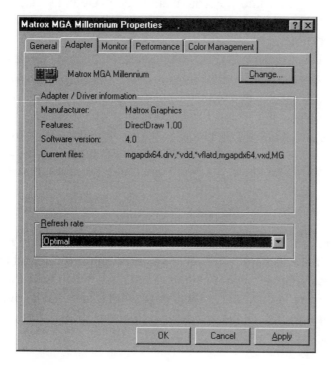

FIGURE 4.6:
The Adapter page at Display Properties ➤ Settings ➤ Advanced. If your adapter is incorrectly identified, change it here.

WARNING If you change to Large Fonts, you will probably need to change your icon spacing, as described in the preceding "Set the Decor" section. You may also find that dialog boxes in some applications do not display correctly, if the application developer failed to design them with large fonts in mind.

If you want accurate on-screen sizing, here's how to get it: choose Other in the Font Size drop-down list. Hold a ruler against the screen, with its zero mark aligned to the zero of the ruler in the Custom Font Size dialog. Drag any part of the on-screen ruler so that the inch marks align with your physical ruler. When you have it right, click OK. You will see a message to the effect that system font changes will not occur until you install the fonts and restart the computer. When you OK the dialog box, you will see another, similar message. Click Yes to continue. Be forewarned: while Windows 98 system fonts resize nicely, many fonts, such as those used in some application menus, will suffer from the resizing that results. Fortunately, you can return to the standard Small Fonts size setting the same way you abandoned it. Open Display Properties, choose Settings, click Advanced, and choose Small Fonts from the drop-down list. So don't be afraid to experiment.

The settings in the Compatibility section of the General page, as well as those on the Performance page, only need to be changed if you have problems with your display. The dialog box explains the settings, and a bit more detail is available if you right-click a setting and then click the What's This button that pops up.

The Color Management tab allows you to fine-tune the colors displayed by your monitor by installing a color profile. Click Add to begin the process. This is mainly of interest to graphic arts professionals who want on-screen colors to come as close as possible to matching colors produced on a printing press.

NOTE One of the cool features of Windows 98 is the ability to support multiple displays. You need a second monitor connected to its own video adapter on your computer's PCI bus. If you have this, and it's properly set up, the Settings page will be replaced by one labeled Monitors. Check the Windows Help index under Multiple Display Support for details on how to set it up.

Effects

The Effects page allows you to change the icons used for My Computer, My Documents, the Network Neighborhood, and the Recycle Bin. You can also set a number of other screen options:

Hide icons when desktop is viewed as Web page   With this option you can hide your desktop icons for a better view of background Active Desktop displays.

Use large icons   Larger icons provide better visibility.

Show icons using all possible colors   This option displays icons in the full color range you selected on the Settings page. If unchecked, icons are limited to 256 colors.

Use menu animations   With this option checked, menus appear to slide open, instead of just appearing in a flash.

Smooth edges of screen fonts   This setting will improve the appearance of large fonts.

Show window contents while dragging   This option should be disabled if your display takes a long time to clear up after you drag a window.

NOTE   **Many of the features included in the Plus! Pack for Windows 95, which had to be purchased separately, are rolled into Windows 98. This includes some of the features on the Effects page.**

Activate Your Desktop

The Web tab of Display Properties is where you go to set up HTML items for your desktop. These could be web pages (especially ones that are updated frequently), or other HTML items, including ones with active elements such as a stock ticker or continuous news or weather feeds. Many such items will only be practical if you have a full-time Internet or intranet connection, or spend lots of time online.

NOTE   **The following sections on setting up Active Desktop elements assume that you already have a working connection to the Internet, whether via a modem or over a local area network. If you had either Windows 95 or Windows 3.1 set up with Internet Explorer as your Web browser, and you installed Windows 98 as an upgrade, you should be ready to go. If you have no Internet service or need to set it up in Windows 98, or if you encounter problems, go to Chapter 6 to get your Internet connection working before you continue with this section.**

Getting Stuff

HTML items can be added to your desktop in several ways. Clicking New on the Web tab (Figure 4.7) will open a dialog asking if you want to connect to the Active Desktop Gallery on Microsoft's Web site. If you answer Yes, you can try out items designed as Active Desktop components. If you like a component, just click the Add to My Desktop button.

WARNING　**If you are connecting to the Internet for the first time after installing Windows 98, you are likely to see a warning message to the effect that file and printer sharing are enabled on your TCP/IP connection. You should follow the recommendation given in the message and disable file and printer sharing on your Internet connection. If you are connecting to a corporate intranet, check with the system administrator.**

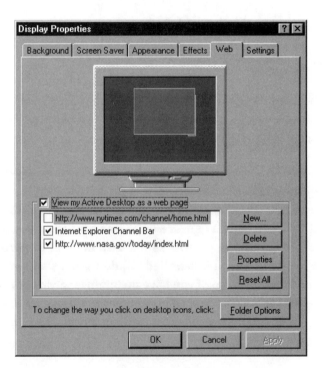

FIGURE 4.7:
Use the Web tab of Display Properties to set up HTML items for your desktop.

You will see a security alert dialog asking if you wish to add a desktop item to your desktop, followed by a confirmation dialog similar to Figure 4.8. If you want to customize the update schedule, click Customize Subscription to start the Subscription Wizard, which is explained in the next section. Otherwise, just OK the dialog. The item will be downloaded and added to your desktop.

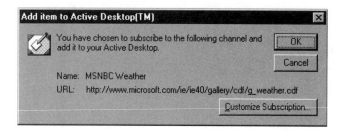

FIGURE 4.8:
Adding an item to your Active Desktop

If you have a Web page in mind that you want to put on your desktop, click No in the Gallery dialog (if it appears) and you will see the New Active Desktop Item dialog. You can type in the web address (Uniform Resource Locator or URL) or click Browse to search for it on your computer. The Browse process starts in your Favorites folder. When you find the site you want, highlight it and click Open to put the URL in the Location box.

If the site isn't in your Favorites folder, you might open Internet Explorer and either search your History folder or go online to find it. When you find the site, highlight the URL in Internet Explorer's address box and copy it with Ctrl+C. Return to the New Active Desktop Item dialog and paste the URL into the Location box with Ctrl+V.

NOTE   Companies that operate their own intranets may require you to include specific intranet pages or active items on your desktop. For example, these might be company or departmental news pages. Your system administrator will have the necessary information on how to set up such items.

Once you have entered the URL you want in the New Active Desktop Item dialog, click OK. Windows 98 will connect to the Web site you specified and present the dialog box shown in Figure 4.8. If the Web site you have chosen does not require you to log in, and you don't want to customize the update schedule, just click OK again. Otherwise, click Customize Subscription to start the Subscription Wizard.

NOTE Don't let the term "subscription" worry you. No commitment or money is involved, and subscribing doesn't send any special information about you to the web site. You are simply telling *your computer* when and how to update the information for your desktop component.

The Subscription Wizard

The Subscription Wizard helps you to set up a simple set of options for how your Active Desktop item will be updated. It starts with the page shown in Figure 4.9. Here you select either scheduled or manual updating, and set the schedule if you wish.

FIGURE 4.9:
Choosing the update schedule for an Active Desktop item

For automatic updating of your Active Desktop item, choose Scheduled. From the drop-down list you then have several choices of update frequency including Daily, Weekly, and Monthly. Items designed for the Active Desktop may also include a publisher's recommended update schedule. You can also create your own schedule by clicking the New button, or modify the schedule you've chosen by clicking Edit. If you use a dial-up connection for Internet access, scheduled updates will only work if you check the box labeled Dial As Needed If Connected Through A Modem.

If you choose to update your item manually, it (and all your other subscriptions) will be updated when you choose Update All Subscriptions from the Favorites menu in Internet Explorer or any open folder.

The Subscription Wizard may have one more page; if the Web site requires you to identify yourself by logging on, enter your user name and password for the site.

TIP
All of the options set in the Subscribe Wizard, and a few more including Unsubscribe, can be found on the property sheet for your subscription. You can get to it by going to the Web tab of Display Properties, selecting the item, and clicking Properties. The Schedule page of this property sheet also has an Update Now button. This is the only way to update a single desktop item (as opposed to updating all your subscriptions).

Whether or not you run the Subscription Wizard, when you OK the Add Item To Active Desktop dialog, Windows will connect to the site you have chosen to download it, and it will be displayed in a window, on the HTML layer of your desktop, as shown in Figure 4.10.

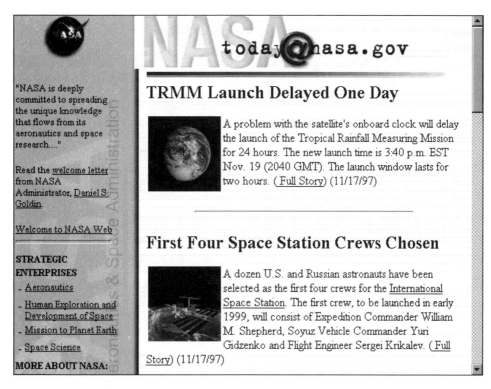

FIGURE 4.10:   A Web site as displayed on the Active Desktop. Notice the absence of space-wasting window borders.

Arranging Your Desktop Items

HTML items on the Active Desktop use a streamlined window design that has very few controls and virtually eliminates wasted space. Normally, these windows have no borders at all. Move your mouse pointer into the window and it grows a very thin border, indicating it is the active window and will respond to your mouse clicks.

To size the window, point to an edge. The border becomes more prominent and your pointer changes to the familiar two-headed sizing arrow. If you point to the top edge of the window, it will sprout a mini-title bar (see Figure 4.11). You can drag this title bar to move the window. It also has two buttons: an x to close the window and a down-pointing arrow that opens a simple control menu.

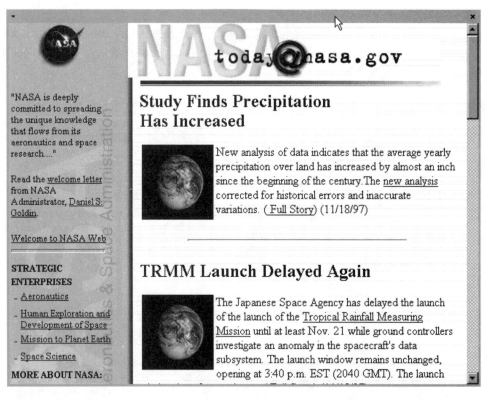

FIGURE 4.11: The mini-title bar only appears when you move your mouse pointer near the top of the window.

HTML items on your desktop are on the bottom of a two-layer desktop (under the "glass," if you will). An HTML item is active when your mouse pointer is in it, but it remains behind any application window or folder that overlaps it. To see the entire HTML item, you will need to move it or move or minimize the window that is obscuring it. You can use the Show Desktop button in the Quick Launch section of the Taskbar to minimize all application windows and folders.

Once you have a clear view of the desktop, you may find that the item you are interested in is partially obscured by another HTML item. Bring the item you want to the top of the stack by clicking any edge of the window.

Items on the desktop's HTML layer cannot be minimized. If you close an item by using the controls on its title bar, you can get it back by returning to the Web tab of Display Properties. Just check the box in front of that item in the list. You can close all of your desktop HTML items by clearing the check mark from the box labeled View My Active Desktop As A Web Page. The items will return when you click the box to put back the check.

The Flexible Taskbar

Like other parts of the desktop, the Windows 98 Taskbar is considerably more flexible than its predecessor. By default, the Taskbar occupies the bottom of the desktop. From left to right, it includes the Start button, the Quick Launch toolbar, the active windows area, and the System Tray.

The active windows area includes a button for each open folder or application on your desktop. This is where windows live when they are minimized. Click a button to restore its window or bring it to the top of the stack. Clicking the Taskbar button of the currently active window will minimize it.

Adjustments

To make your own settings for the Taskbar, click the Start button and select Settings ➢ Taskbar & Start Menu. There are four settings you can make on the Taskbar Options page:

Always on top   Check this box if you want to be able to see the Taskbar even when a program is running full screen. This means you can switch to another program on the Taskbar without having to use the minimize or restore buttons.

Auto hide   Check this box and the Taskbar will appear only when you move the mouse to the bottom of the screen. Both Always on top and Auto hide have to be selected if you want the Taskbar to be available (but not always visible) when running a program full-screen.

Show small icons in Start menu   Check this box and the sample window will show you how the smaller icons look.

Show clock   Remove the check mark if you don't want the Taskbar to remind you of the time.

Besides the clock, the System Tray at the right end of the Taskbar has icons for programs that generally operate in the background. If you have a sound card, there will be a volume control. When your modem is in use, there will be a connection information icon. A fax icon will appear when you are sending a fax, and so on. Click or right-click (in some cases) on these icons to open a small window with information about the current state of the operation.

TIP   **You don't have to leave the Taskbar in its original size or position. Click on a blank portion of the Taskbar and you can drag it to the top or either side of your screen. If it's too wide or too narrow for your taste, move the pointer to the edge of the Taskbar. When the pointer turns into a two-headed arrow, click and drag the edge to resize it.**

And Additions

Apart from the Start button and System Tray, the rest of the Taskbar is now made up of toolbars. This means you can rearrange and add to the Taskbar in many different ways.

You can add any shortcut you like to the Quick Launch toolbar. Just drag it there.

TIP   **If you would prefer larger icons on the Quick Launch toolbar, point to the vertical bar at the left end of the toolbar and right-click. On the menu, choose View ➤ Large. The height of the Taskbar will increase to make room for the larger icons.**

Would you prefer the Quick Launch toolbar beside the System Tray? Click on the vertical bar at the left end of the Quick Launch toolbar and drag it to the right. Drop it where you want it, and notice what happens to the active window area of the Taskbar. Now try dragging the Quick Launch toolbar back beside the Start button. At this point, the active windows area will be compressed at the right end of the Taskbar. Just grab its vertical bar and drag left to give it some breathing room.

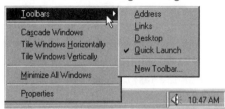

If you right-click in an empty area of the Taskbar, you will get a menu. Select Toolbars, and in the flyout you can add and delete toolbars from the Taskbar.

You probably wouldn't want to remove the Quick Launch toolbar, but you could just by unchecking it on the menu. Check Desktop to add a toolbar that includes all the shortcuts and other icons on your desktop. Such a Desktop toolbar will probably have too many buttons for all of them to fit on the Taskbar. Click the tiny triangles (arrow heads) at either end of the taskbar to scroll through the buttons.

The ultimate in Taskbar flexibility arrives when you click New Toolbar. A browse window opens in which you can navigate to any folder on your machine. When you click OK, the folder's contents appear as a toolbar on the Taskbar. To have enough space for such a toolbar to be useful, drag the upper edge of the Taskbar to enlarge it to two or three rows. Then drag the new toolbar into one of the new rows. Figure 4.12 shows the Finances folder from Figure 3.6, now appearing as a toolbar.

FIGURE 4.12:   Another way of using the customized Finances folder

You can also drag any toolbar onto your desktop, then shape and size it as you like.

Move the toolbar back to the Taskbar the same way. Close it by clicking the x in the upper right corner. To close a toolbar on the Taskbar, right-click on the toolbar and choose Close. Either way, you will see a Confirm Toolbar Close dialog that tells you how to get it back.

WARNING You can close any toolbar, whether on the Taskbar or on the desktop, without affecting the folder on which the toolbar is based. However, deleting an individual item from the toolbar also deletes it from the folder. You can retrieve it from the Recycle Bin, if necessary.

NOTE The active windows area of the Taskbar isn't a toolbar, even though it looks similar to the toolbars you might create. You can move the active windows area around on the Taskbar, but you can't close it or drag it to the desktop.

What's Next

The next chapter expands your view of the Explorer. It has a whole lot more about configuration, and you'll learn some neat tricks that Windows 98 can perform to make your work easier.

EXPLORING IN WINDOWS

Windows Explorer is the part of Windows 98 that gives you an overall view of the drives, folders, and files in your system. Everything that's on your computer or local area network can be found using Windows Explorer. If you are upgrading from Windows 3.1, you will probably use Windows Explorer a lot, because it looks somewhat familiar. After a while, though, you may use it less as you become familiar with alternate ways to get at files and start programs.

In this chapter, we'll cover how Windows Explorer works and the special tricks that it does best.

Starting Out

Windows Explorer offers the traditional way of viewing folders and files located on hard drives and other resources available on your machine (see Figure 5.1). The default Explorer is a two-pane window. When you click on an item in the left window pane, the right pane displays the contents. You can get another look by selecting another choice from the View menu.

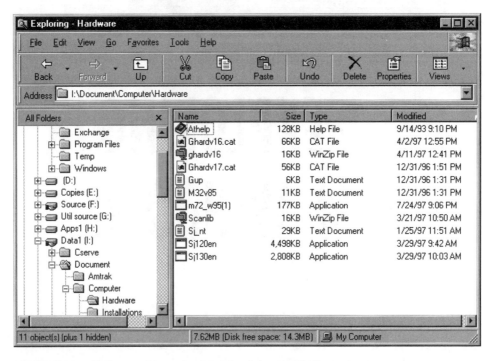

FIGURE 5.1:   Windows Explorer at its most informative: Details view

---

TIP   **More than one instance of Windows Explorer can be opened at a time. In fact, that's often the easiest way to move files from one place to another.**

The Explorer is always available from the Start menu. Click on the Start button, slide the pointer to Programs, then to Windows Explorer, and click.

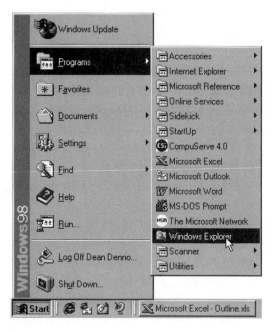

If you find yourself using it often, you may want to put a shortcut to the Windows Explorer on your desktop. Here's a quick way:

1. Begin as if opening Windows Explorer: click Start and slide the mouse pointer to Programs, then Windows Explorer.

2. Using the right mouse button, drag the Windows Explorer shortcut out onto your desktop.

3. When you release the right mouse button, a pop-up menu appears. Choose Copy Here or Create Shortcut Here. (Because it's a shortcut you're dragging, the result is the same.)

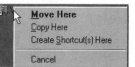

TIP

If you have selected single-click desktop operation, the right pane of Windows Explorer will work that way, too. However, the left pane remains double-click territory. This means you can still click a folder twice, in the left pane only, to rename it.

A Look Inside

Inside Windows Explorer, folders are organized in a fashion that doesn't look all that different from Windows 3.1 or DOS, except that the top level folder/directory is called Desktop and the file names look peculiar.

Extending Yourself

You'll probably notice first that most files shown in Windows Explorer's right pane are missing their extensions. The thinking behind this is that these files are registered (in other words, the system knows what they are and where they came from) and can be activated by merely clicking on them—so why would you need to know the extension?

In a perfect world, of course, you wouldn't. But the Explorer screen shown in Figure 5.2 demonstrates how confusion can arise. There are two files called Capture and three called Imgmgr. Of course, if you look closely, you can probably discern which files are the actual program files, but you may find it more convenient to change the default view by following these steps:

1. Open Windows Explorer.
2. Click the View menu and select Folder Options.
3. Click the View tab, then click the box next to "Hide file extensions for known file types" to remove the check mark. Click OK when you're done.

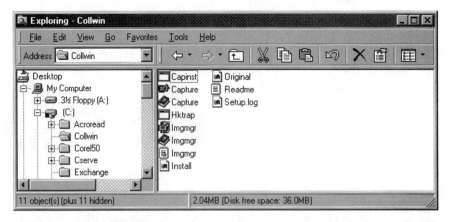

FIGURE 5.2:   In some cases, the lack of extensions can prove confusing—especially when there is more than one file with the same name.

TIP	If you really want to see everything, look under Hidden Files and select Show All Files, so even hidden and system files will show in Windows Explorer.

Of course, many if not most of the programs you'll be using will be started using the Start menu or from the desktop itself, so the file extensions will come to mean less and less from the user's standpoint as time goes on.

Exploring Folders

As with Windows 95, Windows 98 makes it convenient to set up folders that constitute work areas or project areas. For example, the folder in Figure 5.3 contains everything needed to work on this book: various versions of the outline, shortcuts to the printer and a zip utility program, chapters currently in progress, and folders for illustrations and completed chapters. You can make folders for a variety of purposes depending on how you like to work.

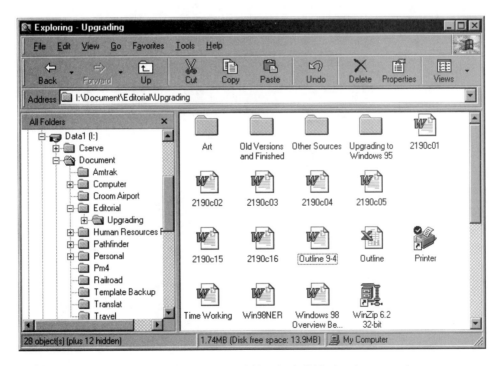

FIGURE 5.3: Use Windows Explorer to set up folders for individual projects or work areas.

NOTE Note the plus and minus signs next to folders. A plus sign means there's at least one more layer of folders that you can see if you click on the plus icon. Click on the minus sign and the lower level will collapse into the upper level.

Windows Explorer is generally the easiest way to pull together and organize the components of such a folder. Once you have it set up, opening it in its own window (as discussed in the "Working with Folders" section of Chapter 3) reduces the amount of space it takes up. Just open My Computer and navigate down to the folder you've set up. To save space, you might remove and re-arrange toolbars, as in Figure 5.4. Depending on your work style, you may find a Details view more useful.

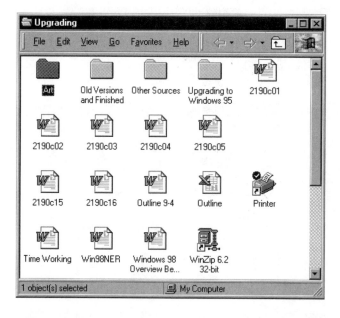

FIGURE 5.4:
The same folder shown in the previous figure, open on the desktop for daily use

Finally, if you don't want the folder open all the time, but want quick access to it, create a desktop shortcut:

1. With the folder open, click the Up button on the toolbar.
2. Using the right mouse button, drag the folder's icon to the desktop.
3. Choose Create Shortcut(s) Here from the menu that pops up when you release the right mouse button.

Moving and Copying Things

The way you work with files and folders, as with everything else in Windows 98, is designed to be consistent and easy to use. You'll use drag and drop to do most things. Once you get the hang of it, it's strictly a no-brainer.

Files and Folders

As in Windows 3.1, you can move an object within a drive by clicking on it with the mouse and then dragging it to its new location. To copy the object, you perform the same action while holding down the Ctrl key. Of course, if you're dragging and dropping across drives, you get a copy of the file or folder no matter what key you're holding down. What a pain.

However, Windows 98 has a much easier way to move, copy, or create a shortcut for an object without having to remember what drive everything's on or what key to hold down for what action. There are basically two methods: one for when you can see the object you want to move and its destination, and one for when the destination is out of sight.

When You Can See It

This is the easiest possible action. To copy or move a file or folder, click it with the right mouse button and drag it to the new location. When you release the mouse button, you can choose Copy, Move, Create Shortcut(s), or forget the whole thing (Cancel).

For a bunch of files or folders, hold the right mouse button and draw a box around the whole bunch. Ignore the pop-up menu that appears when you release the mouse button. Then use the right button to drag the box to the new location. Again, you get the choice of Move, Copy, Create Shortcut(s), or Cancel, next to the outline of the selected objects.

TIP   **You can still select multiple objects in Windows Explorer or any folder by holding down the Ctrl key and clicking them one at a time. If you want to select all the files in a range, highlight the first object, hold down the Shift key, and select the last object in the series.**

And When You Can't

Moving or copying objects is a two-step process when you don't have all the pieces in view. Of course, you can always open two copies of Windows Explorer or open both folders (when you're moving files between folders), but we think the quickest way is to use the right-mouse button menu. Here's how to copy an object:

1. Click the object with the right mouse button and select Copy.
2. Open the folder where you want the copy to go. Right-click on a blank area inside the folder.
3. Select Paste from the menu.

NOTE   **To move an object, right-click it and select Cut from the menu. The object only dims—that is, it doesn't disappear from the old location until you select Paste in the new location to complete the move.**

Multiple Objects

To move or copy more than one object when the destination isn't visible on the screen, just take these steps:

1. Select the group of objects by using the right mouse button to draw a box around them (see Figure 5.5).

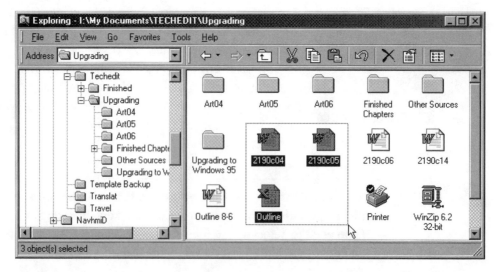

FIGURE 5.5:   One easy way to select multiple objects is to use the mouse to draw a box around them.

2. Release the mouse button. The pop-up menu appears. Select Cut or Copy.
3. Open the destination folder and right-click on a blank area inside the folder. A pop-up menu appears.
4. Select Paste.

TIP   **The keyboard functions of Cut, Copy, and Paste work just as they did in previous versions of Windows. Highlight the object and press Ctrl+X to cut, Ctrl+C to copy, and Ctrl+V to paste.**

Deleting Files and Other Objects

Deleting a file is as easy as selecting it and pressing the Delete key. You can also highlight a bunch of objects, click the right mouse button, and then select Delete from the menu that opens. Unless you've changed the Recycle Bin's default settings, you'll be asked to confirm the deletion.

Deleted files and folders are routinely sent to the Recycle Bin. The exception is files on floppy disks. If you order these deleted, there's no going back (though Windows 98 does notify you of that fact before completing the deletion).

NOTE   **All cut, paste, and delete actions that take longer than a second or two are accompanied by animation. This is a still shot of a file being copied. Some people positively hate the animation, but it does give you some feedback about what's happening.**

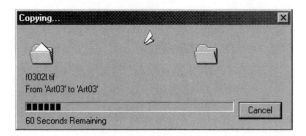

To delete files and have them not go to the Recycle Bin, hold down the Shift key when you press Del or click on Delete. Be aware that this is extinction, and extinction is forever!

Exploring Floppy Disks

Copying files to and from a floppy disk works the same way as with your hard drive. Click the Floppy icon in the left Explorer window to see the contents of the diskette currently in the drive. Windows Explorer also provides the graphical interface for the care and maintenance of floppy disks. If you yearn for DOS, you can also open a DOS window to copy, format, or label a floppy disk.

Making Exact Copies

To make an exact copy of your floppy disk, put the disk in the drive and open Windows Explorer. Click on the icon for the floppy drive with the right mouse button and select Copy Disk as shown in Figure 5.6. The dialog box that opens allows you to select the source and destination drives for your copy operation. It doesn't say so, but these selections must be the same type of disk. For most people, that means the same drive (unless you have two identical diskette drives or two Zip drives).

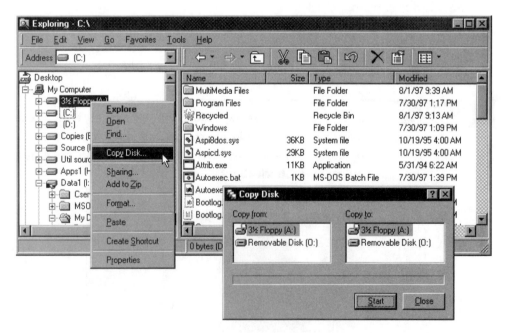

FIGURE 5.6: Windows 98's direct route to copying and formatting floppies

TIP   If you do much work with floppies, you may want to put a shortcut
to the drive on your desktop. Just drag the icon from the left window of the Explorer to your desktop.

Formatting Floppies

Here's how to format a floppy:

1. Put the floppy you want to format into your A: or B: drive as appropriate.
2. Open Windows Explorer.
3. In the left pane of the Explorer window, click once with the right mouse button on the icon representing the floppy drive. A pop-up menu will appear.
4. Select Format from the menu.
5. Select the Format Type and Other options you want:

    Quick: A quick format changes the names of any files on the disk so that they "disappear" as far as the operating system is concerned. This format is very fast (hence the name), but it doesn't check to make sure that the floppy is undamaged. It also doesn't work on new, unformatted disks.

    Full: A full format is necessary for new floppies and desirable for old ones, because it checks for errors and defects on the disk. It's a lot slower, though.

    Copy system files only: This copies system files to a disk that's already formatted without removing any of the files already present. This was a new feature with Windows 95 and allows you to turn any floppy into a bootable floppy.

    Label/No label: Specify whether or not you want to provide a label for the floppy.

    Display summary when finished: This option is on by default. When the formatting is complete, it opens a sheet showing the details of the formatted disk. Clear the box if you don't want to be bothered with this information.

    Copy system files: Check this if you want system files copied to the disk to make the disk bootable.

6. When you're finished selecting options, click the Start button.

WARNING If Windows Explorer (or an open window on the desktop) is showing the contents of the floppy disk, Windows 98 concludes that the floppy disk is in use and therefore it can't be formatted. If you get that message, click on your C: drive icon in the Explorer or close the desktop window showing the contents of the floppy. Then right-click once on the floppy icon and select Format.

Using the Send To Option

When you're working in the Explorer (or any other folder for that matter) and you click on an object with the right mouse button, the menu that opens includes an option called Send To. When you first start using Windows 98, the system will put your floppy drive and other removable media such as a Zip drive on the Send To submenu automatically.

This is pretty handy, as you might guess. But it can be even handier. You can add any application or device you choose. So you can select a file and send it to your word processor or your printer.

As an example, here's how to add the Notepad applet to the Send To menu:

1. Open Windows Explorer. Click on your Windows directory, then click with the right mouse button on the file NOTEPAD. Select Create Shortcut from the menu.
2. Right-click on the shortcut you've just made, and select Cut from the menu.
3. Scroll to the SendTo folder (it's a subfolder under the main Windows folder).
4. Click on the SendTo folder with the right mouse button, and select Paste.

When the menu gets too crowded, open the SendTo folder in the Explorer and delete any extra clutter.

TIP For a quicker way to find the SendTo folder, click once on the Start button and select Run. In the Open box, type in **Sendto** (all one word) and press Enter. The SendTo folder will open on your desktop.

The New File Systems

The original Windows 95 introduced a new file system that has immediate as well as long-term benefits. The mechanics of the DOS file system prevent anything resembling efficient multitasking. DOS was never designed to multitask and every attempt to get around this problem, as in Windows 3.1, was clumsy at best. The new file system introduced with Windows 95 allowed for improvements in performance and for long file names.

An interim update of Windows 95 (available only when pre-installed on new machines) added the new FAT32 file system to reduce wasted space on hard drives over 512 megabytes. Windows 98 includes all of these improvements. We will leave the discussion of FAT32 to Chapter 15 and the installation appendices. The discussion below is pertinent whether or not your machine uses FAT32.

Long File Names

The gnomes that created DOS back in the computer stone age decreed that file names had to follow an 8.3 convention. That is, the main part of the name could only be made up of eight characters (and a number of potentially useful characters were excluded). A three character extension is also part of the name, but the program often usurps those three for its own use.

With Windows 98, files and folders can have names as long as 255 characters. When you give a new file a longer name, the system automatically creates a shortened 8.3 name so your 16-bit Windows and DOS applications have names they can recognize and deal with. For example, Figure 5.7 shows the contents of a Finances folder, and Figure 5.8 shows the same folder's contents in a DOS window with the longer names on the right and the short ones, assigned by the system, on the left.

Windows 98 and any 32-bit applications you add to your system will work with the long file names that you create. Over time, as 16-bit applications are replaced by 32-bit apps, the short names will fade away and not be necessary any more.

Long file names have several nice features:

- The full path for a file with a long name can be as long as 260 characters. The file name itself can be up to 255 characters.
- File names can include spaces as well as characters you couldn't use before, like the comma, semicolon, equals sign (=) and square brackets ([]). However, you still can't use \ / < > : * ? " | in a file name.

• You can use both upper- and lowercase characters in long file names, and the system will preserve them.

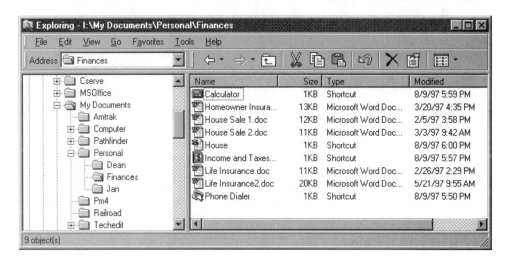

FIGURE 5.7: Here are some programs and files in a Windows 98 folder.

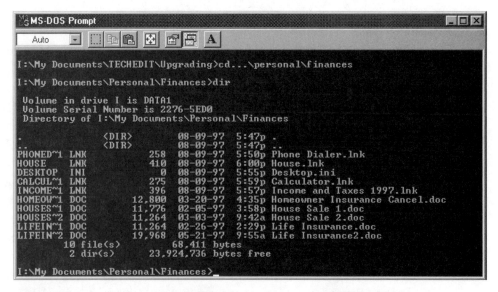

FIGURE 5.8: Here are the same files displayed in a Windows 98 DOS window.

> **NOTE** Long file names are not case sensitive in Windows. If you have to type in a long file name, it's not necessary to remember whether or how you capitalized the name. (Passwords in Windows 98 are case sensitive—as they are elsewhere.)

Finding Files

Windows 98 comes with a very sophisticated file finding tool. It offers a variety of useful functions and usually comes up with what you're looking for.

When You Know the Name

To find a file when you know the name (or part of the name), follow these steps:

1. In Windows Explorer, choose Tools ➤ Find ➤ Files or Folders. (You can also click the Start button, slide the pointer to Find, and then click on Files or Folders.)
2. Type in the file name—either whole or in part. If you only know part of the name, just enter what you know. (For a file that begins with the letters OMY, type **OMY*.*** in the Named text box.)

> **NOTE** If you include a period and extension in the Named box, Find will only list files with exactly the extension you enter. If you do not include a period or wild card character, Find will list every file which has your search string anywhere in its name. For example, entering omy will find every file with omy in its name. To find only files whose names begin with omy, enter omy*.

3. The Look In box tells the program where to search. If you haven't a clue, use the drop-down list or the Browse button to select My Computer, and the program will look everywhere on your system.
4. Click Find Now to start the search.

A window will open at the bottom of the Find Files dialog box showing the results of the search. You can click on a found file in the list and open it or drag it to a new location. If the list is a long one, click on the Name button to sort the files by alphabetical order; click again to reverse the order. Sorts can also be done by folder, size, and type of file.

TIP   To force the program to search for the name exactly as you enter it, including upper- and lower-case letters, open the Options menu and click Case Sensitive.

When You Know Something Else

But what about those many occasions when you don't know enough of the name to perform a search? If you have an idea of when the file was created or when it was last opened or worked on, you'll be able to use the Date function. You can specify a search between two dates or just look for file dates within some previous number of months or days. Specifying a search between two dates is made easier by the nifty new calendar that appears when you click the drop-down arrow of either date box, as shown in Figure 5.9.

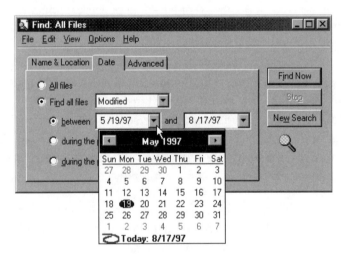

FIGURE 5.9:
The calendar drop-down helps you set up a search based on a file's date.

You can base the search on the date the file was last modified (the most common), the date it was originally created, or the date of last access. This is possible because the new file system maintains these three date/time properties for each file.

NOTE Windows Explorer only shows the date and time a file was last modified. To see the other dates for a file, you have to open its property sheet by right-clicking on the file and choosing **Properties**.

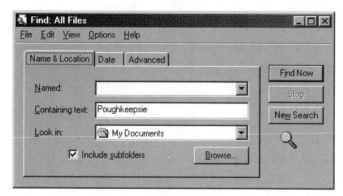

Maybe all you know is that the missing document is a letter written in Microsoft Word and it was addressed to your branch office in Poughkeepsie. Enter the text in the Containing Text box of the dialog, then click on the Advanced tab and select the file type. The drop-down list includes all the file types that are registered with Windows 98 (see the next section).

Searches can be based on even skimpier information. You can leave the Of Type drop-down list on the Advanced tab set to All Files And Folders, and search for files containing a certain word or phrase. Of course, the more you can tell the program, the faster the search will be.

TIP Searches can be conducted for multiple files or file types. For example, to search for all files with names that begin with Jan, Feb, and Mar, you'd enter **Jan*, Feb*, Mar*** in the Named text box. A comma is necessary between file types. A space is optional. If you do not use the asterisk, Find will find all files with these letters anywhere in the file name.

Registering File Types

In Windows 98, you can register a file type to associate it with a particular program. Once a file type is registered, you can double-click a file of that type and Windows 98 will do something with the file. Usually, that means Windows 98 will start the associated program and open the file.

NOTE   **Windows 98 also refers to registered file types as "known." In Windows 3.1, the term was "associated."**

Adding a File Type

Windows 98 does a pretty good job figuring out what files belong to what programs, and most Windows programs register the file types they use when you install them. Still, you may want to add a file type or change the program it's associated with.

To add a file type, follow these steps:

1. Open Windows Explorer, and from the View menu, select Folder Options.
2. Select File Types and click New Type.
3. In the Description of Type box, enter how you want this type of file to be shown in windows that display in Details view. This is for your information, so you can describe it in any way you choose.
4. In the Associated Extension box, enter the three letters that make up this file type's extension (see Figure 5.10). These three letters are important because all files with this extension will display a particular icon and be acted on in the same way as far as the operating system is concerned.

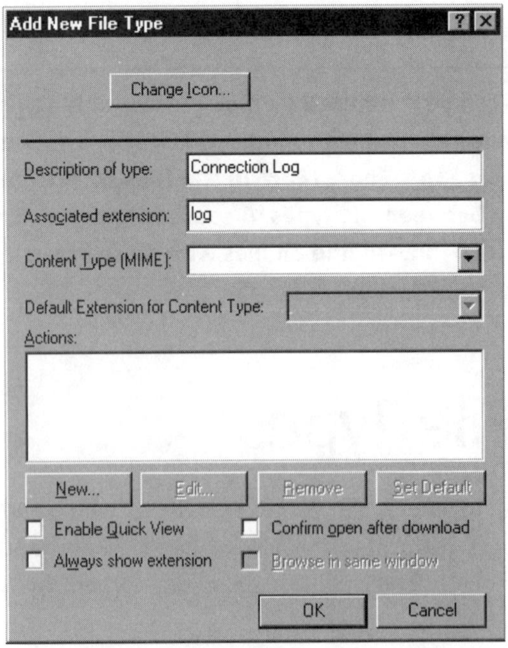

FIGURE 5.10:
Fill in a description of the file type and the file extension.

5. Click the New button. In the New Action box, type in the action you want performed when you double-click files of this type (usually Open) and the application used to perform the action (see Figure 5.11). Use the Browse button to find the exact location of the application you want used. Click OK.

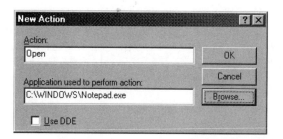

FIGURE 5.11:
Designate the action you want taken and the program that will do it.

6. You can add more actions, if you like, by clicking the New button again. Actions other than just opening the file will generally require command line parameters (also known as switches) after the path and file name for the application. Type them into the text box according to the syntax given in the application's manual or online help. Click Close when you're finished.

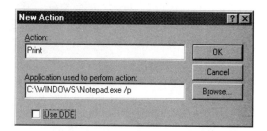

<hr>

TIP   Although it's not documented in either case, /p is the command line switch for Print in both Notepad and Wordpad.

7. Back in the Add New File Type box, the action in bold is the default that will be carried out when you click or double-click a file. It and any other actions you have set up will appear on the menu when you right-click a file.

8. You can click the Change Icon button to select a different icon for the associated files. Figure 5.12 shows the finished window. Click Close when you're done.

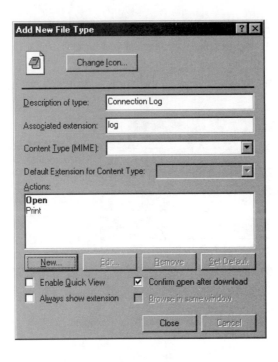

FIGURE 5.12:
Files with the log extension will open (in Notepad) with a click or double-click.

Changing a Registration

To change the registration of a file type, follow these steps:

1. Open Windows Explorer and select Folder Options from the View menu.
2. Under File Types, highlight the type you want to change and click the Edit button.
3. Click New to add a new action, or highlight the existing action you want to change and click Edit.
4. If you're editing, make the change in the Editing action box.
5. When you're finished, select OK or Close several times until you're back on the desktop.

Deleting Registrations

To delete a registration, open Windows Explorer and select Folder Options from the View Menu. Under File Types, highlight the file type you want to unregister and click Remove.

To remove only a specific action, highlight the file type and click Edit. Then highlight the action you want to eliminate and click Remove.

One File Type–Multiple Programs

Most file types are associated with a single program, but there are exceptions. For example, you may have multiple programs that can open bitmapped files (extension .bmp). If you have Paint, Collage Plus, and PaintShop Pro, or another program, you may want to choose which to use each time you open a file.

To have multiple associations, follow these steps:

1. Open Windows Explorer, and from the View menu, select Folder Options.
2. Click the File Types tab. In the Registered file types window, find the file type you want to add another association to and highlight it.

TIP

Unfortunately, you may not know the file type description used for the type of file you want to modify, and there's no automatic way to search the list by extension. You may be able to get a clue by clicking New Type and entering the extension. When you click OK, you will get an error message telling you the file type that is already using that extension. Another trick is to visually scan the list for a likely looking icon.

---

3. Click the Edit button. Shown here are the actions we've just set up for log documents (.log). A log file will open (the action is in bold type) if you click or double-click it. The print action is available from the right-click menu.

4. Click the New button to add an action. In the New Action window, enter the action you want performed as well as the application to perform the action. Here we're adding the option to open the file in Word for Windows.

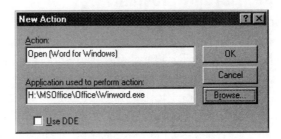

5. Click OK. Back in the Edit File Type window, all the actions will be listed. The item in bold will be the default action. To change the default, highlight the one you want and click the Set Default button. Click Close when you're finished.

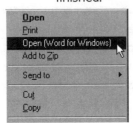

Now a right-click on a log file gives you the additional option of opening the file in Word for Windows. You can add as many associations as you want to clutter up your right-click menu.

NOTE
It's unfortunate that some installation programs register multiple extensions under the same file type description. You can add, edit, or remove actions for all of these extensions, but you cannot make changes to just some of them. The only way to accomplish that is to copy down all the extensions and the actions with the command line for each. Delete the entire file type, then create a new file type registration for each extension separately, with the actions you want for that extension.

Mapping and Sharing Drives

If your computer is connected to others in a local area network (or LAN), the Network Neighborhood icon will appear on your desktop and in the left window of the Windows Explorer. The basics of setting up file sharing over a network are discussed in the Network section of Chapter 11. If that has been done, you can see a list of computers on your network when you click Network Neighborhood in the left window of Windows Explorer.

The Network Neighborhood icon works like any other: click the + to see the list of computers on your network. Click the + beside a computer name to see the list of shared drives on that machine, and click + again to see the list of folders on a drive. When you find the folder you want, click it to show its contents in the right window, as in Figure 5.13. In some cases, you may have to enter a password.

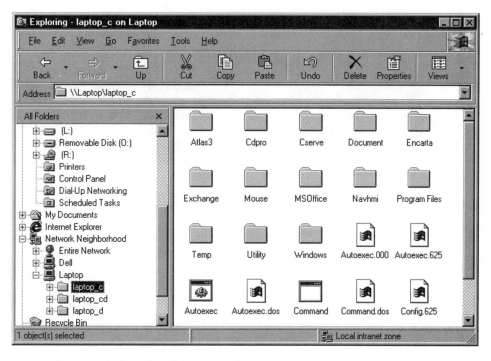

FIGURE 5.13:   Exploring a shared drive on another computer

Mapping a Drive

Explore your network for a while and you will probably realize that, although it works well, it's a slow process. You have to go through several steps just to find the right drive on another machine, and then you may still have to navigate several layers of folders to find the one you need.

Windows 98 allows you to shortcut the process of navigating to the drive you need. It's called drive mapping, and it allows you to set up a drive on another computer to look like a local drive on your computer. Here's how:

1. Use Windows Explorer to find the drive to which you want to connect.
2. On the Tools menu, select Map Network Drive.
3. Accept the default drive letter shown in the top box, or select another from the drop-down list.
4. In the second box, begin by typing two backslashes (\\). See Figure 5.14.
5. After the backslashes, type the network name of the computer, as shown in the left window of Windows Explorer. In our example, the name is **Laptop**.

FIGURE 5.14:
Mapping a drive on another computer to a drive letter on your computer

6. After the computer name, type a single backslash, followed by the share name of the drive, again as shown in Windows Explorer. In our example, the drive name is **laptop_c**.
7. If you want this mapping to be re-established every time you log on to your computer, check the box labeled Reconnect at logon.
8. Click OK.

The mapped drive will now appear in Windows Explorer and in My Computer as if it were on your own computer, as in Figure 5.15. The icon indicates that it is a network drive. You can get there with a single click. If you want a shortcut on your desktop, just drag it there from the Explorer left window.

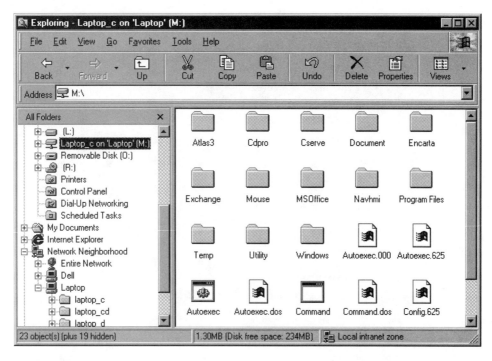

FIGURE 5.15:   The drive named laptop_c on the machine called Laptop has been mapped as drive M:.

Sharing a Drive or Folder

How do you give others access to drives or folders on your computer? Once again, the network must already be set up with facilities for file sharing, as described in Chapter 11. If it is, do this:

1. Navigate to the drive or folder you want to make available to others on your network.

2. Right-click on the drive or folder and choose Sharing from the pop-up menu.

3. On the Sharing page of the property sheet, select Shared As, as shown in Figure 5.16.

4. Accept the default Share Name or change it to something that others will understand. Share names are limited to 12 characters.

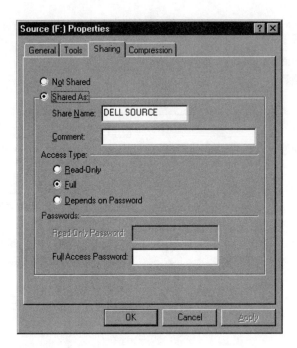

FIGURE 5.16:
Sharing a drive
with other users
on your network

5. Indicate what type of access you want others to have, and enter a password if you want to limit access. Remember that if you grant full access, others will be able to change the files on your computer.

6. OK the revised property sheet.

The drive or folder you have chosen to share will now appear under the name of your computer when others on your network open their Network Neighborhood. If you specified a password, they will need it to gain access.

What's Next

In the next chapter, we'll take a first look at the Internet and Windows Explorer's twin, the Internet Explorer. You'll find that the two Explorers are very closely related.

BROWSING FAR AND NEAR

The Internet is a worldwide collection of computer networks that are linked to one another by high-speed digital data connections. The Internet's best-known component is the World Wide Web. Many companies have recently begun to build internal networks, called intranets, which are modeled on the Internet. Intranets aid corporate communications and teamwork, and are relatively simple to build and maintain because they use well-established Internet technology.

The basic tool for exploring the World Wide Web and using other services of the Internet or your corporate intranet is called a browser. Two browsers dominate the market: Netscape Navigator and Microsoft Internet Explorer. Guess which one is usually included with Windows 98!

However, Internet Explorer, version 4.0, isn't merely *included* with Windows 98. It forms an integral part of the Windows 98 desktop; it can even *replace* the desktop, if you are so inclined. Even if you choose to use Netscape Navigator as your Web browser, you will still need to set up Internet Explorer if you want to take advantage of Active Desktop features.

To start Internet Explorer, click this icon on the desktop, or the smaller version of it on the Quick Launch toolbar.

If you already have an Internet account, and Windows 98 knows about it, Internet Explorer will start and automatically connect. In that case, you can skip the next section and go on to Starting Out.

Getting Connected

If you don't already have a connection to the Internet, or if Internet Explorer doesn't know about it, the Internet Connection Wizard will start. You can also start the Wizard yourself, either from the Start menu under Programs ➤ Internet Explorer or by clicking the desktop shortcut Connect to the Internet. As you can see in Figure 6.1, the Wizard will help you do one of two things: either choose an Internet service provider and set up a new account, or enter the necessary information so Internet Explorer can connect to an account you already have.

Opening a New Account

If you don't have an Internet connection and you want Windows 98 to help you open an account with a service provider, choose the top option and click Next. The Connection Wizard will dial a toll-free phone number and connect to the Microsoft Referral Service to download information on Internet service providers in your area.

TIP   **The Internet service providers listed are primarily ones with a national network of access phone lines. If you prefer to sign up with a local service, you may need to contact them directly for information. A local service may provide their own setup software, or they may give you the necessary information to set up the account yourself. In this case, go to the section on Using an Existing Account for instructions on how to enter the information they give you.**

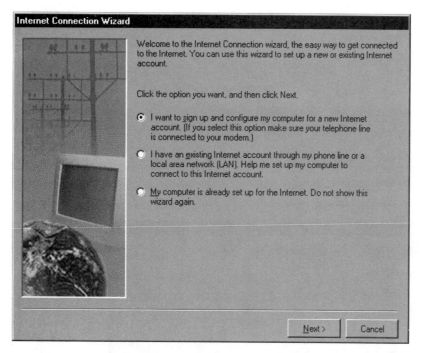

FIGURE 6.1: Starting out with the Internet Connection Wizard

After a few minutes, your modem will disconnect and the list of Internet service providers appears in the Connection Wizard. Click on each provider in turn to see detailed information about the service. When you decide on a provider, be sure it is highlighted and click Next. Fill in the information requested and click Next again to connect to the service you have chosen and sign up for an account. Because each service has its own sign-up procedure, you'll have to rely on their instructions and support if you need help.

Using an Existing Account

If you already have an account with an Internet service provider, choose "I have an existing Internet account…." Click Next, and the Internet Connection Wizard will begin asking you for the necessary information to connect to your existing account.

The next dialog box is designed to weed out users of online services: America Online, AT&T WorldNet, CompuServe, Prodigy Internet, or The Microsoft Network. If you use one of these for your Internet access, choose the second option. Otherwise, choose the first. If you tell the Wizard you use the Internet via an online service, and click Next, you will simply be advised to configure your online service by opening it from its desktop icon or the Online Services folder.

If you tell the Wizard that you use an Internet service provider or local area network for Internet access, the next question (as shown in Figure 6.2) is whether you connect over a phone line or via a local area network (LAN). If you have a modem installed in your computer and use it to connect to the Internet, that's a connection over a phone line. If your computer is connected to a local area network that has an Internet or intranet connection, choose the second option. You will need to ask your network system administrator for the information you need to set up your connection.

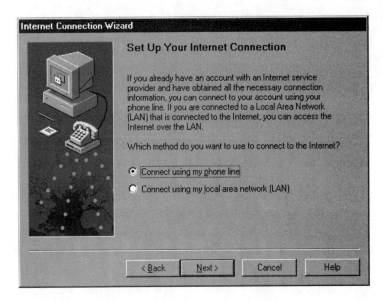

FIGURE 6.2:   If your Internet connection is not an online service, what is it?

Assuming you use a modem to connect, you would choose "Connect using my phone line" and click Next. If you have more than one modem installed on your computer, the Wizard will ask which one you want to use for this connection. Select it from the drop-down list and click Next. Make sure "Create a new dial-up connection" is selected, and click Next again. The following chart lists the information you will need to complete the Wizard, and where to get it. ISP means your Internet service provider.

Internet Account Setting	Where to Get It	Your Setting
Phone Number	ISP	
User Name (logon name) and Password	Chosen when you signed up for service with the ISP	
Connection Name	You decide	
Internet Mail		
Display Name	You decide	
E-mail Address	ISP	
Incoming & Outgoing Mail Servers	ISP	
E-mail Account Name & Password	Chosen when you signed up for service with the ISP	
Friendly Name for E-mail Account	You decide	
Internet News		
Display Name	You decide	
E-mail Address	ISP	
News (NNTP) Server	ISP or special news server	
News Server Account Name & Password	Operator of news server (if required)	
Friendly Name for News Account	You decide	

Working through the Wizard

In each dialog of the Wizard, fill in the information requested, using your information from the chart. When you have filled in all the information for a dialog, click Next to continue.

The phone number, user name, and password are the ones you use to dial in and log on to your account. After entering this information and clicking Next, choose Yes to change advanced settings if you need to set the connection type (PPP or SLIP), a special logon procedure, or IP or DNS server addresses. In most cases, you will not need to change these settings. Just click Next again.

Enter a connection name. This is simply a name to identify this set of dial-up information on your computer; you can choose any connection name that makes sense to you. Click Next to go on to setting up your Internet mail account.

For Internet Mail, the display name and e-mail address are what will appear in the From: field of mail you send. In many cases the e-mail account name and password will be the same as your user name and password. However, they may be different, especially if your Internet service provider allows for multiple e-mail addresses on one account.

NOTE **Outlook Express is Internet Explorer 4's new companion program for handling Internet mail and newsgroups. You should complete the Internet Connection Wizard's sections on Internet mail and newsgroups only if you intend to use Outlook Express as your Internet mail and newsgroup client. If you have another program and intend to continue using it, bypass these sections of the Wizard by choosing No when it asks whether you want to set up mail and news accounts. Using Outlook Express is discussed in Chapter 8. See Appendix A for options regarding fax capability, which is not included in Outlook Express.**

The next information the Wizard will ask for is the addresses of your mail servers, as shown in Figure 6.3. After that, you only need to choose a friendly name for your e-mail account. As with the connection name, the friendly name is used only on your computer, to identify the account to you, so it can be anything you like.

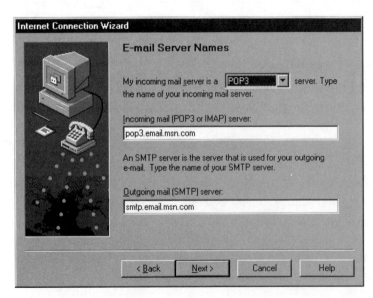

FIGURE 6.3: Once you have the information, the Internet Connection Wizard helps you put it in its place.

The Internet News settings provide access to news groups, one of the most popular resources on the Internet. Once again, the display name and e-mail address are what will appear in the From: field of items you post in a news group. The news server address identifies the news server you want to use. Most often, this will be the server designated by your Internet service provider, but it could be a special or private server. In this case, the server may require you to log on; check the box labeled "My news server requires me to log on" and provide your account name and password for that news server after clicking Next. Once again, the friendly name can be whatever you choose.

Finally, you can set up an Internet directory service if your account includes this service and you have the necessary information from your service provider. If you don't know whether you have a directory service, just accept the default of No and click Next. Click Finish, and you're done. Now when you click the Internet Explorer icon, the browser will start and connect to your service provider.

TIP

Don't worry if you don't have all the information you need to set up mail, news, or directory services. You can skip a service by choosing No when the Wizard asks if you want to set up that service. When you have all the information, return to the Wizard by choosing Programs ➢ Internet Explorer ➢ Connection Wizard on the Start menu. Choose "I want to set up a new connection...," then "Connect using my phone line." Next choose "Use an existing dial-up connection" and select the connection from the list. Click Next, choose Yes, and click Next again to continue through the Wizard, making changes or adding your new information.

Starting Out

The three most popular functions on the Internet are browsing the Web, sending and receiving e-mail, and participating in newsgroups. We'll cover Web browsing here, and leave e-mail and newsgroups to Chapter 8.

When you first start up Internet Explorer, it logs you on over your network or dial-up connection to the Internet and goes to the Microsoft home page, as shown in Figure 6.4. This is a big web site with lots of information on Microsoft products, including Windows 98 and Internet Explorer. It also has a variety of support tools arranged by product and free downloadable software. At some point, you will probably want to become familiar with it.

WARNING The first time you connect to the Internet after installing Windows 98, you are likely to see a warning message to the effect that file and printer sharing are enabled on your TCP/IP connection. You should follow the recommendation given in the message and disable file and printer sharing on your Internet connection. If you are connecting to a corporate intranet, check with your system administrator.

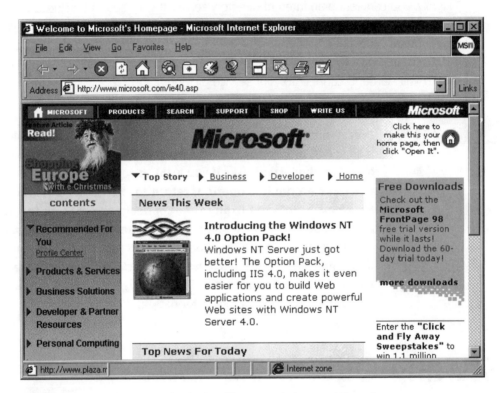

FIGURE 6.4:   Internet Explorer begins by taking you to its home at Microsoft.

If finding more ways to play with your software is not the task of the moment and you want to go somewhere else on the World Wide Web, just click in the address box and type the URL (*Uniform Resource Locator* or Internet address) of the site you'd like to visit. Press Enter and Internet Explorer will take you there.

Most companies that operate a Web page can be found by entering **www.*company-name*.com**. For example:

www.corel.com is the Corel home page.

www.honda.com is the American Honda Motor home page.

www.kentuckyfriedchicken.com is the KFC home page.

NOTE | **If you are familiar with Internet addresses, you may be aware that the full address should have http:// in front of the www. Internet Explorer knows that just as well as you do, so you can save your fingers from typing the http://.**

Many government agency sites are a bit harder to find, but not all; for example, **www.nasa.gov** is an easy way to begin checking out pictures from the Hubble telescope, news from Mars, and plans for upcoming space shuttle launches.

Once you are at your desired Web site, navigate through it by clicking the buttons and other links provided on the site. Any place where your mouse pointer changes to a hand is a link that will take you somewhere, either within the Web site or to another site.

The Standard Toolbar

Using the Internet effectively requires a lot more than just getting to one site and following the links it may provide. To help you get around more quickly and easily, Internet Explorer has several toolbars. This is the standard toolbar:

To save screen space, we have removed the labels from the toolbar in most of our figures. You may want to do the same, especially if you don't see all the buttons shown here. Right-click on the bar and choose Text Labels to toggle them off.

The Back and Forward arrows operate just as they do in a folder or a Windows Explorer window: they take you back to where you were last, or forward again if you've already gone back. The down arrows beside the buttons allow you to pick from a back or forward list.

The Stop button tells Internet Explorer to stop downloading the current page. This is useful if the page has graphics or for some other reason is taking a long time to load, and you decide you don't want to wait for it all. Just click Stop (or press the Esc key) and move on.

Refresh tells Internet Explorer to re-load the current page. Use it if you suspect you didn't receive the entire page due to communication problems, or if you are looking at a page offline (that you previously downloaded) and suspect the contents may have changed. The keyboard shortcut for Refresh is F5, just as in Windows Explorer.

TIP   **Perusing web pages doesn't always have to be done online. If you want to work through a site carefully, but don't want to tie up your phone line for a long time, just move through the site quickly. Go to another page as soon as Internet Explorer finishes loading the current page. (You can tell this by the progress bar at the bottom of the Internet Explorer window.) When you have downloaded all the pages you want, find the Connection icon in the System tray at the right end of the Taskbar.**

Right-click the icon and select Disconnect from the menu. You will be disconnected from your service provider, but you can go back and explore the pages you downloaded because they are cached on your hard disk. If you click a link to a page that wasn't cached, Internet Explorer will ask if you want to go online to download it.

The Home button has become the victim of confusing terminology. It takes you to your Internet start page, which by default is the Microsoft home page. You can change your start page on the General tab of the Internet Options dialog, reached via the View menu.

The next four buttons (Search, Favorites, History, and Channels) each open a bar on the left side of the Internet Explorer window. Click the same button again to close the bar. Later in this chapter, we will come back to the Search, Favorites, and History functions. Channels are discussed in Chapter 7.

The Full Screen button gives you the maximum possible area for viewing web pages. It not only maximizes the Internet Explorer window, it also removes the menu bar and toolbars (except the standard toolbar). The same button restores the window to normal configuration.

The Mail button opens a menu for direct access to your e-mail program and Internet newsreader.

The Print button sends the current page to your default printer. Finally, the Edit button opens FrontPage Express, to which we will return in the next chapter.

NOTE   **You set the programs to be used for mail and news in the Internet Options dialog box, described later in this chapter. Windows 98 includes Outlook Express to perform these functions if you have no other e-mail or newsreader program. Outlook Express is described in Chapter 8.**

More Toolbars

Internet Explorer has two additional toolbars besides the Standard toolbar, as shown in Figure 6.5. The Address Bar contains only the combination box where you can enter any Internet or intranet address (URL) or the path to a folder on your own machine or your local area network. You can use the box's drop-down list to return to a site you recently visited, or to navigate the resources on your machine or Network Neighborhood.

FIGURE 6.5:   This is the default toolbar arrangement. You can probably do better.

The Links toolbar gives you instant access to any sites included in the Links folder. Drag its vertical handle to the left to see the contents of the Links toolbar. As installed, the Links toolbar can take you directly to several different pages of the Microsoft Web site. Adding your own links is described in the Favorites section later in this chapter.

As in folders and Windows Explorer, you can rearrange the toolbars in Internet Explorer. Just click on the vertical bar at the left end of any toolbar and drag it around the toolbar area just below the title bar. To remove a toolbar, right-click it, then click on the checkmark for that toolbar to toggle it off. You can move the menu bar just like a toolbar (though you can't delete it).

Here's a toolbar arrangement we like because it fits everything into the smallest possible space. We've removed the text from the Standard toolbar by unchecking Text Labels under View ➤ Toolbars. Note the small triangle (arrowhead) at the right end of the Links toolbar. It serves to scroll through the toolbar, because not all of its buttons are visible in the space we've given it.

Disconnecting

Disconnecting from the Internet is especially important if you use a single telephone line both for Internet access and for more traditional purposes. It's also important if you pay connect-time charges or long-distance tolls for access. However, the designers of Internet Explorer and Windows 98 don't seem terribly interested in this issue. Exiting Internet Explorer in most cases will not disconnect your dial-up Internet connection or hang up your modem.

Internet Explorer will disconnect after the connection has been idle for a period of time that you can specify. Go to View ➤ Internet Options. Click the Connection tab, then the Settings button. One of the options in the Dial-Up Settings dialog box that appears is "Disconnect if idle for xx minutes." The default is twenty minutes. You might want to shorten this time, but you still wouldn't want to rely on this method of disconnecting when you know you're finished.

To be sure you are not connected when you don't want to be, keep an eye on the System Tray at the right end of your Taskbar. If you see this Connection icon, you are connected. To change that situation, right-click the icon and choose Disconnect.

TIP You can also double-click the Connection icon to open a small dialog box with information about your connection. In particular, it will tell you the actual speed of your current connection.

Menu Miscellany

On the View menu, you can change the size of the fonts Internet Explorer uses to display Web pages. You can also change the character set to view pages written in other alphabets.

Similar to folders and Windows Explorer, the last item on the View menu is options, in this case Internet Options. It opens the Internet Properties dialog where you can set preferences for an enormous variety of functions, including content ratings and the amount of hard disk space to allot for temporarily storing (caching) Web sites. It also has controls for security levels, which will be discussed in Chapter 7. The General page includes controls for colors to use, languages, and accessibility functions for those with limited vision, as well as more detailed control of fonts than that offered under View ➤ Fonts.

Click Connect on the Connection tab of Internet Properties to use the Connection Wizard to modify your Internet connection settings or to set up a new connection. The Settings button on the same page allows you to choose among Internet connections if you have more than one. After choosing the one you want to use, you can click Properties to change the settings for that connection.

On the Programs page of Internet Properties, you can select the e-mail program you want to use for Internet mail. The drop-down box labeled Mail should list any e-mail programs installed on your computer, as well as Outlook Express, which comes with Internet Explorer. The program you choose here will open when you ask Internet Explorer to switch to mail, either with the toolbar Mail button or with the Go menu. Also on the Programs page, you can set your preferred programs for reading Internet newsgroups, making Internet phone calls, and retrieving personal information. We will discuss some of the other settings in Internet Properties later, under the topics they relate to.

TIP   **You can change Internet Explorer options without starting the program first. Just right-click its icon and choose Properties.**

Internet Explorer's Help menu is more extensive than most. In addition to the usual help files, it offers direct access to an online Web tutorial, support, and a variety of pages from the Microsoft Web site. It even has a link to a Microsoft site for downloading Internet Explorer updates.

It's My Favorite

Internet Explorer has several ways of reducing the number of times you have to type in a long Internet address, thus making it easier to find your way back to a site you like. One is Favorites.

 Click this button to open the Favorites bar along the left side of your Internet Explorer window.

The Favorites bar starts out with some default contents, but the important thing is that you can add whatever you wish. If you think you may want to return to a site you are visiting, click Add to Favorites on the Favorites menu. This will open the dialog box shown in Figure 6.6, which offers several choices of how to set up this particular favorite site.

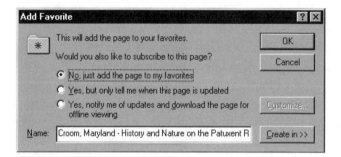

FIGURE 6.6:
What kind of Favorite do you have in mind?

Subscriptions

Besides adding the current page to your Favorites, the dialog also asks whether you would like to subscribe to the page. The default choice "No, just add the page to my favorites" works the way Favorites did in previous versions of Internet Explorer: it adds the site to your list of favorites. It will appear on the Favorites bar, and you need only click on it to go to the site.

The second choice is "Yes, but only tell me when this page is updated." With this choice, the site will be added to your list of favorites, and Internet Explorer will automatically monitor the site for changes. When a change occurs, you will be notified by the addition of a small red sunburst at the upper left corner of the page's icon.

Finally, you can choose "Yes, notify me of updates and download the page for offline viewing." This tells Internet Explorer to check the site for changes and automatically download any changed pages. This way, you always have the current version cached on your hard disk, where you can explore the site without having to connect to your Internet service provider, and without having to wait for slow downloads.

NOTE Does this subscription stuff sound familiar? It should, if you read Chapter 4 on setting up the Active Desktop. Favorites subscriptions work the same way.

With either kind of subscription, you can click the Customize button to set additional options. If you want more definite notification of changes, Internet Explorer can send you an e-mail message. You can enter your user name and password, if the site is one that requires you to log on. And, for a full subscription, you can set the update schedule.

TIP Remember, if you use a modem to connect to the Internet, you have to check the box labeled "Dial as needed if connected through a modem" to allow Internet Explorer to go online automatically and carry out scheduled updates.

To check the status of all your subscriptions, choose Manage Subscriptions on the Favorites menu. The Subscriptions folder that opens will tell you such things as when a subscription was last updated, and whether the update was successful. To change the settings of a subscription, right-click on it and choose Properties from the menu.

Favorite Favorites and Other Favorites

If you use the Internet extensively, or if you just like to have a quick way back to each site that interests you, you may find your list of favorites becoming unwieldy. Internet Explorer helps solve this problem by allowing you to group your favorites, just as you do with files on your hard disk.

By default, new favorites are added to the Favorites folder. As shown in Figure 6.7, clicking the Create In button will expand the Add Favorite dialog box to include a new window showing the folder structure within Favorites. It starts with several folders, including Channels and Links. Highlight the folder where you want your new favorite, and OK the dialog.

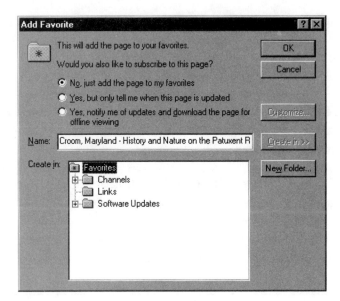

FIGURE 6.7:
You can put your new favorite in the Favorites folder, or in another folder within Favorites.

To create a new folder, highlight Favorites (or another folder where you want to create the new one) and click the New Folder button. Enter a name for the folder and click OK. The new folder will be highlighted in the Add Favorite dialog box as the location of your new favorite, so you can click OK there, too, and you're done.

> **TIP** To reorganize or delete existing favorites, including in the Channels and Links folders, choose Organize Favorites on the Favorites menu.

The default folders within Favorites (the ones you didn't create) have special purposes. The contents of the Channels folder appear on the Channel bar on your Active Desktop, and also on the left side of the Internet Explorer window when you click Channels on the toolbar.

Items in the Links folder appear on the Links toolbar, described earlier in this chapter. You can add the Links toolbar to any folder or Windows Explorer window with the View ➤ Toolbars ➤ Links command.

> **TIP** If you were at a site recently but failed to add it to your Favorites list, you can find it again by clicking on the arrow next to the address field to open a drop-down list of recent URLs. If you don't find it there, check out the next section on using the History bar.

Going Back in History

Internet Explorer maintains history files so that you can return to a Web site you have visited recently, even if you don't know its URL and didn't put it in your Favorites folder. Click the History button on the toolbar to open the History bar, or choose Explorer Bar ➤ History on the View menu.

Figure 6.8 shows Internet Explorer with the History bar open. Sites you have visited during the current week are organized by day. Sites you visited longer ago are organized by week. Click a day or week to see the list of sites you visited. Clicking a site will open a list of individual pages.

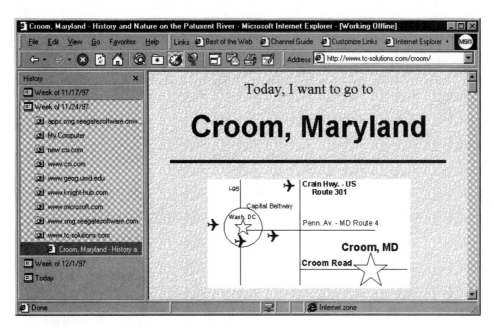

FIGURE 6.8: Internet Explorer keeps track of where you've been recently.

When you click a Web page in your history list, Internet Explorer goes there if you are currently online. Otherwise, it opens the page from the cache it keeps on your hard disk. If you want to update the cache to the current version of the page, click the Refresh button on the toolbar or press F5.

The General page of the Internet Options dialog (View menu) allows you to set the number of days links are stored in your history folder. The default is twenty days. You can also clear your history file here.

Searching

Knowing how to get back to a place you've been before is helpful, but how do you find what you want in the first place? Unless you already know the URL of a site that has the information you want, you will probably need to use a search engine.

Internet search engines are located at Web sites, and each of them can be reached by entering its URL, just like any other Web page. But since you may not know these URLs off the top of your head, Internet Explorer has built-in links to several of the most popular search engines. Click the Search button to open the Search bar for access to these links.

Select a search engine from the drop-down list and it will open in the Search bar (see Figure 6.9). You can enter the word or words you want to search for; in some cases there are other options you can select.

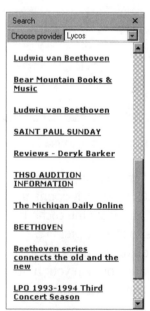

FIGURE 6.9:
The Search bar with a subject entered and with the results of the search

When you are ready, click the Search (or similar) button and the search engine goes to work. It will return a list of links to sites that include the words you searched for. Just click a link to go to that Web site or page. The advantage of using the Search bar is that you can keep the list of search results visible in the bar as you visit the sites.

What are the differences between the search engines? Some search the keywords assigned to Web sites, some search for individual pages within sites, and some search the entire text of pages. Each uses its own set of rules on how to conduct a search, and they offer different degrees of user control over those rules. Some also include indexes organized into topics and sub-topics. Some search services offer subjective reviews or ratings of the sites they cover, and others just try to index everything they can find.

The best way to determine which search engines will best serve your needs is to experiment. Conduct the same search using different services, and compare the results.

In some cases, clicking the search engine title at the top of the Search bar will open a more extensive version of the search page in the main Internet Explorer window. Here you can find out more about search options and get help on how to use the service. You can gain access to a wider variety of search engines by clicking "List of All Providers" in the Choose Provider drop-down list. This opens a Web page that lists search engines and directory services in a number of different categories.

TIP   **Unless you are experienced or have better luck than most, you probably won't find exactly what you're looking for on your first try. Try different search services, and pay special attention to the options that determine exactly how your search is carried out.**

Local Browsing

As we've mentioned several times before, Internet Explorer can now be used as your Windows 98 interface, replacing the desktop. This is probably a good idea only if most of your work is Internet or intranet based. It makes a few operations such as moving files a bit less convenient, but in exchange you get complete consistency of operation between your machine and your Internet or intranet environment.

To try Internet Explorer in place of the desktop interface, just start it up. There's no need to go online for this experiment, so click Cancel if your modem starts dialing, and click Work Offline or Stay Offline. (Your configuration determines which of these you see.) Maximize Internet Explorer using the conventional Maximize button in the top right corner of the window (not the Full Screen button on the toolbar).

The quickest way to begin browsing your computer's resources is to choose My Computer on the Go menu; if you only want to look at documents stored in your My Documents folder, choose My Documents from the Favorites menu. You can also type any local path in the Address bar. For example, if you want to see the root folder of drive D:, type **d:** and press Enter. Internet Explorer recognizes **d:** as a path on your computer and adds **** to complete it.

Internet Explorer displays the contents of the selected folder just as if you had opened that folder on the desktop. Figure 6.10 shows My Documents being displayed. Notice that the Standard toolbar has changed to show buttons appropriate to working with files on your computer. As a matter of fact, this Standard toolbar is just like the one in the Windows Explorer.

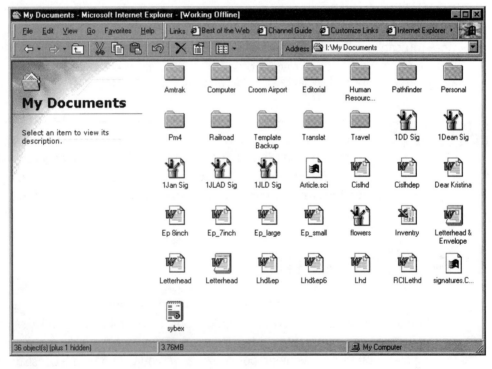

FIGURE 6.10: Internet Explorer browsing My Documents

A few other things also change when you tell Internet Explorer to browse your computer. For example, the drop-down list in the Address bar lists the resources in My Computer, instead of the URLs of Web sites you've recently visited. Also, the last item on the View menu is now Folder Options instead of Internet Options. This means you have access to all the usual functions of the Folder Options dialog: the detailed settings available on the View tab, and the File Types tab for making or changing file associations, as discussed in Chapter 5.

Navigate around your computer just as you would using a folder window on the desktop. Drill down one level at a time by opening folders shown in the current window. Move up one level at a time using the Up button on the toolbar, or move up multiple levels using the drop-down list in the Address bar.

Moving and Copying

You can move and copy files and folders just as explained in Chapter 5, with one condition: you almost never can see the object and its destination at the same time, so you have to use this method:

1. Highlight the object (file, folder, or shortcut).
2. Right-click the object and choose Cut to move it or Copy to copy it.
3. Open the destination folder and right-click in a blank area of it.
4. Select Paste from the menu.

You can select multiple objects, too. Use the method that fits what you want to do:

- Drag a box around the objects.
- Click an object, then use Shift + click to select another object and all those in between.
- Hold Ctrl while selecting multiple items one at a time.

Floppy Disks

To check the contents of a floppy disk in Internet Explorer, choose My Computer from the Go menu and open the disk. To copy or format a floppy, right-click on its icon in My Computer and choose your operation from the menu, as shown in Figure 6.11. Details of these operations are covered in Chapter 5.

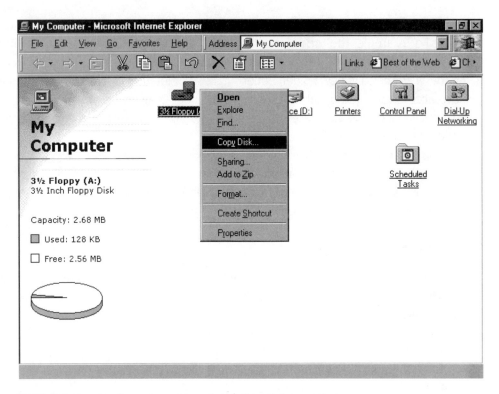

FIGURE 6.11: Copying or formatting a floppy disk with Internet Explorer

Taskbar Supreme

You might have begun to wonder how you are going to start programs conveniently without access to the shortcuts on your desktop. There are several answers to this question.

The first is that if you frequently use a variety of programs, it may not be a good idea to try to use Internet Explorer as your interface. Perhaps you should go back to the desktop, remembering that it, too, is now rich in browser-like features.

The second answer is that you still have access to the Taskbar. You can start any installed program from the Start menu, though you may have to go through a couple of layers to find it. Also, you can return temporarily to the desktop (by restoring Internet Explorer to a non-maximized window) and drag important shortcuts into the Quick Launch toolbar on the Taskbar.

Finally, you can right-click in a blank area of the Taskbar. Under Toolbars on the menu, choose Desktop.

This will create a new toolbar on your Taskbar, containing all the shortcuts that are on your desktop. Remember that you can resize and rearrange the Taskbar and its toolbars, for better usability.

Are You Convinced?

If you've experimented with Internet Explorer as your interface and decided you prefer it to the Windows 98 desktop, there's an easy way start it whenever you start Windows:

1. Click the Start button.
2. Move your mouse pointer to Programs, then to the Internet Explorer folder, then to the Internet Explorer program shortcut.
3. With the right mouse button, drag the Internet Explorer shortcut to the left, then to the StartUp folder. When the Startup folder opens, drag into it and release the right mouse button. See Figure 6.12.

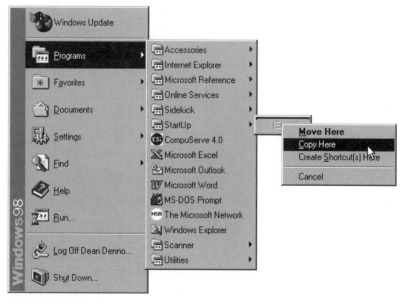

FIGURE 6.12: Putting a shortcut to Internet Explorer in the StartUp folder

4. Choose Copy Here from the menu that appears when you release the right mouse button.

5. Right-click on the new Internet Explorer shortcut, and choose Properties from the menu.

6. Set the Run box to Maximized, and OK the Properties dialog.

Now you will immediately see your preferred interface whenever you start Windows 98.

What's Next

There's lots more to Internet Explorer 4.0 than we can discuss in a book about Windows 98. (For a thorough expose on the subject, see the Sybex book *Mastering Internet Explorer 4*, by Gene Weisskopf and Pat Coleman.) On the other hand, you may need to know more than the bare basics. The next chapter takes up several more features of Internet Explorer and related programs that may be important to you depending on how and how much you use the Internet.

CHANNELS AND OTHER INTERNET GOODIES

In this chapter, we take up several Internet and Internet-related features of Windows 98. The channels feature is a method of delivering Internet content, which you have selected, to you so you can peruse and enjoy it at your leisure, without waiting for slow downloads. Channel technology is one of the major efforts being made to simplify Internet use, while increasing the commercial value of the medium to content providers. Several hundred channels ranging from news to entertainment should be available by the time Windows 98 goes on sale.

Many new uses of the Internet raise security concerns. Whether you are sending a credit card number for shopping or transmitting business data to a co-worker or client, you want assurance that your message is safe from prying eyes. You also want to keep your own computer or network safe from both viruses and accidental damage that might be caused by downloaded programs. Internet Explorer 4.0 offers several features to assist you with maintaining security.

Perhaps you are one of the many people interested in building a Web page for either Internet or intranet use. We'll show you the basics of doing this with FrontPage Express.

Finally, we'll tell you how to use NetMeeting for Internet phone calls and conferences. If you have a sound card with microphone, you can talk. With a video camera, you can make it a video phone call. And, without either, you can still have a live conference, exchanging messages and drawings to collaborate on projects.

Internet Channels

In spite of the enormous growth in popularity of the World Wide Web in recent years, it is still far from being part of most people's everyday lives in the way television, radio, newspapers, and magazines are. Part of the reason is that many people still think of computers as difficult to use, and of the Internet as one of the things that's "hard." Channels are an attempt to change that perception.

The Channel Bar

A channel is just a Web site, but one with several special characteristics. One of these is that it's listed in a Channel Guide such as the one maintained by Microsoft on its Web site. This means that you can get to a channel without having to know or enter its Web address (URL). You can also add channels to the Channel bar on the Windows 98 desktop. Then, when you click one, Internet Explorer will start in its full-screen channel mode and open the channel.

Besides several specific channels, the channel bar includes category headings such as Entertainment, News and Technology, Business, Lifestyle and Travel, and Sports. Click one of these buttons and Internet Explorer will list some of the channels available in that category. Click the one you want and you will be connected.

Finally, there's the Channel Guide button. The first time you click it, you will be offered the option of viewing an explanation of what channels are and how they work. Choose Yes, and let the active HTML page cycle through its explanations a few times, until you have absorbed the information. Then move your mouse pointer to the left side of the screen so the channel bar re-appears, and click the Microsoft Active Channel Guide button.

This will start your Internet connection and take you directly to a Microsoft-sponsored listing of available channels, as shown in Figure 7.1. You can look at the day's featured channels, browse the channels in a category, or search for channels that interest you. When you find one, just click to go there.

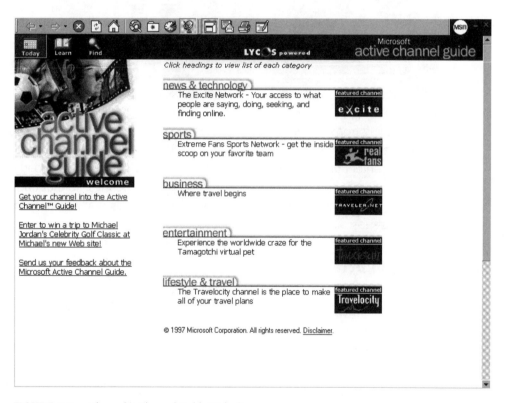

FIGURE 7.1:   Microsoft's Channel Guide Web site

TIP

The special full-screen view shown in Figure 7.1, without title bar or menu bar, is the default for channel viewing. You can click the Full-screen button to change the view to a normal Internet Explorer window.

When you find a channel that you want to visit again easily, click the Add Active Channel button displayed on the page. This will open the dialog box in Figure 7.2. Select the subscription option you want. (Subscribing is described in the next section.) When you OK the dialog, the channel will be added to your channel bar.

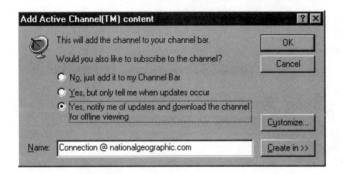

FIGURE 7.2:
Add to your channel bar and subscribe if you wish.

While choosing from hundreds (or eventually thousands) of channels is a far cry from using the full richness of the Internet, it provides a simple and direct way to get started. Many content providers are clearly hoping that channels will both broaden the appeal of the Internet and focus users on their particular offerings. To that end, easy access is only the beginning of what channels offer. Channels really come into their own when you subscribe.

Subscribe for Better Access

When you subscribe to a channel, you tell your computer to download the channel's content automatically at regular intervals, and to store that content on your computer. Then you can view the channel when you wish, without having to wait for slow downloads. The provider of a channel includes a recommended update schedule, which you can accept or modify to suit your needs.

To subscribe to a channel, open it from the channel bar or channel guide and click the Add Active Channel button. You can accept the default to have the channel downloaded automatically, or choose only to be notified of new content. If you choose to have the channel downloaded, the next download will be scheduled as recommended by the provider of the site.

If you want control over the download schedule of a subscription, go to the Favorites menu in any folder or Explorer window and choose Manage Subscriptions to open the Subscriptions folder. Right-click on the subscription you want to change and choose Properties from the pop-up menu. Choose the Schedule page of the subscription's property sheet, as shown in Figure 7.3.

TIP As noted in Chapter 4, subscribing simply tells your computer to download content automatically. No information is sent to the channel provider by the act of subscribing. However, some channels, like some other Web sites, require you to give certain information in order to have access to the site. Such channels require you to log on with a user name and password, so that information you give once doesn't have to be repeated every time you request access to the site. If you are concerned about how information you provide may be used, contact the channel provider.

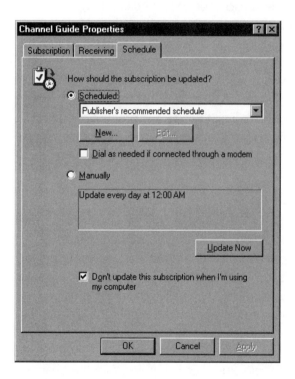

FIGURE 7.3:
Setting the download schedule of a channel subscription

The subscription shown in the figure has scheduled downloads on the channel Publisher's Recommended Schedule. The window in the middle of the property sheet describes the schedule: Update every day at 12:00 AM (midnight). To change the schedule, select an alternate from the drop-down list, or click the New button to create one from scratch. You can use the Edit button to change any existing schedule except the publisher's recommended one.

TIP   **If you prefer, you can set the update schedule when you first subscribe to the channel. Click the Customize button in the Add Active Channel Content dialog shown in Figure 7.2. The dialog boxes you will see will be a bit different from Figure 7.3, but they offer the same options.**

If you use a modem to connect to the Internet, you will also need to check the box labeled "Dial as needed if connected through a modem", to allow updates to happen automatically.

 If you want the subscription to be updated only when you decide to do it, choose Manually. You can then update the subscription by clicking the Update button on the toolbar of the Subscriptions folder.

 To update all of your subscriptions at once, click the Update All button, or go to any Favorites menu and choose Update All Subscriptions.

The other pages of the subscription property sheet allow you to Unsubscribe if you wish, and to limit the type and amount of material that will be automatically downloaded. For example, click the Advanced button on the Receiving page to specify whether you want Sound and Video items downloaded.

Where Do You Want It?

You have several options for viewing the channel content that's been downloaded: full-screen, in Internet Explorer, as part of your Active Desktop, or as a screen saver. Full screen is probably the best for channels that you want to see only when you choose to view them. Just click the channel's button on the desktop channel bar, and you've got it. If you've chosen not to keep the channel bar on your desktop, you can click the Channels icon in the Quick Launch section of the Taskbar to open the full-screen channel viewer. It includes a channel bar.

 There are two ways to view a channel in a normal Internet Explorer window. If Internet Explorer is already running, click the Channels button on the toolbar, then choose your channel. If you've already opened the channel and are viewing it full screen, click the Full Screen button to return to a standard Internet Explorer window where you can select the channel you want.

The easiest way to put your favorite channel in a window on your Active Desktop is if it offers an Add to Active Desktop button. Click the button, OK a couple of confirmation dialogs, and the channel will appear on your Active Desktop. In some cases, you won't get the entire channel, but only a specific item that the channel provider has designated as an Active Desktop item.

If you want the channel on your desktop and there is no Add to Active Desktop button (or the button doesn't do what you want), you'll have to go through a slightly more involved procedure:

1. Open the channel.
2. If you are in the full-screen channel viewer, switch to a standard Internet Explorer window by clicking the Full-Screen button.
3. Highlight the channel's URL in the address bar. Press Ctrl+C to copy the address to the Windows clipboard.
4. Right-click on the desktop and choose Properties.
5. On the Web page of Display Properties, click the New button.
6. If a dialog appears asking if you want to connect to the Microsoft Web site to look at Active Desktop items, click No.
7. The New Active Desktop Item dialog box appears. Click in the box and press Ctrl+V to paste in the channel address from the clipboard.
8. OK the dialog. Read the "Add item to Active Desktop" dialog box that appears. If the site requires you to log in, click the Customize Subscription button, then click Next to enter your user name and password.
9. When you click OK, Windows will connect to the site and download the necessary components to establish the desktop window.

You can modify the window just like any other Active Desktop item (see Chapter 4). The subscription properties are accessible via Manage Subscriptions on any Favorites menu, as described in the previous section.

Finally, some channels offer the option of displaying as part of the Channels screen saver. If the channel offers this option, a dialog box will appear when you subscribe, asking whether you want the channel included in the screen saver. To change the settings of the Channels screen saver, open Display Properties and choose the Screen Saver tab. Make sure the Channel Screen Saver is selected and click the Settings button to open the Screen Saver property sheet shown in Figure 7.4. If you have more than one channel included in the screen saver, you can determine how long each will be displayed. You can also choose whether or not to play the channel's background sounds, and what action will close the screen saver.

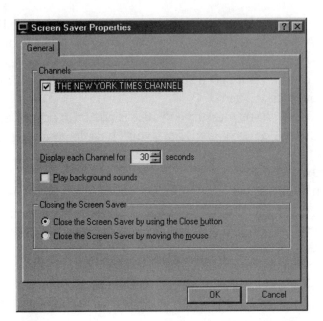

FIGURE 7.4:
Setting properties
for the Channels
screen saver

TIP **Remember, you don't have to subscribe to a channel to view it, but if you find yourself connecting to a channel frequently you should subscribe to avoid the long waits while downloading new content.**

That's the story on using channels. It's fairly short because channels have been well designed for ease of use. Don't let the brevity of this section mislead you; channels promise to be very valuable Internet resources.

WARNING **Though channels should be easy to use, many of the channel designers are still learning how to do it. The result is that a fair number of them don't actually work the way they are supposed to. Even the Channel Guide operated by Microsoft has had problems. So if you have trouble with a channel, don't assume it's caused by something you've done. Patience will probably be required in this arena for some time to come.**

Security and Convenience

The Internet is not a single entity. It is a worldwide system of networked computers that operates without any centralized authority, except for the setting of essential technical standards. This is what makes it so valuable. Nearly anyone can establish a Web site, post whatever information they wish on the site, include links to sites they feel are related (or just interesting), and invite feedback from users.

The same characteristics that make the Internet a valuable resource also make it an open frontier where the only real security lies in actively protecting yourself and learning from those you trust. Popular uses of the Internet cover a wide variety of features. Personal e-mail, newsgroup discussions, large amounts of public information, entertainment and advertising, shopping, distribution of computer software, exchange of confidential business information, and online meetings are all part of the Internet. All of these functions can be carried out with Internet Explorer and related programs, and each involves its own security considerations.

In this section, we will discuss some of the security and convenience features that are part of Internet Explorer. These features relate mainly to using Web sites (including channels), limiting access from your computer to certain types of sites, checking the identity of sites you deal with, and protecting personal information such as credit card numbers.

Internet Explorer's Zones

When you connect to a Web site, Internet Explorer places limits on what will be downloaded from that site, and may prompt you for permission before allowing certain types of downloads. The limits are designed to protect your computer and data from being damaged by software that may be part of the Web site. You control the limits by assigning the site to a zone in Internet Explorer.

By default, all Web sites are assigned to what Internet Explorer calls the Internet zone. The zone appears at the right end of the status bar at the bottom of the Internet Explorer window. If you don't have a status bar in Internet Explorer, click Status Bar on the View menu.

The medium security settings that apply to the Internet zone will require your agreement before downloading and running some types of Java and ActiveX software. The settings also prevent the use of some types of ActiveX and Java that are considered more risky.

WARNING In the constant search for ways to do more with Web sites, two systems have been developed to allow sites to include small programs that are downloaded to your computer to provide such features as animation, sound, and information gathering. One is Java, developed by Sun Microsystems, and the other is Microsoft's ActiveX. Like any other software, Java applets and ActiveX controls could disrupt your computer or data if they are badly written. They could also be used to cause your computer to do things you don't want, like transmitting information from your computer without your authorization. This makes it important to allow programs to be downloaded only from sites you know and trust.

If you want to allow more freedom in the use of Java and ActiveX from a particular site, with fewer OK's from you, you can assign it to the Trusted Sites zone, which has fewer security restrictions. You should do this only if you are confident that the site is maintained by responsible people who will not attempt to invade your computer for illicit purposes, and who keep their own site secure so it can't be used for purposes they don't intend. By default, only secure server sites are accepted as Trusted Sites.

1. Choose Internet Options from the View menu.
2. Click the Security tab.
3. Choose "Trusted sites zone" from the drop-down list, as shown in Figure 7.5.
4. Click the Add Sites button.
5. Type the site's URL into the box labeled "Add this Web site to the zone." By default, this must be a secure server using the **https** protocol. The result should look like Figure 7.6.
6. Keep the check mark in the box at the bottom, unless you have made the possibly risky decision to include a non-secure site in your Trusted Sites.
7. Click OK twice.

TIP It isn't yet clear exactly how the specific security settings of Internet Explorer's Internet zone will work out in practice, so we are going to make a conservative recommendation: Use Trusted Sites only for sites maintained by people with whom you have some sort of relationship. This might include sites run by the company you work for, or by clients or contractors. Keep all others in the Internet zone, at least until you have solid reasons to treat them with greater confidence.

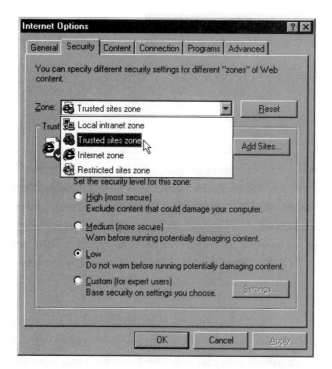

FIGURE 7.5:
Making security
zone settings

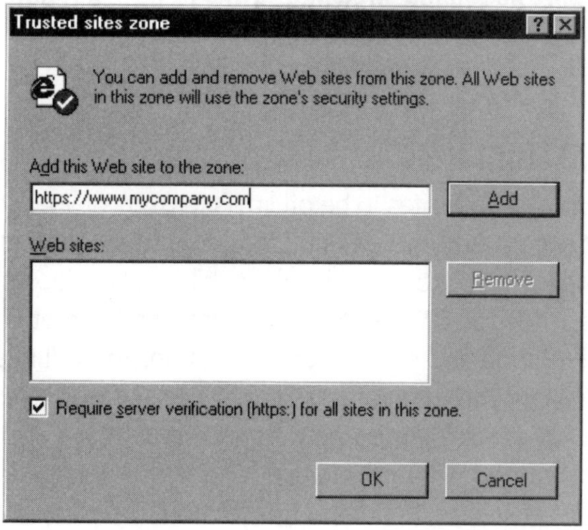

FIGURE 7.6:
Adding a site to
the Trusted
Sites zone

You can also assign sites to the Restricted Sites zone in order to apply a higher level of security restrictions. This greatly restricts the downloading of active content from the site. You should use this designation for sites whose motives or competence you find suspect, but which you still want to visit. The procedure for adding a site to the Restricted Sites zone is the same as for Trusted Sites, except that you should choose Restricted in step 3.

Internet Explorer also has a fourth security zone called the Local Intranet zone. This can be used in companies that operate their own intranet. Sites are assigned to this zone by your intranet system administrator.

NOTE When you select a zone on the Security page of Internet Options, as in Figure 7.5, the radio buttons show you the default security level for that zone. You can change it, though it's hard to see why you would. You can also select Custom and set the individual security levels for more than a dozen different types of interaction with a Web site. Doing this is strictly for Web experts who know their way around with Java and ActiveX.

WARNING Another essential element of security relates to all exchanges of files with others, not just over the Internet. Virus scanning software is essential. Windows 98 does not provide this function, so you should install reliable antivirus software from a reputable software publisher. And keep it up-to-date.

You Can't Get There from Here

If you want certain types of Web sites to be off limits to users of your computer, you can make use of the Content Advisor feature. Generally, the feature is intended to allow parents to limit the Internet sites to which their children have access.

To enable the Content Advisor, choose Internet Options on Internet Explorer's View menu. Choose the Content tab and click the Enable button. You will need to choose a password, which will allow you future access to change settings. After you OK the password, the Content Advisor dialog box opens as shown in Figure 7.7.

The ratings system included with Internet Explorer is the Recreational Software Advisory Council's rating service for the Internet, called RSACi. The system allows you to specify acceptable levels of profanity (language), nudity, sex, and violence. Click on each category in turn and use the slide control to set the level that is acceptable to you. The bottom of the page gives a more detailed description of each setting as you select it.

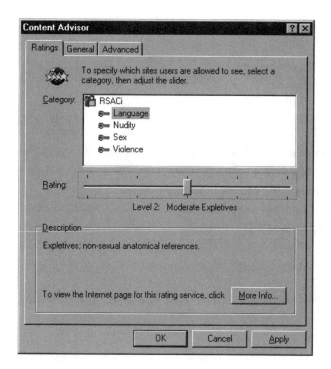

FIGURE 7.7:
Setting content limitations

If you simply choose settings and OK the dialog, users of Internet Explorer on your computer will be limited to visiting sites that have been rated by the RSACi system and that meet the acceptability levels you have set. Attempting to view a site that does not meet these criteria will open a dialog box explaining why Content Advisor will not allow the site to be opened. You can bypass the restriction by entering the password you chose when you set up Content Advisor.

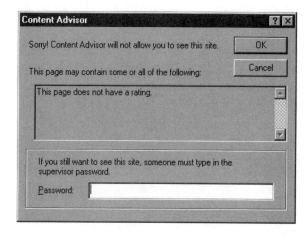

Working this way can be very limiting, because many useful (and completely inoffensive) sites carry no rating. In a simple test, we had to enter the password several times to open the home page at **www.toyota.com**, and four more times to view the page offering photos of the 1998 Corolla. Needless to say, there was nothing the least bit offensive on either page.

NOTE   **A more efficient way to work unrestricted would be to disable Content Advisor when you are using the Internet, then re-enable it before leaving your computer unattended. Just return to the Content tab of Internet Options, click the Enable/Disable button, and enter your password.**

You can consider changing settings on the General and Advanced tabs of the Content Advisor dialog to reduce such problems. On the General page, you can select an option to allow users to see unrated sites. However, this seems to defeat the purpose of using Content Advisor. The General page is also where you can change the Content Advisor password.

The Advanced page of the dialog is where you can install a rating system other than RSACi. You would obtain such rating system software from a company or organization that provides it. Install it according to the instructions provided with the software, then go to the Advanced tab of the Content Advisor dialog to tell Content Advisor to use the new rating system. Some rating systems make use of ratings bureaus, which can also be selected on the Advanced page.

Identification Certificates

A big potential problem when conducting business over the Internet is making sure people and organizations are who they say they are. Certificates are one method of dealing with this problem. Certificates are issued by certifying authorities. The Certificates section of the Content tab (Figure 7.8) in Internet Options allows you to control the certificates used and accepted by Internet Explorer on your computer.

Use the Authorities button and the Publishers button to specify which kinds of certificates Internet Explorer should accept. If you connect to servers that perform client authentication by means of personal certificates, use the Personal button to import the certificates you need.

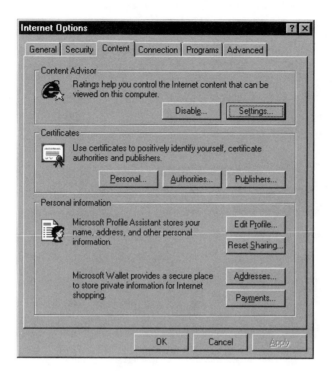

FIGURE 7.8:
The Content page is a bit of a grab-bag.

Handing Out Your Profile

Many Web sites gather information about their users by requiring you to register before gaining access. The information you give may be used only for demographic studies to orient the site's advertising, or it may be used to compile mailing or phone lists for use by the site provider or for sale to others. It is important to pay attention to what information you give out about yourself, and how that information may be used.

Profile Assistant can help you easily provide the information you want to give out and concentrate on the question of how it will be used. On Internet Explorer's View menu, choose Internet Options, then the Content tab. Click the Edit Profile button and you will see the tabbed dialog shown in Figure 7.9.

As you work your way through the tabs, you are actually creating a Windows Address Book entry for yourself. When you are finished, click OK. With your permission in each case, Profile Assistant will send this information to Web sites that request it, usually the first time you visit such a site. The request from a Web site for your Profile Assistant information should specify what information is being requested and how it will be used. Consider carefully before you agree.

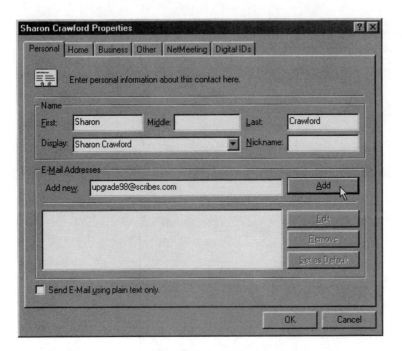

FIGURE 7.9: Enter information that you are willing to give to Web site operators.

NOTE   **Using Windows Address Book is explained in Chapter 8.**

Shopping

With the growth of shopping by Internet, it has become more and more necessary to have secure methods of transmitting confidential information like credit card numbers. Some vendor sites switch to a secure connection when requesting payment information. It's probably true that sending information in this way to a reputable vendor is no more risky than giving the same data over the phone, or handing your credit card to a waiter you don't know. But not everyone sees it that way, and it's not very convenient to pull out your credit card and enter its numbers along with your name, address, and phone number every time you want to make a purchase online. Online is supposed to be convenient, after all!

Enter another of Internet Explorer's little companion programs, Microsoft Wallet. It, too, lives on the Content page of the Internet Options dialog. Click the Addresses button to open the Address Options dialog shown in Figure 7.10.

FIGURE 7.10:
Wallet identifies
address entries by
"display names"
that you select.

Clicking Add allows you to enter a new address in the form shown in Figure 7.11. You can also import an address from the Windows Address Book by clicking the button at the top. Begin by creating an entry for yourself, with your home or business address. Identify the entry by entering a display name in the box at the bottom.

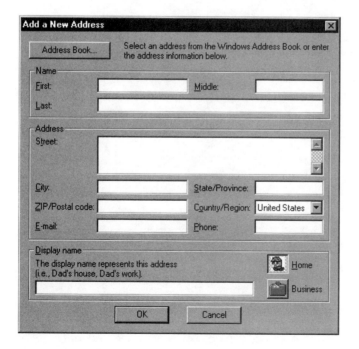

FIGURE 7.11:
Create entries
for shipping
addresses you
want to use for
Internet shopping.

Entries you create here will be added to the Windows Address Book. They will also appear in Wallet's list of addresses, identified by their display name, as shown in

Figure 7.10. For example, the "Jan at Chimney Hill" entry is for a friend who sometimes uses our computer to place orders for supplies she wants shipped to the farm where she boards her horse. When you are finished, click OK to return to the Content page of Internet Options.

The Payments button opens a Payment Options dialog box similar to Address Options. There's an important difference between address options and payment options: all payment information is stored on your computer in encrypted form, and is accessible only with a password that you will create. Here's how to enter payment information:

1. Click the Add button.

2. Select the type of credit card from the list. (As of this writing, acceptable cards are Visa, Mastercard, American Express, and Discover.)

3. Click Next to open the dialog box shown in Figure 7.12.

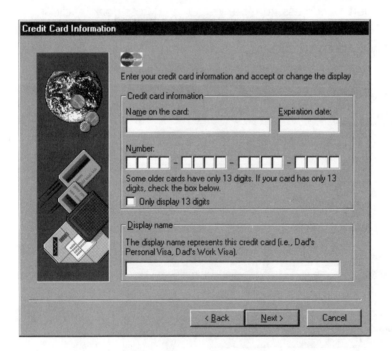

FIGURE 7.12:
Fill in the information for a credit card you want to use for online shopping.

4. Enter your credit card information, and a display name to identify the entry.

5. Click Next to move on to the billing address for this credit card. You can choose among the address entries you already created, or create a new address entry.

6. Click Next again to choose a password for the credit card information. After entering the password a second time to confirm, click Finish.

You can enter more credit cards if you wish, and you can give each entry the same password or use different passwords. Different people using the same computer should each use their own password(s).

Now, when you place an order from a Web site that supports Microsoft Wallet, you can simply choose the appropriate shipping address and credit card from your Wallet (by its display name). No need to type it all over. Of course, you will need the password that unlocks the credit card information.

Creating a Web Page

There are several reasons why you might want to create a Web page. You might want to post it on the World Wide Web to attract clients to your business or interesting people to correspond with. Another reason, requiring an interactive Web page, is to gather information from users of the page. Or you may want to create a Web page to customize the view of a folder on your computer, perhaps for the benefit of others who have access to that folder over a local area network or intranet.

A book about upgrading to the Windows 98 operating system is not the place for a full course in the many considerations that go into producing and maintaining a Web site. Nor are the tools available in the Windows 98 package really intended for that purpose, though they could serve for a simple site. In this section, we will demonstrate the production of a simple group of linked Web pages using FrontPage Express, to give you an idea of the possibilities. After that, we will discuss a few other options and some of FrontPage Express's shortcomings.

A Simple Web Page

Producing a simple Web page involves several steps: entering and formatting text, then adding graphic elements and hyperlinks. FrontPage Express, shown in Figure 7.13, is more than capable of handling these elements, and makes the whole process fairly simple.

For our example, we will create a Web page about a historic airport near the community of Croom in eastern Prince George's County, Maryland. Besides a couple paragraphs of text, we will incorporate links to two related Web sites. We'll have one photograph on the page and links to several others, as well as a link to a related page containing the text of the historic marker at the airport site.

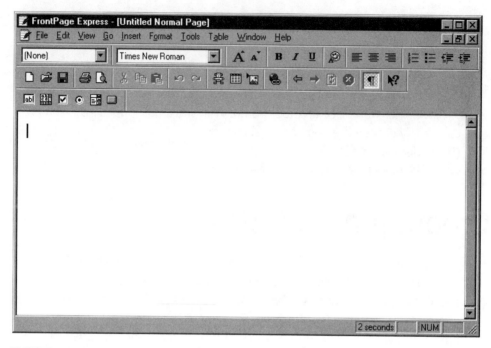

FIGURE 7.13: FrontPage Express is a basic tool for creating Web pages.

This Web page is not intended to stand alone as a Web site. It will be incorporated into an existing site that consists of a Croom home page and related pages. However, one of the great things about the design of the Web is that the same tools and methods are used at all levels. A home page can be created with exactly the same tools we will use, though it would likely consist of more elements. You can regard this example as a sort of cookbook. Follow along, substituting your own text, graphics, and hyperlinks, and you can create whatever Web page you like.

NOTE   First, we did some preliminary work not related to FrontPage Express. We used a scanner and basic image-editing software to scan photographs that we wanted to use. We cropped them and saved them as GIF files in a folder we called Croom Airport.

Start with FrontPage Express

Begin by opening FrontPage Express from the Start menu under Programs ➤ Internet Explorer. Just under the menu bar is the Formatting toolbar; below that is the Standard toolbar. The Forms toolbar is the small one. Because forms are beyond the scope of what we can cover in a book about Windows 98, we went to the View menu and unchecked Forms, so that toolbar will not appear in the remaining illustrations.

Most of the buttons on the Formatting and Standard toolbars are probably familiar from your use of word processors or Internet Explorer, so we've only labeled a few of them. Some serve functions that are beyond the scope of this book. Pause your mouse cursor over any button to see a pop-up label.

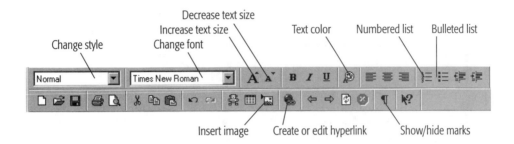

Entering Text

Because our page will begin with a heading, we chose Heading 1 from the Change Style drop-down list, then typed the heading. It looked like Figure 7.14.

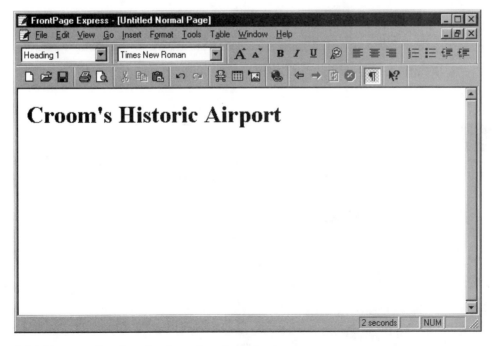

FIGURE 7.14: Choosing a heading style and entering the text

Next, we pressed Enter to move to the next line and typed in two short paragraphs of text. FrontPage Express shifted automatically to Normal style, so we didn't need to change the style for the text. To lend a bit of visual variety, we went back and selected the heading, then changed its typeface to Arial. The result is shown in Figure 7.15.

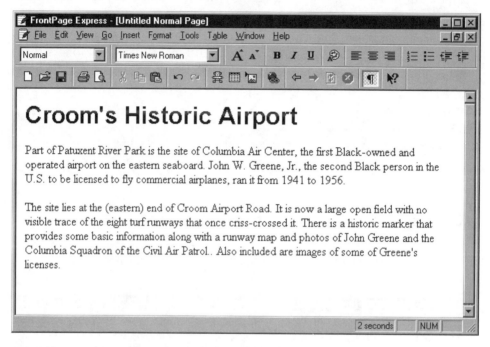

FIGURE 7.15: The text of our simple Web page is complete.

FrontPage Express lists all the fonts available on your system in its Change Font drop-down list. You should only use those that you are sure will be available to users viewing your page.

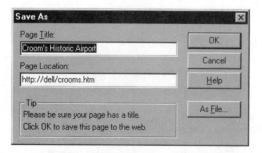

At this point, it was time to save our work. Choosing File ➢ Save (or clicking the Save button) gave us the dialog box at left.

FrontPage Express has the ability to save directly to your Web server, if you have the necessary permissions, but our situation required saving to a local file. The Page Title is how the page will be referenced in such things as favorites and history lists, so we titled it Croom's Historic Airport (just like the heading) and then clicked As File. This opens a standard Save dialog box, and we saved the file as airport.htm in the Croom Airport folder we created earlier.

TIP   If FrontPage Express gives you an error message when you use File ➤ Save, try File ➤ Save As instead.

Adding a Photo

We decided the photo on this page should be between the two paragraphs of text, so we put the cursor at the end of the first paragraph and pressed Enter to create a new line. Then we clicked the Insert Image button on the Standard toolbar to open the Image dialog box shown in Figure 7.16.

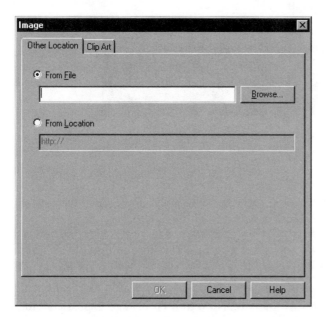

FIGURE 7.16:
Insert an image file by browsing from this dialog.

The Browse button in the Image dialog defaults to the folder where the current file is saved, so finding the file we wanted was easy, because it was in the same folder as the page file. As soon as we clicked Open, the file was inserted on the page, which then looked like Figure 7.17.

FIGURE 7.17: The Web page with a photo inserted

TIP

Photos and other graphics are slow to download. Some might say that this photo is too large. We felt it was OK because it's the only photo on the page. You probably would not want to use multiple images of this size. Note that FrontPage Express' status bar (at the bottom of the window) gives an estimate of download time for the page as you create it.

We decided the photo should have a caption, so we pressed enter to insert a line of text just below it. After typing the caption, we selected the line and made it bold by clicking the Bold button on the Formatting toolbar. This set it off from the rest of the text.

Hyperlinks to Other Web Sites

Next we created the links to other Web pages. The first is to a Web site with information about Patuxent River Park. We selected those words by dragging over them with the mouse, then clicked the Create or Edit Hyperlink button on the Standard toolbar.

This opens the Create Hyperlink dialog box shown in Figure 7.18. We typed the full address for the link in the URL box and clicked OK. After creating a second link on the words Columbia Air Center, the upper part of the page looked like Figure 7.19. The hyperlinks appear in blue, just as they will when the finished page is opened in a Web browser. However, the cursor does not change to a pointing hand when it's over these hyperlinks. That is because the links are not live when working in FrontPage Express. They will be live when the page is opened in a browser.

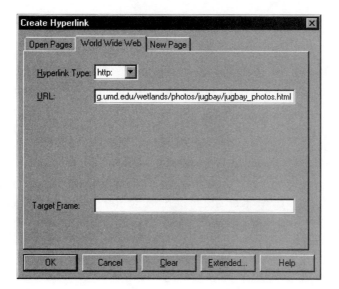

FIGURE 7.18:
Inserting the URL for a hyperlink

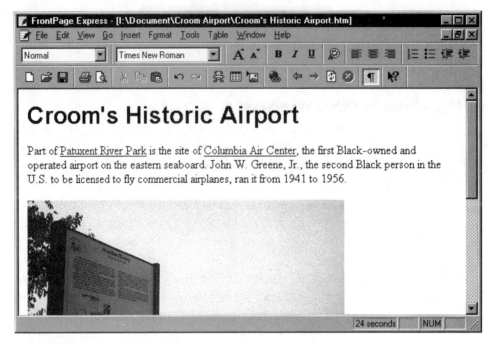

FIGURE 7.19: The underlined words have hyperlinks.

Links to Our Additional Material

All that remained to do at this point was to create links to the remaining items we wanted to include: another photo of the site (from a different location) and details from the historic marker. These would be photos of John W. Greene, Jr., the Columbia Squadron of the Civil Air Patrol, and the runway layout of the airport. Finally, we wanted to include the text of the historic marker.

The photos of Greene and the squadron were the simplest because they required no captions. All we had to do was create hyperlinks to the image files. Because they are stored in the same folder as the Web page, no path or directory information is needed. We highlighted the text that was to be linked (John W. Greene, Jr., in the first case) and clicked the Hyperlink button. We changed the Hyperlink Type to (other) and typed the name of the file in the URL box. That's it!

The photo of the site and the runway layout each required a caption, so each had to be put on its own page. These are simple pages consisting only of a single inserted image and the caption text.

TIP When creating links to related files and pages, it's a good idea to stick to all-lowercase file names. Windows 98 (and Windows NT) don't care if a file name is uppercase and the link to it is lowercase, but other operating systems do. Since many Web servers run on the Unix operating system, you could run into trouble with mismatched cases. If you keep everything lowercase, you won't have a problem.

FrontPage Express makes it easy to create such pages linked to your starting page. We selected the text for the link, in this case the words "eight turf runways." We clicked the Hyperlink button, then the New Page tab in the dialog. Figure 7.20 shows the dialog box without any changes having been made. We just accepted the defaults for Page Title and URL and clicked OK. This opened a New Page dialog, where we again accepted the default Normal Page and clicked OK.

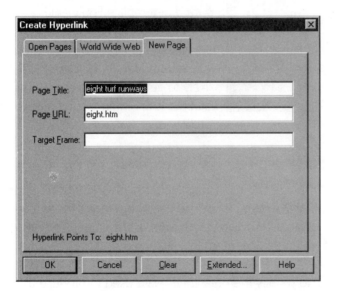

FIGURE 7.20:
Creating a new page linked to the page you are working on

FrontPage Express opened a new, blank page. The first step was to save it with File ➤ Save As in the same folder as the rest of the project. Then we simply inserted the photo and typed the caption, just as we described above for the photo on the main page. The process was the same for the page containing the text of the historic marker, except there was no photo to insert.

That's all there was to it. We sent the entire contents of our Croom Airport folder to the administrator of the Web site, who graciously agreed to post it for us. Since it is a sub-folder within an existing folder named croom, he simplified the name of our folder to airport. You can see the finished pages at www.tc-solutions.com/croom/ airport/airport.htm.

Creating More Complex Pages

FrontPage Express includes several very useful wizards and templates to aid in construction of more complex Web pages. These include forms for gathering information from Web site users and a template for creating a personal home page. Choose File ➤ New to open the New Page dialog and select the wizard or template you want.

Unfortunately, FrontPage Express also has several shortcomings. One of them is that if you select New Web View Folder, you are likely to get an error message. The next section has more information on this and related problems.

Customizing a Folder

Taken together, FrontPage Express (in its Help system) and the Customize This Folder Wizard claim that you can customize the appearance of a folder by using FrontPage Express to create an HTML page. Unfortunately, although FrontPage Express is a released product (as part of the Internet Explorer 4.0 package), the claim is untrue at the time of this writing. If you don't mind digging into HTML programming, you can use FrontPage Express to modify the default template used to produce the Web view of folders on your computer. This process is a bit more complex than it should be, because of bugs in the first release of FrontPage Express.

To modify the Web view of a particular folder on your computer, open the folder and choose View ➤ Customize This Folder. In the Wizard that appears, choose Create or Edit an HTML Document, then click Next twice. If FrontPage Express starts and opens the file called Folder.htt, as shown in Figure 7.21, you are in luck. An important bug has been fixed in the version you have, and you can skip the numbered steps below.

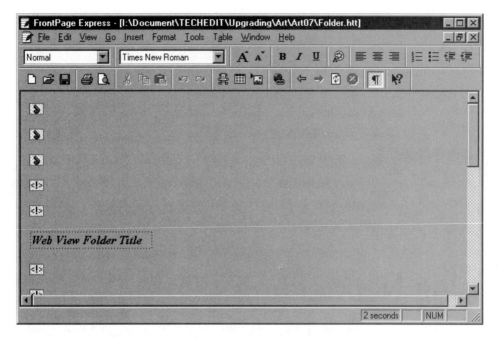

FIGURE 7.21:   The default folder template, as opened by FrontPage Express

If, instead of FrontPage Express, you see Folder.htt open in a Notepad window, don't despair. Do this:

1. Close Notepad and click Finish when the Customize This Folder Wizard reappears.

2. Go to View ➤ Folder Options. On the View page, be sure Show All Files is selected.

3. Open FrontPage Express with Start ➤ Programs ➤ Internet Explorer ➤ FrontPage Express.

4. Choose File ➤ Open, then click Browse.

5. In the second Open File dialog, choose Hypertext Templates (*.htt) in the Files of Type drop-down list.

6. Navigate to the folder you want to customize.

7. Open the file Folder.htt. It should look like Figure 7.21.

Now you can use FrontPage Express to modify the template. However, you will need to know more about HTML than we can teach you here. If you want to study HTML, try choosing View HTML to see the entire template. Or you can right-click on each element as displayed in FrontPage Express, and choose HTML Markup Properties to study the contents of each item separately.

Our best advice for customizing folders is to experiment, and don't be afraid of the consequences. You can always get rid of what you've done and return to the default template. Choose View ➤ Customize This Folder, and choose Remove Customization. Click Next and Finish until the Wizard is done, and you will be back where you started.

> **TIP** For more information on the status of FrontPage Express and how to get it to work as it's supposed to, click the Web button in FrontPage Express Help to connect to Microsoft's support site for Internet Explorer and its related programs.

Using NetMeeting

NetMeeting is another part of the Internet Explorer 4.0 package included with Windows 98. NetMeeting allows you to call other people over the Internet or a local area network. You can talk to a person you have called if you both have sound cards with speakers and microphones. You can also send and receive video images, if you have the necessary hardware. Without any special hardware, you can share applications, draw on a shared whiteboard, and send and receive files and text messages. Audio and video are limited to two participants at a time, but the other functions can involve a larger group.

Because the servers used by NetMeeting maintain directories of who is logged on, you can also go looking for someone with whom to chat. We'll tell you how to do this, and also how to avoid it, if that's your preference.

Like FrontPage Express, NetMeeting has far too many capabilities for us to cover them all in a book about Windows 98. We'll get you started and tell you where to find additional information.

Starting NetMeeting

Start NetMeeting by finding it on the Start menu under Programs ➤ Internet Explorer. If it's not there, you need to install it:

1. Choose Start ➤ Settings ➤ Control Panel.
2. Open Add/Remove Programs and click the Windows Setup tab.

3. In the Components list, select Communications.
4. Click the Details button.
5. In the Components list, put a check in the box by Microsoft NetMeeting.
6. Click OK twice.

The first time you start NetMeeting, you will see a series of dialog boxes. The first one gives a brief list of the things NetMeeting can do. Click Next and you will see the dialog in Figure 7.22, asking you to choose a directory server. Microsoft operates several such servers, and several non-Microsoft servers are also on the drop-down list. You can also type in the address of any other appropriate server.

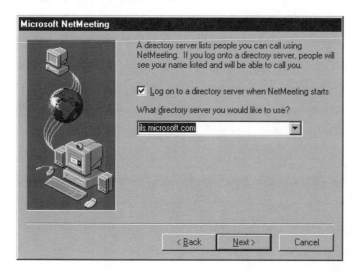

FIGURE 7.22:
Tell NetMeeting what server you want to use for calls.

NOTE **The important thing to understand is that you and the person (or people) you want to call must all be logged on to the same server. Unless the person you are calling stays logged on to a particular server at all times, you will have to arrange your meeting in advance. That means agreeing on what server to use and when. You also need to know the e-mail address of the person you want to call.**

After choosing your server, click Next and you will be asked for your name, e-mail address, location, and comments. You have to enter an e-mail address and first and last names, but they can be real or otherwise. Location and comments are strictly optional. When you log on, the information you entered will be listed in the directory on that server. The next dialog asks you to categorize the information you just gave as personal, business, or adults only. Your information will be visible in the server directory only to people who choose the category you designate.

NOTE   **If you are looking for anonymity online, you can use virtually any character string as your "e-mail address." It doesn't even have to look like a valid address. Whatever string you use essentially becomes your logon name for that server and will be used to make connections through the server, as long as you are logged on. Of course, if you want people to be able to find you by your name and e-mail address, you should use your real ones.**

Clicking Next again moves you along to tell NetMeeting what kind of network connection you have: modem, ISDN, or local area network. After you confirm your connection type, NetMeeting starts the Audio Tuning Wizard. First you set the volume of your speakers, as shown in Figure 7.23. Click Test to hear a sample sound and move the slide control to the volume you like.

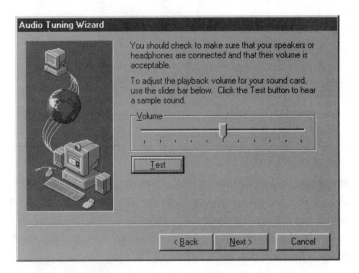

FIGURE 7.23:
Setting your speaker volume for NetMeeting

The next dialog in the Wizard asks you to read aloud a short text sample, so that NetMeeting can set the input volume of your microphone. Once you've done this, click Next, then Finish, and NetMeeting itself will start.

Using the Directory

NetMeeting will automatically log on to the server you selected and download the directory of people currently logged on. Your screen will look like Figure 7.24.

FIGURE 7.24: You can call anyone who is logged on, if they accept the call.

Here's how to read the directory. The icons to the left of each e-mail address give the current status of that user. For a key to the meaning of these icons, click the Category drop-down list. Making a selection in the category list will also determine what directory entries you see.

A speaker icon to the right of the e-mail address indicates that the person is equipped for audio connection. You will be able to talk to him or her. The box with a lens in the next column represents a video camera; it indicates the person is equipped for video.

Remember when you designated your information as either "business" or "personal," when setting up NetMeeting? That determines how you show up in the directory. If you chose "business," your information remains invisible to someone who chooses "personal" in the Category box. Likewise, you see only directory listings that match your selection in the Category box. Selecting "All" allows your list to include people who designated their information as "Adults Only."

The remaining columns contain the information each person gave when logging on. You may want to enlarge the window or change the column widths to get a better view of the information. These columns work as they do in Windows Explorer. Change column width by dragging the boundary between column headers. Sort on a column by clicking its header; click again to reverse the sort.

You are not limited to the directory of the server where you are logged on. Click the Server drop-down list and make another selection. NetMeeting will download and display the current directory of that server, while keeping you logged on to the server you originally chose.

TIP **Where you are logged on determines what directory you are listed in, but you can make a call to anyone in any directory, or without using any directory.**

Making a Call

To call someone listed in a directory, highlight the name and click the Call button on the toolbar. You will see the dialog shown in Figure 7.25. The necessary information is already entered, so just click Call in the dialog box.

You can also call people without first finding them in a directory. You need to know both the name of the server where they are logged on for Internet calling and their e-mail address. Click the Call button and enter the information in the address box. The server name goes first, then a slash (/), then the e-mail address, as shown in Figure 7.25. Leave the Call Using setting at Automatic and click Call.

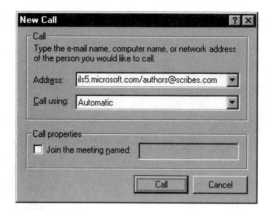

FIGURE 7.25:
Making a call with
NetMeeting

NOTE   **NetMeeting connects to the Internet automatically only when you start it up. If you are running NetMeeting, but are not currently connected to the Internet, you will have to initiate the connection manually. If you use a modem to connect, do this by opening the Dial-Up Networking folder (Start ➤ Programs ➤ Accessories ➤ Communications). Click your Internet connection to start it.**

If someone calls you, you will hear a telephone ringing and a small dialog box will open on your screen. It tells you who is calling and asks whether you want to accept the call.

When the connection is made, your NetMeeting window will change to display the status of the current call. This is shown in Figure 7.26.

Sometimes it takes a few seconds for the direct audio connection to be made. If you are left wondering what's going on, click the Chat button on the toolbar to initiate written communication. The Chat window is shown in Figure 7.27. It will open on the screens of all participants in the call.

TIP   **Remember, if you join a call already in progress by calling one of the participants, you create a multi-person call. Voice communication and video will only be available to two participants at a time, but everyone can use the other facilities such as Chat.**

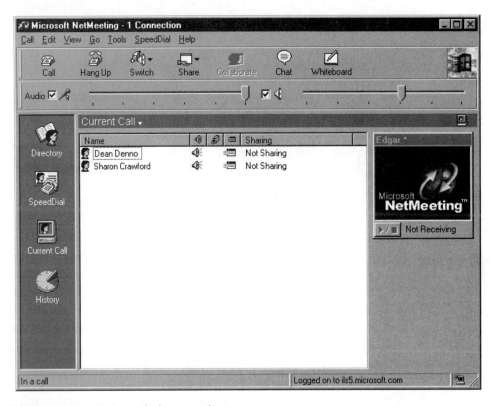

FIGURE 7.26: You've made the connection!

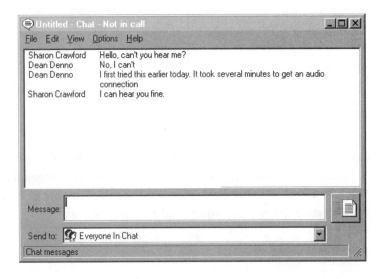

FIGURE 7.27:
Written communi-
cation is always
available via Chat.

Type your message in the box at the bottom. Press Enter or click the button to the right of the Message box to transmit your message to all other participants in the call. In a multi-party call, you can send a message to one person only by selecting the recipient from the Send To drop-down list.

Working Together

Once you have established a connection, you can share applications if you wish. This allows the other person to see what you are doing on your computer, in any applications you choose to share.

To share an application, first start it if it isn't already running. Then choose the application from the list that appears when you click Share on the toolbar. A window will open on all other connected computers, which will be a duplicate of the application window on your computer. Other participants in the call will see anything you do in that window, whether it's editing text or pulling down a menu.

Because the other computers display only a copy of what is on your screen, they do not need to have the program installed. You can share any program installed on your machine, without worrying about whether others have it.

NOTE Application sharing, like voice and video, places a substantial load on the network connection. If you are using a dial-up connection and try to share a graphics program, for example, you are likely to get very poor audio performance.

There's another level of collaboration available, as well. Click the Collaborate button and anyone can work in the shared application(s). Only one person can be in control at a time. Whoever is not in control sees a dimmed mouse cursor carrying the initials of the person who currently has control. Take control by clicking your mouse. Shifting control can be a slow process, however, and it requires the cooperation of others to *not* click their mice.

Other NetMeeting Functions

By default, anyone you call and anyone from whom you accept a call is added to your SpeedDial list. This means you can call them again without having to find them in a directory and without having to manually enter the server name and e-mail address in the New Call dialog box. Open your SpeedDial list by clicking SpeedDial in the Navigation Icons column at the left side of the NetMeeting Window. Make a call by double-clicking the entry you want. Of course, the call can only be completed if the person you are calling is logged on to the server.

You can also create SpeedDial entries manually by clicking the SpeedDial button on the toolbar.

TIP   **You can gain some window area at no real cost by removing the check mark from Navigation Icons on the View menu. You still have access to the same views by choosing from the drop-down list below the microphone volume slider.**

Because NetMeeting sessions can place heavy loads on both your network connection and your processor, NetMeeting includes an accessory called Intel Connection Advisor. This starts automatically along with NetMeeting, and it puts its icon in the System Tray at the right end of the Windows Taskbar.

Double-click the icon to open the window shown in Figure 7.28. The Audio tab is particularly helpful. It tells you how much audio is being lost, how much delay is occurring in audio transmission, and how much audio data is being transmitted. With a bit of experience, you will come to know both your own and your network connection's limitations in relation to these figures.

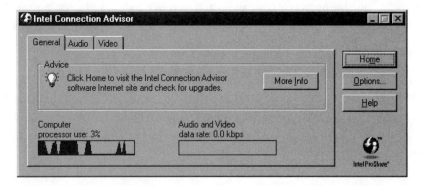

FIGURE 7.28:   Connection Advisor can help you figure out why sharing is slow, or why your audio is breaking up.

When you want to change the information NetMeeting uses, choose Tools ➤ Options to open the tabbed dialog in Figure 7.29. If you make heavy use of NetMeeting, you may want to select the option on the General page to "Run when

Windows starts and notify me of incoming calls." The General page is also where you can change the type of network connection you are using.

FIGURE 7.29:
Changing
NetMeeting
options

The page tabbed as My Information lists the information about you that is posted to the server directory when you log on. You can make any changes you wish, including changing your category (business or personal).

TIP   **You can also get direct access to My Information from the Call menu.**

The Calling tab in Options is where you can change the server you log on to. It also has an option to not list yourself in the server directory. This means that you will receive calls only from people who know your e-mail address and know you are logged on, perhaps by pre-arrangement. This page of the dialog also includes several SpeedDial options.

You can get more information on NetMeeting use and ongoing improvements by visiting the Web site at **www.microsoft.com/netmeeting/**.

What's Next

In this chapter we've discussed a broad variety of Internet-related functions, but there's lots more to come. The next chapter will cover what is probably the most universal of Internet uses, Internet mail. We will also discuss the use of newsgroups, which is handled by the same software as Internet mail.

INTERNET MAIL
AND NEWS

Windows 98 comes with an entirely new mail system. As is to be expected, this is both good news and bad news. In this case, it's mostly good. If you're upgrading from Windows 95, and you like or need the Windows Messaging System (Exchange), you can keep using it. If you haven't been using Exchange, you probably won't miss it.

Users who are connected to a local area network, including company intranet users, can continue using their current e-mail system. Home and small office users for whom e-mail means Internet mail will find the new Outlook Express far easier to set up and use than Windows 95's Exchange. Outlook Express also allows you to use Internet newsgroups (the Usenet). The only real drawback is that there is no built-in fax capability. We'll discuss that problem in Appendix A, "Installing for Windows 95 Users."

Internet Mail

Windows 98 and Internet Explorer are designed to work with your preferred e-mail program. The installation routine checks your system for installed e-mail programs, and lists them in the Mail drop-down box on the Programs page of the Internet Options dialog (on Internet Explorer's View menu). If you upgraded from Windows 95 with Microsoft Exchange installed, it will appear on the list as Windows Messaging. Outlook Express, which is part of the Windows 98 package, is also on the list. The program you choose from this list is the one that will start when you click Mail on Internet Explorer's Go menu.

Internet Explorer also has a Mail button that opens a small menu of mail functions. It can give you direct access to a few functions of some e-mail programs. From the menu, you can read your mail or open a New Message window to type a message. If you wish, the new message can include either a link to the Web site currently open in Internet Explorer, or a copy of the current page. Of course, you can also open your mail program directly, either from the Start Menu or from a shortcut on the desktop.

Starting Outlook Express

If you don't already have an e-mail program, Outlook Express can handle your Internet mail very nicely. If you have Microsoft Exchange (left over from Windows 95) but find it complicated and difficult to use, give Outlook Express a try.

NOTE   **In spite of the similar name, Outlook Express is not a scaled-down version of Microsoft Outlook. If you have Outlook (a part of the Office 97 suite), you can use it for your e-mail if you prefer, though it can't work with newsgroups. If the only e-mail you use is Internet mail, you may find Outlook Express easier.**

To set Internet Explorer to start Outlook Express, do this:

1. Right-click the Internet Explorer icon.
2. Choose properties, then the Programs tab.
3. Set the Mail drop-down list to Outlook Express.
4. Set the News drop-down list to Outlook Express, unless you have another newsreader you prefer.
5. Click OK.

Now, Internet Explorer will open Outlook Express when you choose Mail from the Go menu or when you choose an operation from the menu under the Mail button on the toolbar. You can also start Outlook Express from its desktop shortcut, from the Quick Launch section of the Taskbar, or from the Start Menu (Start ➤ Programs ➤ Internet Explorer ➤ Outlook Express).

Figure 8.1 shows the Outlook Express main window, which is designed like a Web home page. Besides the usual menus and toolbar, there are six icons in the right pane that you can click for a quick route to the most common functions:

- Read Mail opens your inbox so you can read your messages.
- Read News opens the list of newsgroups to which you have subscribed. (Newsreader functions are described later in this chapter.)
- Compose a Message allows you to create a mail message.
- Address Book opens your address book.
- Download All connects to your Internet mail service and downloads all your new mail messages.
- Find People allows you to connect to an Internet directory service (white pages) to find someone's e-mail address.

The three buttons across the top of the right pane are links to Microsoft's Web site. The first two take you to the Outlook Express and Internet Explorer areas, while the third links to a more general page. Clicking one of the bars will start Internet Explorer and connect to the site.

The left pane of the Outlook Express main window gives you direct access to your Inbox, which holds received mail until you delete it, and the Outbox, which holds messages you have created until you connect so they can be transmitted. There are also folders for items you've sent, items deleted from your Inbox, and items you've composed but decided not to send yet (drafts). The left pane also lists any news servers that you have set up in Outlook Express.

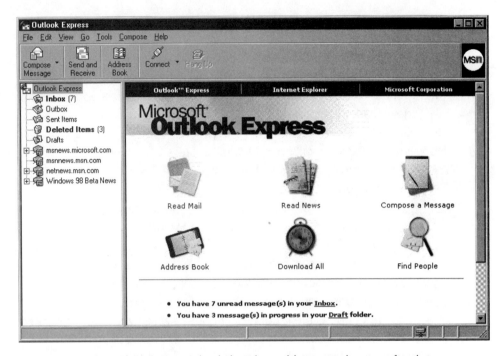

FIGURE 8.1: The Outlook Express main window gives quick access to important functions.

Adding an Internet Mail Account

To handle your e-mail, Outlook Express needs information about your Internet (or company intranet) mail account(s). If you already set up your Internet mail account along with your Internet access for Internet Explorer (in Chapter 6), you can probably skip this section. You will need to enter the information for your account if you haven't already done it, or if you have more than one Internet mail account that you want to use with Outlook Express.

Before you begin, read through the steps to make sure you have all the necessary information.

1. In Outlook Express, choose Tools ➤ Accounts.

2. Click the Mail tab. Any accounts you have already set up will be listed here, as shown in Figure 8.2.

3. Click Add and choose Mail to set up a new account in Outlook Express. The Internet Connection Wizard will start.

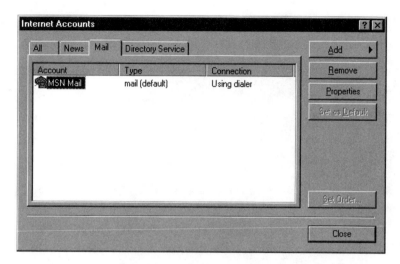

FIGURE 8.2: Use the Internet Accounts dialog to manage your Internet mail, news, and directory service accounts.

4. Enter the name you want to appear in the From field of messages you send from this account. Click Next.

5. Enter your e-mail address for this account. This is the address you chose when you established the account with your service provider. Click Next.

6. Enter the e-mail server names given to you by your service provider. There are separate servers for incoming and outgoing mail. Set the incoming mail server type (in the drop-down box) to either POP3 or IMAP, to match the beginning of the server name. Click Next again.

7. Enter your logon name and password for this e-mail account (Figure 8.3). If the e-mail account is part of a package with Internet access (from an Internet service provider), the logon name and password are probably the same as for your Internet access. Click Next to continue.

8. Enter a "friendly name" for this Internet mail account. If you have multiple accounts, this is the name that will help you tell them apart. For example, use names like "Bob's Personal E-mail" or "Mary's Work Mail." Click Next again.

9. Choose your method for connecting to the Internet. If you connect via a local area network or choose to connect manually, this is your last entry. Click Next, and then Finish. If you want Outlook Express to dial automatically to connect, choose "Connect using my phone line," then click Next.

FIGURE 8.3:   The Internet Connection Wizard steps you through the process
of setting up an Internet mail account in Outlook Express.

10.   To use a connection that is already set up on your computer, choose it from
the list and click Next, then Finish. If you need to set up a new connection,
choose "Create a new dial-up connection," and click Next.

11.   Continue through the Wizard. You will need to enter the phone number you
dial to connect to your Internet mail provider, your user name and password,
and a name for the connection. Don't change the advanced properties
unless you know you need to. Finally, click Finish.

Outlook Express can now connect to your Internet mail account to send and
receive mail. If you need to change (or just check) any of the information you entered,
re-open the Internet Accounts dialog, highlight the account name, and click the
Properties button. You can also use the Internet Accounts dialog to remove an account
you no longer need.

Reading Your Mail

Clicking the Read Mail icon in the main window takes you to your Inbox, shown in
Figure 8.4. You can also get there by clicking the Inbox in the left pane of the Outlook
Express window. Then click the Send and Receive button on the toolbar to tell Out-
look Express to connect to your Internet service provider and get your mail.

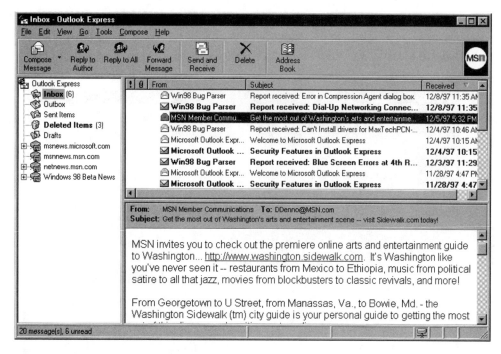

FIGURE 8.4: The Outlook Express Inbox

Outlook Express pops up this dialog box to show the progress of your e-mail connection. The dialog will disappear after your mail has been downloaded, but Outlook Express will not automatically disconnect from your Internet service unless you check the "Hang up when finished" box. Clicking the Details button will expand the dialog to tell you exactly what Outlook Express is doing.

In the Inbox, your messages are listed in the upper pane, with unread messages in bold. You can change the order of messages by clicking a column heading to sort messages according to that column. Click the heading again to reverse the sort order.

When you highlight a message header in the upper pane, the message itself appears in the lower preview pane. Double-click on a message header to open the message in its own window for easier viewing. This view is shown in Figure 8.5. As you can see, Outlook Express is not limited to plain text e-mail. It also handles messages formatted in HTML, which means you can vary fonts and colors and include links and graphics—as long as the people you are writing to use e-mail software that can handle HTML messages.

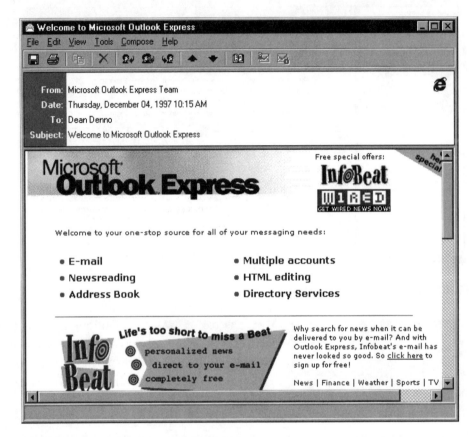

FIGURE 8.5: Reading your mail in Outlook Express

TIP You don't have to find out ahead of time what e-mail programs your correspondents use, and whether they can display HTML messages. Anyone whose software can't handle HTML will still receive your message, but it will be displayed as plain text.

The Inbox view will be most useful if you receive lots of e-mail and need to decide which messages to read by quickly checking the subject and sender. Otherwise, you may find it simpler to just double-click your first new message and work in the mail reader window (like Figure 8.5) from there on. The toolbar gives you quick access to the most common operations.

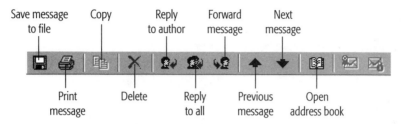

Work your way through your messages using the Next and Previous message buttons. As you read each message, Outlook Express will mark it as Read in the Inbox by changing its entry to normal type instead of bold. To delete a message, click the Delete button instead of Next; Outlook Express will automatically move on to the next message.

Replying

To reply to a message, click the Reply to Author button. Outlook Express opens a reply window like the one in Figure 8.6. The sender of the original message is automatically entered in the To field, and the original subject is copied to the Subject field with "Re:" in front of it. The entire original message is copied to the text area, so that the person you are replying to can easily refer to their original message. You get a blank line at the top of the text area, with the cursor already there, so you can just start typing.

TIP If the message you are replying to was a long one, it may be a good idea to delete parts of it from your reply. You can put >> and << around the parts of the original that you leave and put your reply paragraphs between the remaining paragraphs of the original, to create a point-by-point reply for the sake of clarity.

If you create your reply by clicking the Reply to All button (instead of Reply to Author), your reply will be sent to all the people listed in the To and Cc fields of the original message.

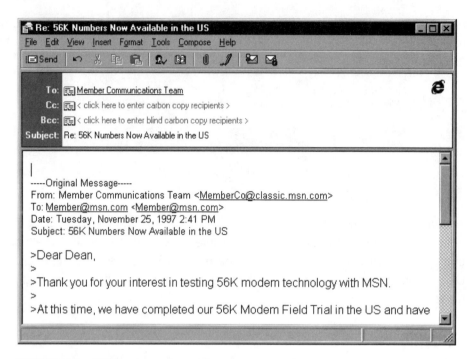

FIGURE 8.6: Replying to a mail message

When you are finished typing your reply, just click the Send button on the toolbar to put the reply in your Outbox. It will be transmitted the next time you connect to your mail service by clicking Send and Receive in the Outlook Express main window. Because most of the controls in the reply window are the same as in a new message window, we'll discuss them in the next section.

NOTE If the message to which you are replying used HTML formatting, your reply message will also use HTML by default. Outlook Express will provide a formatting toolbar in the reply window. Its use is discussed in the Fancy section below. If you wish, you can use the Format menu to change the reply to Plain Text.

Sending a New Message Plain...

There are several ways to open the New Message window shown in Figure 8.7. From the Outlook Express start-up window, click the Compose a Message icon. From the same window or the Inbox or Outbox, click the Compose Message button on the toolbar. If you're reading your mail in its own window, choose New Message on the Compose menu.

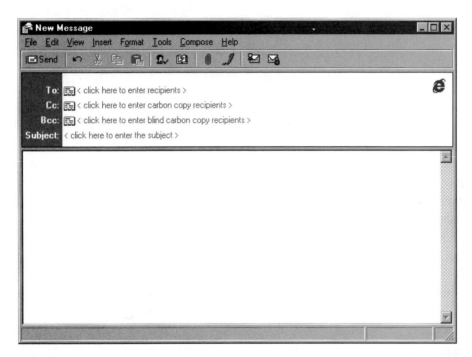

FIGURE 8.7:   Composing a new message in Outlook Express

Click in the To field to type the name of the person to whom you are writing; the name has to match an entry in your Address Book. (We'll discuss the Address Book later in this chapter.) Or you can click the icon that looks like a Rolodex card in the To field to select your addressee from the names in your Address Book. Repeat this procedure for the Copy (Cc:) and Blind Copy (Bcc:) fields, if you wish.

TIP   As in many other parts of Windows 98, if you rest your mouse pointer on one of these fields, you will get a pop-up help message. In this case, it tells you that you can enter multiple names, separating them with commas or semicolons.

Fill in the Subject field, and then move on to typing the body of your message. Once again, there's a toolbar to help you with the most common operations.

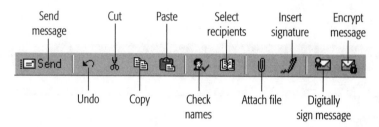

If you've entered one or more names in the To or copies fields, and want to be sure they are really in your Address Book, click the Check Names button. If you've entered a name for which there is no match, you'll be able to choose the correct name from your Address Book or create a new entry. The Select Recipients button offers an alternate way to fill in the To and copies fields. You may find it quicker if you need to fill in several names.

Use the Attach File button to attach a file to your message. The file will appear as an icon in a separate window below your message. Outlook Express calls this button "Insert File," but that's a misnomer.

When you finish typing your message, click the Send button to put it in your Outbox. Outlook Express will then connect to your Internet service to transmit it.

> **NOTE** If you prefer you can use Send Later on the File menu to just put the message in your Outbox. It will be transmitted the next time you click the Send and Receive button, or the next time Outlook Express automatically logs on, checks for mail, and logs off. See the section, "More Outlook Express Options," later in this chapter, on how to control this feature.

Or Sending Your Message Fancy

To dress up your messages to catch the recipient's eye, you can use HTML's graphics and formatting abilities. Outlook Express comes with over a dozen types of stationery, which include background, graphics, and appropriate fonts. Start an HTML message by choosing Compose ➤ New Message Using or by clicking the down arrow just to the right of the Compose Message button on the toolbar in Outlook Express's main window.

You will then see this menu, though the specific stationery items on it may vary. Choose the one you want to use. Click More Stationery to open a browse window listing all the stationery files in the Stationery folder, or choose No Stationery to create a message from scratch with HTML formatting.

The New Message window opens with your chosen stationery (or none), and with a formatting toolbar at the top of the message text area, as shown in Figure 8.8. Fill in the To, Copies, and Subject fields the same as for a plain text message. Then move your cursor into the message body area, and do just about anything you like! You can accept the ready-made text and add your own information, or you can delete what's been provided and just use the background.

FIGURE 8.8: Using ready-made stationery to dress up your message

> **TIP** Once you've started a message, you can change it from plain text to HTML by choosing Rich Text (HTML) on the Format menu.

Most of the controls on the formatting toolbar will be familiar to anyone who has used a Windows word processor. The best way to discover the details is by experimenting. Here are a few buttons that may not be familiar. If you don't see all of these buttons on your toolbar, enlarge your message window.

Button	Purpose
	Styles menu: select a predefined paragraph style
	Font color
	Insert a horizontal line
	Insert a hyperlink
	Insert a picture

Remember that a hyperlink has to be attached to text. The Insert Hyperlink button is available only when you highlight the text to which you want the hyperlink attached.

Of course, you'll probably find that it's much easier to send most of your e-mail as plain text. Stationery and HTML formatting are nice tools to have when you want to make a message special.

Signing Your Message

There are two kinds of signatures commonly used in e-mail, and neither of them has anything to do with your pen-and-paper signature. If security is an issue, you can sign your message with a digital ID, by using the Digitally Sign Message button. We'll discuss digital IDs, which are also used for the Encrypt Message function, in the next section.

The more common kind of signature is simply text. It generally consists of your name and whatever else you might want to use to close your messages. For example, one of the authors of this book has recently been using a signature that reads: "Sharon

Crawford, Unindicted co-conspirator * Upgrading to Windows 98 (Sybex 1998) * Running Back Office Small Business Server (Microsoft Press 1998) * Running Microsoft Windows NT Server 4.0 (Microsoft Press 1997) And sole perpetrator Windows 98: No Experience Required (Sybex 1998)."

A signature line can also be short and simple, or can extend to such elaborate efforts as using text characters spaced out over several lines to simulate a written signature or other graphic.

To create your signature line, return to the Outlook Express main window.

1. Choose Tools ➤ Stationery.
2. On the Mail tab, click the Signature button to open the dialog in Figure 8.9.

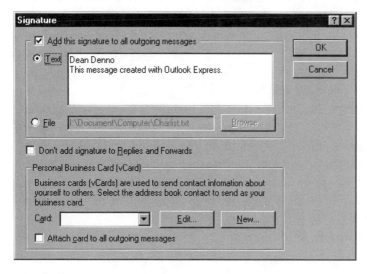

FIGURE 8.9:   Setting up your signature and business card

3. Check the box to "Add this signature to all outgoing messages."
4. For a simple signature like the one shown, choose the Text radio button and enter the signature lines you want.
5. If your taste runs to the more elaborate, you can choose File to have a file inserted as your signature. You can also choose whether your signature should be used when you reply to or forward a message.
6. When you are finished, click OK twice.

Once you set up a signature, it is automatically included any time you open a new message window in plain text mode. The insertion point is placed above the signature, so you can just type your message and the signature will always be at the end. If you choose to also use your signature with replies and forwards, you should pay attention to where it is automatically placed in such messages.

The Insert Signature button does what its name says: inserts your signature text at the current insertion point in your message. However, because signatures are designed to be added automatically at the appropriate place, you probably won't make much use of it.

Adding a Business Card

In the Signature dialog box, you can also set up a business card to be transmitted with e-mail messages. The card is sent as an attachment in a standard format called vCard. The information included on your card comes from an entry in your address book. Because you may not want it to include the same information you use for other purposes, you should create a special Address Book entry called My vCard (or some such).

1. Click Tools ➤ Stationery.
2. On the Mail page, click Signature.
3. In the Personal Business Card (vCard) section of the dialog (Figure 8.9), click New.
4. Enter whatever information you want included in your e-mail business card. You are creating an Address Book entry. (For more information, refer to the Address Book section later in this chapter.) Click OK when you are finished.
5. In the Signature dialog box, check "Attach card to all outgoing messages," if that is what you want. Click OK twice.

If you did not choose to attach your business card to all messages, you can attach it to individual messages by choosing Insert ➤ Business Card when composing a message.

 When someone sends you a message with a vCard attached, you will see a file card icon in the header area of the message reading window.

Click it to open the vCard attachment, which will appear as an Address Book entry. There's also a button to add the information to your Address Book.

Digital IDs

A digital ID allows you to prove your identity to others with whom you correspond electronically. A part of your digital ID also allows others to encrypt messages they send you. Digital IDs work in conjunction with the S/MIME standard for secure electronic mail.

Personal digital IDs generally are tied to a particular e-mail address. If you have more than one e-mail account set up in Outlook Express, make sure the default account is the one for which you want a digital ID. Check this on the Mail tab of the Tools ➤ Accounts dialog.

Here's one way to get a digital ID:

1. Open Outlook Express's Tools ➤ Options dialog.

2. On the Security page, click the Get Digital ID button. This will start Internet Explorer and connect you to the certification page of Microsoft's Internet Explorer Web site.

3. Read the information provided, then click the VeriSign Get Your ID Now button to connect to their site.

NOTE **As of this writing, VeriSign is Microsoft's preferred provider of digital IDs, and is offering free 60-day trial digital IDs for use with Outlook Express.**

4. You may see a Security Alert explaining that you are about to use a secure Internet connection. You have to click OK to continue. When you get to the VeriSign site, you will see a Security Warning asking, "Do you want to install and run 'Microsoft Certificate Enrollment Cab'…." You must answer Yes to continue. A form will open with your name and e-mail address already filled in. Read any information about optional features and decide whether you want them. Read the explanation of the challenge phrase, and enter one (like a password).

5. There are several more options to decide on, including the possibility of getting a full-featured permanent digital ID for a modest fee. After you have chosen your options, click the Accept button at the bottom of the page. You can then continue working in Internet Explorer, or exit and disconnect if you wish.

6. After leaving the VeriSign site, wait a few minutes. Close the Options dialog in Outlook Express if it's still open. Then click Send and Receive. You will receive an e-mail from VeriSign with further instructions.

7. When you read VeriSign's message, it will include a Next button. Click the button to connect again to the VeriSign Web site.

8. When you see the message that your digital ID has been successfully generated, click the Install button. (You may have to scroll to the bottom of the page to see the message and button.) After a few seconds you will see a message that your digital ID has been installed in Outlook Express. Close Internet Explorer and disconnect from your Internet service if you wish.

9. Return to Outlook Express and choose Tools ➤ Accounts.

10. Select the e-mail account for which you just obtained the digital ID, and click Properties.

11. Choose the Security tab, and check the box labeled "Use a digital ID when sending secure messages from: [your e-mail address]", as shown in Figure 8.10.

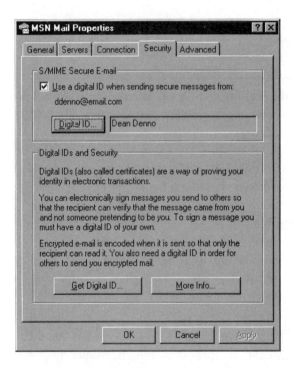

FIGURE 8.10:
Associating your digital ID with your e-mail account

12. Click the Digital ID button. You will see a list of the personal certificates installed on your machine. If this is your first digital ID, there will probably be only one.

13. Highlight the new certificate and click OK twice, then Close.

You can now use the Digitally Sign Message button in a message compose window. The digital signature serves to prove your identity and the authenticity of your message to those who receive it.

When someone sends you a digitally signed message, its icon in the Inbox will include a red ribbon seal.

When you view the message, you will first see a help message explaining the digital signature. You can check the box at the end of the help message if you don't want to see it in the future. Then click the Continue button to see the message content.

NOTE   Digitally signed messages are also indicated by the words "Digitally signed and verified" in addition to the red ribbon seal in the message header area.

Encrypted E-mail

If you want to be able to send encrypted e-mail to the person from whom you have received a digitally signed message, you need to add that person's digital ID to their record in your Address Book.

1.   Open the signed message and choose File ➤ Properties.
2.   On the Security tab, click "Add digital ID to Address Book." This opens the property sheet for the entry, if the person is already in your Address Book. Otherwise, it creates a new entry with the name, e-mail address, and digital ID.
3.   You can add or change whatever information you wish, as described in the Address Book section later in this chapter. Look on the Digital ID's tab to confirm that the digital ID has been added.
4.   Click OK twice.

WARNING   If the person who sent the digitally signed message has more than one e-mail address and the message was sent from an address not listed in your Address Book, you will need to manually enter the e-mail address in step 3. Also, the process is likely to fail if you have multiple address book entries for the same person. Multiple e-mail addresses for the same person are not a problem when adding the digital ID as long as they are stored in the same Address Book record. To send an encrypted message to someone with multiple e-mail addresses, you will have to set their default e-mail address to one for which you have a digital ID.

You can now use the Encrypt message button on the compose window toolbar to encode messages to this person.

When someone sends you an encrypted message, it will be marked with a lock icon. When you try to read the message, the first thing you will see is a help message explaining encrypted e-mail. If the message has been properly encrypted by someone to whom you gave your digital ID, Outlook Express will decrypt it automatically. Click the Continue button at the end of the help screen to view the message.

Using the Mail Folders

The left pane of the Outlook Express main window offers a tree view of the folders used to organize your mail and newsgroup messages. Click any folder to open it. Here is a brief description of the folders:

Inbox is where incoming e-mail lands. Whether you read it or not, it stays in the Inbox until you put it somewhere else.

Outbox is where outgoing e-mail and newsgroup messages are held. When the messages are transmitted (uploaded to the servers), they are moved out of the Outbox to Sent Items.

Sent Items holds copies of messages you have sent.

Deleted Items keeps copies of items you have deleted from other folders. If you want this folder emptied automatically when you quit Outlook Express, you can set this option on the General page of Tools ➤ Options.

Drafts is a folder you can use to hold messages for future use. The only way messages get to the Drafts folder is if you put them there. You can do this with File ➤ Move to Folder in a compose window, or by dragging and dropping them.

News Servers are listed by the friendly name you assign, as described in the next section.

You can create new folders by right-clicking in the upper part of the pane (above the news servers). This is one good way to create a filing system to organize your e-mail. Move messages by dragging them from the upper right pane to the folder where you want them. You can also create copies with the File ➤ Copy to Folder command in a compose window.

NOTE Outlook Express folders are not Windows 98 folders, and can only be used within Outlook Express.

Get Your News Here

An important part of the Internet is the Usenet, composed of thousands of newsgroups. A newsgroup is like a community bulletin board: Anyone can post anything. The only restraints are self-imposed, based on the topic and decorum (or lack thereof) of the particular newsgroup. There is no assurance of accuracy, quality, or even authenticity of postings, except the responses of other participants in the newsgroup.

Newsgroups are hosted on news servers, also called NNTP servers (for Network News Transfer Protocol). Your Internet service provider should give you access to at least one news server. The total number of public newsgroups on the Internet is near 20,000, but some news servers carry only a few thousand of these.

NOTE Some news servers are limited to special purposes. For example, as part of the beta test of Windows 98, Microsoft operated a news server open only to beta test participants. It hosted over a hundred newsgroups devoted to discussing various features of the operating system and its accessories.

Programs that allow you to read newsgroup postings and post your own messages are called newsreaders. Outlook Express is a newsreader as well as an e-mail program. If you have another newsreader installed, you can set which program Internet Explorer opens when you use its Go ➤ News command. In Internet Explorer, choose View ➤ Internet Options ➤ Programs. Set the News drop-down list to the newsreader you prefer. Of course, if you choose a newsreader other than Outlook Express, we can't help you here with how to use it. You probably already know. In that case, you can skip the next section.

Adding a News Server

The process of reading and creating newsgroup postings is very similar to e-mail, so it's appropriate that Outlook Express handles both operations. The first step in gaining access to newsgroups is to tell Outlook Express what news server to use.

1. Look at the left pane of the Outlook Express window. Any news servers you have already set up will be listed here.

2. If you need to set up a new server, choose Tools ➤ Accounts.

3. In the Internet Accounts dialog, click the News tab.

4. Click Add and choose News. The Internet Connection Wizard will start.

5. Enter the name you want to appear in the From field of messages you post. Click Next.

6. Enter your e-mail address. This allows other newsgroup participants to send you private e-mail, as an alternative to responding in the newsgroup. Click Next.

7. The dialog box shown in Figure 8.11 appears. Enter the news (NNTP) server name given to you by your service provider. If this is a private server that requires users to log on, check the box at the bottom. Click Next again.

FIGURE 8.11: Entering your news server name

8. If you checked the log on box, a dialog will appear where you enter your logon name and password. Fill these in and click Next, or skip to the next step if you don't have to log on.

9.   Enter a "friendly name" for this news server. This is the name that will identify the server to you in Outlook Express. Click Next again.

10. Choose your method for connecting to the Internet. If you connect via a local area network or choose to connect manually, this is your last entry. Click Next, and then Finish. If you want Outlook Express to dial automatically to connect, choose "Connect using my phone line," then click Next.

11. The necessary connection should already be set up on your computer, so choose it from the list and click Next, then Finish. If you need to set up a new connection, choose "Create a new dial-up connection," click Next, and continue with the Wizard.

12. When you are done, click Close in the Internet Accounts dialog. You will see a message asking if you want to download newsgroups from the server you just added. Click Yes.

NOTE   **If you need more information about setting up a connection, refer back to the discussion and table in the "Getting Connected" section of Chapter 6.**

Finding Your Interests

Once you have set up your news server, you need to find out what newsgroups it contains. If you just completed step 12 above, the list will be downloaded. Otherwise, highlight the news server in Outlook Express's left pane, and answer Yes to the question that appears about viewing a list of available newsgroups. Outlook Express will connect to the server and download the list. The list of newsgroups will appear as shown in Figure 8.12.

It would take you a long time to look through this list for the ones that might interest you. But you can enter a keyword in the box at the top to limit the view. There are over 18,000 entries on this particular list, but entering **wine** in the box cuts the list to eight. You can also enter multiple keywords, separated by spaces, to see only groups whose names contain all of your keywords. When you find newsgroups you want to check out, highlight them and click Subscribe.

When you think you're done, click the Subscribed tab and check over your list. Then OK the dialog box. The news server should still be highlighted in the left pane. Now go to the Tools menu and choose Download this Account. Outlook Express will connect to your server and download the headers of approximately the last 300 messages posted in each newsgroup to which you have subscribed.

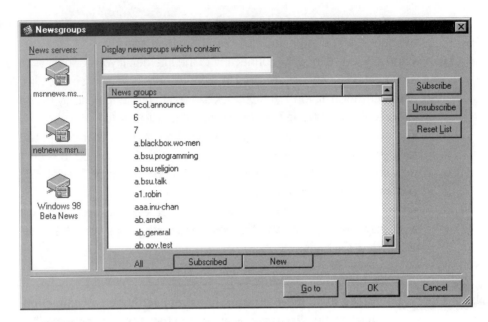

FIGURE 8.12: Finding newsgroups that interest you

TIP **You can return to the Newsgroups dialog box to change your subscriptions by clicking the News Groups button on the toolbar.**

Now click the + beside the news server name in the left pane of Outlook Express. This will expand the folder to list all the newsgroups to which you subscribed. Click a group and the upper right pane will list the message headers. You can change the sort order of the list by clicking the column headers. If you are still online, clicking any message header will download the text, which will appear in the lower right preview pane. A + beside a message header indicates there are replies. Click the + to see the list of replies.

Getting Messages

If you disconnected after getting the headers, clicking a header will produce a message in the preview window that the message is not cached and you need to connect to the server. Here's how to do it efficiently, and with minimal online time:

1. Hold down Ctrl as you look through the list of headers. Click each header that interests you. Don't expand the lists of replies; just click the one visible header (for the original posting).

2. When you are finished, choose Tools ➤ Mark for Retrieval ➤ Mark Message.

3. Choose Tools ➤ Download this Newsgroup.

4. In the dialog that appears, accept the default Get Marked Messages, and click OK.

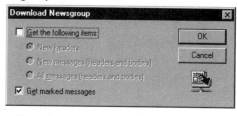

5. Outlook Express will again connect to your news server and will download the full text of the messages you selected, including replies.

6. If you now look closely at the list of headers, you will see that the icon for those you chose to download has changed from a half page (header only) to a full page, indicating that the full text has been downloaded and cached for you to read when you wish. See Figure 8.13.

7. As with e-mail, click on a header to read the message in the preview window. Double-click to open the message in a separate window.

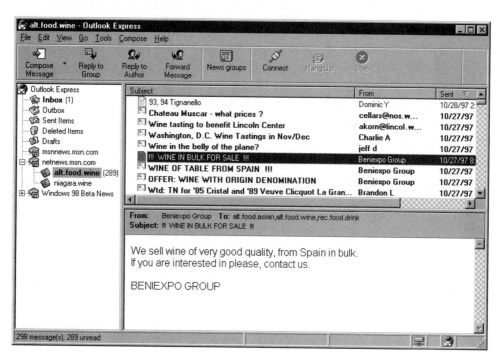

FIGURE 8.13: Full text has been downloaded only for selected messages.

These are the icons used in the header listing to indicate the status of the message text. "Cached" means the text has been downloaded and stored on your machine, so it can be read without going back on line.

Icon	Meaning
	Message not read or cached
	Message read (online) but not cached
	Message cached but not read
	Message cached and read

NOTE **If you want to keep messages after you have read them, you will need to change an Outlook Express setting. Go to the Advanced tab of Tools ➢ Options, and remove the check mark from the box labeled "Don't keep read messages."**

Reading and Replying

You can read newsgroup messages in several ways, depending on your Internet connection and your preferences. If you have a full-time connection or don't mind staying online, you can use the header pane to select messages, which will appear in the preview pane. Or you can double-click a header to open the separate message-reading window, shown in Figure 8.14. Navigate by using the Next and Previous buttons on the toolbar, or equivalent menu commands or hotkeys. There are also Next Unread Message and Next Unread Thread commands under Next on the View menu.

If you prefer to download selected messages as described above, you still have two ways to view them. You can use the header pane to select and the preview pane to read. If you prefer to read messages in a separate window, first go to the View menu in the Outlook Express main window. Under Current View, choose Downloaded Messages. Now when you double-click a header to open the message-reading window, you can navigate just among the messages you downloaded, without having to bother with all the other headers.

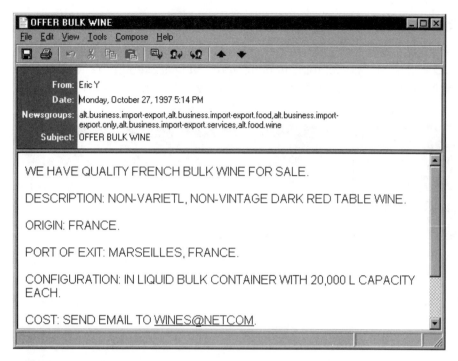

FIGURE 8.14:   Reading newsgroup postings in their own window

---

NOTE   **There are many possible ways to organize your newsgroups. For additional helpful hints, look at Outlook Express's Help, especially the Tips and Tricks section.**

In replying to a newsgroup posting, you must first decide whether you want to reply with a posting in the newsgroup or by private e-mail. To reply with a posting, click the

 Reply to Group button on the toolbar. If you are using the Outlook Express main window, the button is labeled. At left is the version you will see in the message-reading window.

 The Reply to Author button allows you to compose an e-mail message that will be sent only to the author of the posting.

Either way, the reply window is very similar to the one used for replying to e-mail, as discussed earlier in the chapter. When you click the Post button, the message will be placed in your Outbox. It will be transmitted the next time you connect to your news server.

Posting a New Message

Posting a new message in a newsgroup is easy with Outlook Express. In the main window, be sure the appropriate newsgroup is highlighted in the left pane. Click the Compose Message button to open the window shown in Figure 8.15.

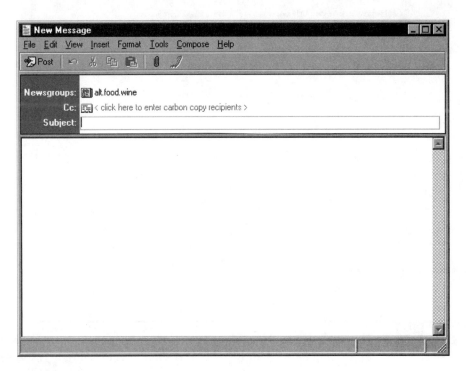

FIGURE 8.15: Creating a new message for your newsgroup

The cursor is already in the Subject field, so you can just enter the subject, then use the Tab key to move to the text area and start typing your message. If you want to post to multiple newsgroups, click the icon in the Newsgroups field and select from a list of the newsgroups to which you subscribe. You can use the Cc field to send copies as e-mail to anyone listed in your Address Book.

When you are finished, click the Post button on the toolbar. The message will be placed in your Outbox, to be posted to the newsgroup the next time you connect.

TIP **Etiquette is important in newsgroups. Pay attention to the tone of discussion if you want to be sure that your contributions will be welcome.**

More Outlook Express Options

Outlook Express offers far too many options for us to discuss all of them. Choose Tools ➤ Options to open the Options dialog, which has seven pages. You should explore them; you may find useful features you hadn't imagined. We will cover only a few of them here. Remember that you can get an explanation of any option by right-clicking it and then clicking the What's This button that appears.

The first option on the General page is how often to automatically check for new messages. If you leave this option checked, Outlook Express will check your mail server as often as specified here, whenever you are connected to the Internet. If you use dial-up Internet access and want Outlook Express to connect automatically to check for new messages, you will also need to check "Automatically dial when checking for new messages" on the Dial Up page of Options.

If you frequently write more than one message at a time and want them collected for sending at the same time, go to the Send page of Options and remove the check mark from "Send messages immediately." The Send button will then place your message in your outbox, to be sent the next time you click Send and Receive.

To get Outlook Express to automatically hang up your modem after sending and receiving messages, go to the Dial Up page and check "Hang up when finished sending, receiving, or downloading."

Windows Address Book

Though the Windows Address Book can serve broader purposes, its most effective use is likely to be limited to Internet-based communications. For example, it is nicely integrated with Outlook Express and Internet Explorer, but it can't use the Windows Phone Dialer to dial a phone number.

You can open the Windows Address Book from the Start Menu by going to Programs ➤ Internet Explorer ➤ Address Book. It can also be opened from Outlook Express's main window toolbar, or from the Go menu in Internet Explorer. Figure 8.16 shows how the Address Book opens.

As in similar Windows programs, you can sort on a column by clicking the column header button. Click the button again to reverse the order. A small pointer indicates which column is sorted, and whether it is ascending or descending. You can also go to View ➤ Sort By to set whether sorts on the Name column are done by first or last name.

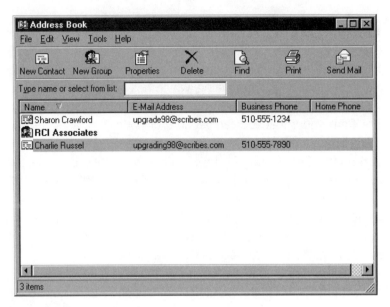

FIGURE 8.16: Good for e-mail, OK for phone numbers

Adding Contacts

Click the New Contact button to create a new record in the Address Book. This opens the dialog box in Figure 8.17.

On the Personal page of this dialog, you can enter the person's name and nickname. The display name will identify this record in the Address Book. Also on this page, enter the person's e-mail address. If there is more than one, click Add after entering the first e-mail address; this will put the address in the list box and allow you to enter the next address.

On the Home and Business pages, you can store the person's home and business addresses and phone numbers, including fax, pager, and cellular numbers, as well as company, job title, and department. There are also fields for personal and business Web page addresses.

The Other page allows you to include free-form notes about the person, and the NetMeeting page stores information needed for Internet phone calls and conferencing, using the Microsoft NetMeeting software that is part of the Internet Explorer 4.0 package. Finally, the Digital IDs page stores the codes used for digital signatures and encrypted e-mail.

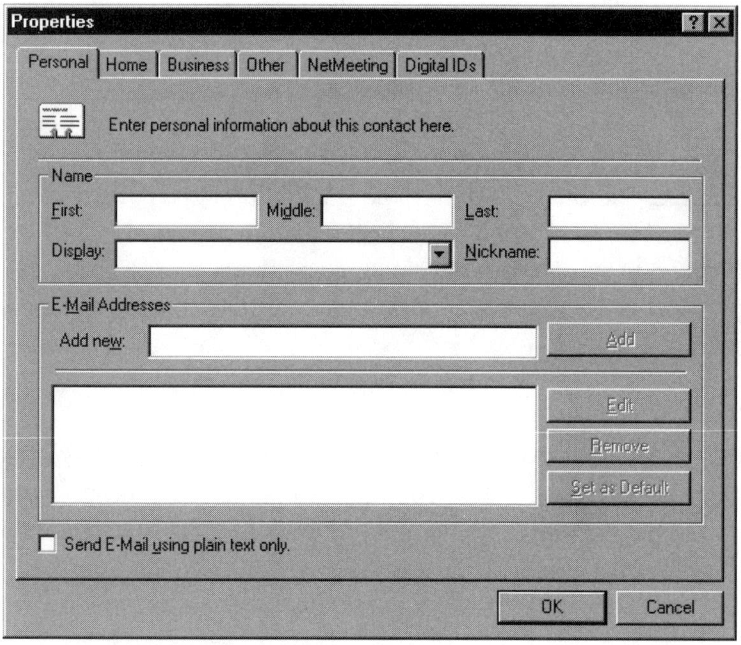

FIGURE 8.17: Entering information for a new contact

Besides storing information about individuals, you can create groups to use as mailing lists. Click New Group on the Address Book toolbar. Give the group a name and select the individuals you want to be part of the group.

Using Address Book Information

You will probably most often use Address Book information in Outlook Express. When composing a new message, clicking the Address Book button on the toolbar or any of the file card icons in the To: or copies fields allows you to choose recipients from your Address Book. If you choose a group, all of the group's members will receive the message.

On the General page of Outlook Express's Tools ➤ Options dialog, you can choose whether to "Automatically put people I reply to in my Address Book." The default is yes. If you prefer not to put everyone with whom you have an incidental exchange of e-mail in your address book, remove the check mark. You can still easily add any sender or recipient you choose. When you open a message to read it, you can right-click on the From, To, or Cc fields and choose Add To Address Book from the menu.

Internet Explorer's Profile Assistant uses Address Book to store information about you. You can then use Profile Assistant to quickly send such information to Web sites that request it. More details on this are in Chapter 7.

You can open Address Book itself to make use of the full range of information you have stored there. Unfortunately, the initial view shows only the person's name, default e-mail address, and business and home phone numbers. For any other information, you must double-click the entry and choose the tab you need in the Properties dialog. Once there, you can copy out information you need, or edit the entry. If you have entered personal or business Web page addresses, you can use the Go button beside the entry to open the page.

What's Next

All the great Internet features we've been discussing in this chapter (and the previous two) don't do you any good unless you have access to the Internet. In the next chapter, we'll discuss how to sign up for Internet service or for the more extensive features available from an online service.

INTERNET AND ONLINE SERVICES

So, you've survived nearly to the turn of the millennium without using the Internet, but you're starting to think it's time. Or perhaps you're an experienced Internet user wondering whether you should sign up for one of the more elaborate online services.

We will discuss these and related questions first, and then go on to the mechanics of signing up for service from one of the providers whose software is included with Windows 98.

What Type of Service?

Three kinds of companies currently offer dial-up access to the Internet. There are national (and international) Internet service providers, which have access phone numbers throughout the U.S. and perhaps some other countries as well. There are local Internet service providers, which offer access from a very limited geographical area. And there are online services, which offer special discussion forums, libraries, and databases in addition to Internet access.

National Internet Services

For most people, the most important advantage of national Internet service providers is that they offer local phone numbers for access in most cities. If you travel and want your e-mail and Internet access to travel with you, this can be extremely important.

On the other hand, a large national or international company may not be able to provide the kind of personal service that smaller, local companies may offer. You shouldn't need technical support very often, but if getting it requires you to pay for twenty minutes of jumping through voice-menu hoops and waiting, you may want to look elsewhere.

Many of the large Internet service providers will give you software that automatically sets up a new account and configures your system to use it. If the automatic configuration doesn't work for Internet Explorer 4.0, they should still be able to give you the information you need to configure manually, as explained in Chapter 6.

Remember that Chapter 6 also tells you how to use the Internet Connection Wizard to get information on, and sign up with, a variety of mostly national Internet service providers. In addition, AT&T WorldNet has chosen to include its sign-up software right in the Windows 98 package.

NOTE   Most of the Internet discussion in this book is oriented to Microsoft's Internet Explorer 4.0, because it is a part of Windows 98. However, if you prefer Netscape Communicator (the successor to Navigator 3.0), there's no reason you can't use it. Any Internet service provider should be able to give you the necessary information to configure it for their service. The one thing you shouldn't do is settle for an older version of either program.

Local Internet Services

You don't have to choose only between large national companies for Internet service. Most cities and even many smaller towns have local companies that offer access to the Internet. If you can find a good one, it might be your best option.

You may find that a local company can give more personal attention to any problems you may face in setting up your service. And if you want help with a larger project such as setting up and maintaining a Web site for a home-based business, a good local service may be much better than a larger company.

Unfortunately, there are also some really bad apples among local Internet service providers. Companies that don't have enough modems and phone lines to handle the demand or don't have enough capacity in their connection to the Internet backbone will prove to be frustrating time wasters.

Before you sign up with a local Internet service provider, ask friends and colleagues who have been using local services. Occasionally, local newspapers or computer user magazines may provide reviews and comparisons. The same sources may list local user groups where you can ask about the reputation of particular services.

NOTE Many local telephone companies and some cable TV companies are also getting into the Internet access business. Some phone companies offer access packages that include an ISDN line and adapter, for faster access than you can get with any modem. The fastest home Internet access is via TV cable systems. It is currently available only in a few limited areas, but if you live in one of those areas you should probably check into it.

Online Services

Online services offer a variety of special features in addition to e-mail and Internet access. Each of the four major online services has its own history, strengths, and weaknesses. All of them have extensive networks of access phone numbers in the U.S., and varying degrees and methods of access in other parts of the world.

America Online (the biggest) and the Microsoft Network (the newest) are attempting to make the online medium a whole new experience, using television as their inspiration. AOL also has very popular chat services. CompuServe (or CSi) focuses on business users and computer professionals, with bigger libraries of downloadable files than any other service. It also offers extensive extra-cost services. Prodigy Internet is basically a national Internet service provider that includes some special features such as chat facilities. It also aggregates some Web content for easier access.

All of the online services attempt to make the online experience easier for newcomers than just jumping into the Internet. That alone is reason enough for some new users to prefer them. In addition, all now use either Internet Explorer or Netscape Navigator (or both) for Internet access, so you are not limited to their specialized interfaces.

TIP   **Whether you choose an online service or an Internet service provider, wait a month or two before getting your e-mail address printed on business cards and letterhead. If the first service you try doesn't provide what you need, take your business elsewhere.**

The Online Services folder is shown in Figure 9.1. Open the file About The Online Services for some useful information, including customer service and technical support phone numbers for all of the services.

FIGURE 9.1:
Online services sign-up central. The Microsoft Network icon is on the desktop.

The rest of this chapter gives a description of each of the services that comes with Windows 98, along with instructions for setting up a new account at each. You can also use the online services icons to re-install software for a service with which you already have an account.

Remember that whenever you are online your phone line will be in use, calling the access number you chose when you set up the online service's software. If this is not a local call the toll charges from your phone company can run up very quickly. When signing up with any of these services, you will probably want to have your phone book handy to check your local dialing area, especially if your area doesn't include a major city.

WARNING Although the services generally provide free trial periods, they require you to provide billing information, usually a credit card number or checking account information, when you sign up. It's up to you to cancel your account if you decide not to keep it. Otherwise, the charges will start appearing automatically after the free trial expires, whether or not you actually use the service.

America Online

America Online (AOL) is the biggest and in many respects the glitziest of the online services. It provides a supportive "home" community for people new to the online world. AOL's chat groups are well organized and generally civil, and have a consistent level of participation. AOL also features more online chats with celebrities than any other service.

AOL has an excellent collection of online periodicals including *Rolling Stone* and *@Times*, which includes more of *The New York Times* than is available on the paper's Web site. AOL also develops original content such as Parent Soup and a series of regional guides. Many of these services are now also available on the Web, but the AOL version is often more complete.

Like the other online services, AOL handles members' e-mail to and from any Internet address. It also offers additional e-mail services that only work between AOL members. For example, you can call a message back before it has been read by the addressee, or send Instant Messages that pop up on the screen of friends who are currently online. Also, AOL allows several e-mail addresses per account; family members living apart can exchange e-mail while sharing a single AOL account. AOL software also provides "flash sessions," which allow the user to quickly upload finished e-mail and newsgroup messages, and download waiting e-mail and marked files. This minimizes time online, and allows you to automate the process and do something else while downloading.

AOL's selection of downloadable software, drivers, and other files is less than what CompuServe offers, but is still adequate for most users, and the download process is simple. The service's biggest drawback is also the one for which it has been in the news: not enough network capacity for its huge, and still growing, number of sub-scribers. That situation has improved since its worst period in late 1996 and early 1997, but still presents some difficulties.

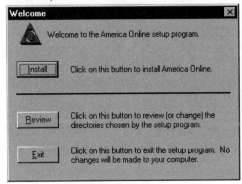

To sign up for America Online, open the Online Services folder and click the AOL icon. First, choose U.S., Canada, or UK service. If the processor in your com-puter is not a Pentium or better, AOL will tell you that they do not recommend using their software with anything less. Choose not to install this version and the setup exits without any fanfare. The next dialog box allows you to print a copy of the America Online Quick Reference Guide, if you wish. Next comes the Welcome dialog shown here. Click Review if you are already an AOL subscriber and want your screen name(s) and preferences copied from an old installation of AOL on your machine. Review also allows you to specify the installation directory for AOL.

Clicking Install sets up the AOL software on your machine. This takes only a couple of minutes. After exiting the install program, click the new AOL icon to start the soft-ware. It will first connect to a toll-free number and download a list of local access num-bers. AOL has lots of local numbers, including quite a few that will work with new 56K modems. Try to find both a primary and a secondary number that are local calls; you may want to have your phone book handy if you don't know all the details of your local calling area. After you pick two phone numbers the AOL software will disconnect. Then click the Sign On button, as shown in Figure 9.2, to connect via one of the local numbers and sign up for service.

AT&T WorldNet

Although its software is included in Windows 98's Online Services folder, AT&T WorldNet is not an online service. It is a national Internet service provider, and so is not really comparable to the other services described in this chapter. If you don't feel you need the special facilities and resources offered by the online services, AT&T WorldNet might be a good option.

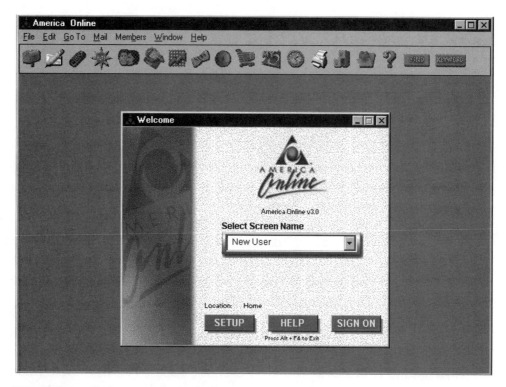

FIGURE 9.2: Signing on to AOL for the first time

One of the big attractions is that the service is free for up to five hours of use a month for your first year—if you sign up from a phone line that has AT&T as its long-distance service. Otherwise, the monthly, hourly, or unlimited access rates are similar to those of the online services.

Begin the sign-up process by clicking the AT&T WorldNet icon in the Online Services folder. Follow the instructions; eventually, if you decide to go ahead, the software will dial a toll-free number to carry out the enrollment procedure. Be sure to read the Service Agreement and Operating Policies. Then continue through the pages of the setup, providing requested information and clicking Next to move on.

When you are finished, you'll be using Internet Explorer as your Internet browser. When you log on, you will initially be connected to the AT&T WorldNet home page.

CSi (CompuServe)

CompuServe, now going by the name CSi, is the oldest of the major online services. Although it was recently bought out by America Online, the new owners have promised to continue to operate it as a separate service.

Besides e-mail and Internet access, CSi offers a broad array of well-attended forums where discussions often involve novices as well as those experienced in the given subject matter. From computers to pets to women in aviation, the range is great. The software also makes it easier to follow a particular discussion thread than with other online services or Internet newsgroups. The software also includes a filing cabinet where you can stash e-mail and forum messages under subject headings you create.

CSi was the first online home of many computer and software companies, and still has the widest array of downloadable software and driver files. Many companies continue to sponsor support forums on CSi even as they also set up Web pages for the same purpose.

CSi's greatest strength is in business services. It has such resources as the Newspaper Archives, which is much more extensive than anything available in one place on the Web. It also has a wide range of searchable business databases, many of which involve extra fees for use. The Business Database Plus holds over two million articles, available at fees that are quite reasonable in a business context. Many of the business services and databases use older-style plain text interfaces. They may take some getting used to, but their power lies in their content.

CSi recently introduced unlimited service pricing for the first time. Although it's a few dollars more per month than the other services, it's easily worth it if you need the kind of resources that are available only here.

Install CompuServe software by clicking the icon in the Online Services folder. Early in the process you get the chance to view the Readme file; it's a good idea to do so. Then choose Express installation unless you want to be able to specify the drive and directory where CompuServe software will be installed. The Custom option allows you to specify this, and also what type of connection to use. You will need to restart your computer after the files are installed.

Clicking the CompuServe 4.0 icon at this point will start the software. Click the Signup button for a new account or Setup if you already have a CSi account. If your computer already has an older version of CompuServe software, the connection settings will be taken over automatically.

For a new account, read the Signup Wizard initial screen and click Next. The list that appears (Figure 9.3) gives you an idea of CSi's worldwide access network. You should understand, however, that access in many countries involves communications surcharges.

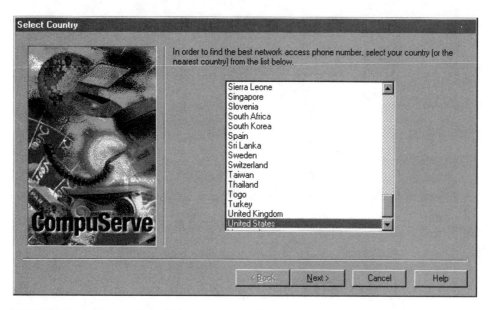

FIGURE 9.3: CSi access is available in many countries.

The Wizard then asks for information about your phone line, and connects to a toll-free number to find the closest local access numbers. After choosing an access number, continue the sign-up process. When you are finished, the CompuServe opening screen looks like Figure 9.4.

FIGURE 9.4:   CompuServe's opening screen takes you directly to a variety of services.

Prodigy Internet

Though the original Prodigy service attempted to provide unique content to attract users, the current Prodigy Internet is basically a national Internet service provider with a few extras. If you want some guidance as you get started using the Web, Prodigy Internet may have what you're looking for. Prodigy's service uses your browser rather than special software. In the case of the setup included with Windows 98, that means Internet Explorer 4.0. It also adds a special configurable toolbar for faster access to your favorite features.

Prodigy's major unique service is content aggregation. Under the motto, "untangle the Web," it assembles a collection of Web sites in ten different subject areas. The subjects include music, travel, and computing, and the selected sites have been screened for the quality of their contents and for reliability and ease of use. Prodigy users contribute to the ratings that are a part of this process. It can help you find excellent sites within some subject areas without getting lost on the Web.

Signing up for Prodigy Internet is similar to signing up with an Internet service provider, as described in Chapter 6. Clicking the icon in Online Services starts Internet Explorer and opens a cached Web page with a variety of information buttons and another button to Sign Me Up (Figure 9.5). Clicking it starts the Internet Connection Wizard and connects to Prodigy's secure server for the sign-up process.

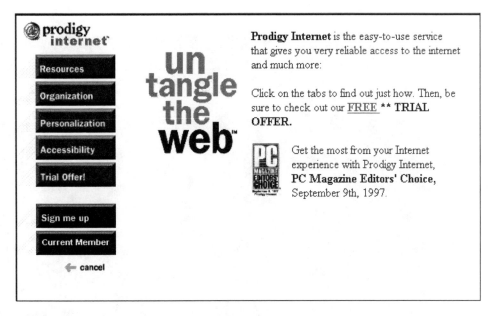

FIGURE 9.5: Prodigy Internet's information page

The Microsoft Network

Microsoft's own entry into the online service arena, The Microsoft Network (MSN) is a very slick attempt to show what can be done in the field, making heavy use of animation and sound. Unfortunately, this pushes the limits of what can be done with a modem connection.

In addition, the content is fairly limited and uneven. Some of the best is on the channels in the area called On Stage. Some of the channel content, and much of the additional content created by MSN, is available to anyone at **www.msn.com**, or at specific sites such as **cartalk.msn.com** for National Public Radio's favorite auto mechanics.

There are several useful services in the Essentials area, including the well-known Expedia travel service. Here again, most of it can be reached without an MSN membership.

Windows 98 gives MSN an edge over the other online services by putting its setup icon on the desktop rather than in the Online Services folder. Part of the software is included with Windows 98 and will be set up when you click either icon. After re-booting your machine, the setup program will connect to MSN, sign you up for service, and download more software to complete the installation. When the process is complete, the opening screen looks like Figure 9.6.

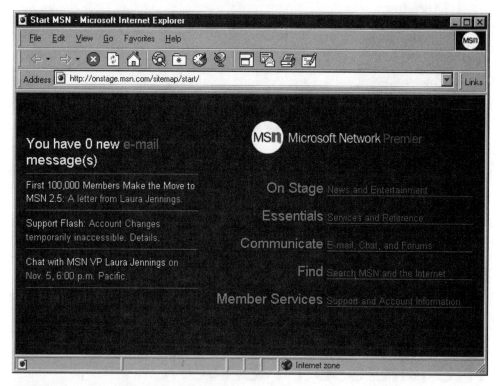

FIGURE 9.6: The Microsoft Network's startup screen

What's Next

Whether in the Internet Connection Wizard or the Internet Options dialog, you've probably encountered Dial-Up Networking by now. We'll discuss it in detail in the next chapter when we talk about Road Warriors. The setup will be essentially the same whether you're connecting to the Internet, or connecting to your office network from home or while on the road.

FOR ROAD WARRIORS

In the previous chapter, we showed you how to install software and open an account with an online service or an Internet service provider. In this chapter, we're going a step further, showing you how to configure Dial-Up Networking so you can connect to your company's network (or any other, for that matter) via Windows 98. We'll also show you how to set up a Briefcase to keep your mobile files and your base system files synchronized.

NOTE   **This chapter assumes that Windows 98 has automatically installed and set up your modem. If you just bought your modem and haven't yet set it up, do that first using the Modems icon in the Control Panel. Chapter 11 has more on this.**

Dial-Up Networking

Dial-Up Networking is Windows 98's system for using a modem to connect to the Internet or to your office network. If you set up an online service account as described in Chapter 9, you are already using Dial-Up Networking, even though you may not have encountered the name. The same is true if you used the Internet Connection Wizard to set up a modem connection to your Internet service provider, as described in Chapter 6.

If you use either an online service or a national Internet service provider, you will need to set up a connection to the local access phone number when you go on the road. Or perhaps you are on the road and need to consult a file on your office computer. To do this, you'll first have to create the dial-up connection.

NOTE   **The machine to which you are connecting must be a server, or at least configured so that it can act as a server on demand. See "Creating a Dial-Up Server," later in this chapter.**

Creating a New Connection

Creating a new connection to a server, whether it's your Internet Service Provider or your computer at work, is simply a matter of following the Wizard and answering a few questions.

To create a new Dial-Up Networking connection:

1. Open the Dial-Up Networking folder in My Computer. You can also select it under Programs ➢ Accessories ➢ Communications on the Start menu. This will open up the Dial-Up Networking folder. In Figure 10.1 you can see some of the connections that were set up when we installed the online services discussed in Chapter 9.
2. The first time you open the Dial-Up Networking folder, you may only see the Make New Connection icon. Click it to start the Make New Connection Wizard.
3. Replace the default name My Connection with a name that will describe the connection you are setting up, as shown in Figure 10.2. If your computer

has more than one modem, choose the one you want from the drop-down list. Click the Next button.

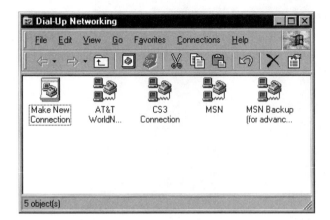

FIGURE 10.1:
Use the Start menu to get to the Dial-Up Networking folder.

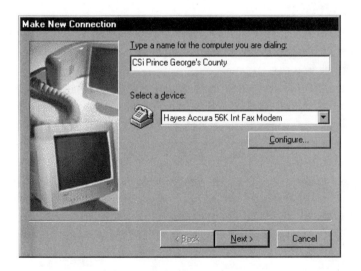

FIGURE 10.2:
Each connection you create needs a name that identifies it to you.

4. Type in the phone number for the new connection, as shown in Figure 10.3, and click the Next button.

5. Click the Finish button and you'll have a new icon for the connection in the Dial-Up Networking folder.

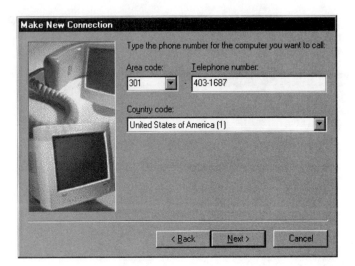

FIGURE 10.3:
Each connection, even if it's a local number, needs full information about area and country codes.

Using Your Connection

If your new connection is to a Windows NT Remote Access Server, or an Internet Service Provider that supports PPP, or, in fact, most systems you will be connecting to, using it is easy. Just follow these steps:

1. Click the new icon in your Dial-Up Networking folder, and the Connect To dialog box shown in Figure 10.4 should open. (If it doesn't, go to the Connections menu in the Dial-Up Networking folder. Choose Settings and put a check in the box labeled "Prompt for information before dialing.")

FIGURE 10.4:
Connecting to a remote system is accomplished in this dialog box.

2. If your user name on the remote system is different from your current Windows 98 user name, you will need to change the User name box to whatever your name is on the remote system.

3. Enter your password. If you want to have Windows 98 save your password for this remote system, check the box.

WARNING **Don't let Windows 98 store your password unless you're confident that no one else has access to the computer you're currently using. You'll always have an opportunity to type in the password if you don't have Windows 98 save it.**

---

4. If your current location doesn't appear in the Dialing From box, choose it from the drop-down list. If it's not there, refer to the Adding New Locations section later in this chapter.

5. Click on the Connect button and you'll see the Connecting To status box.

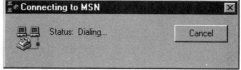

6. Once you're connected, you can use the shared files, printers, and other resources of the other computer just as if you were right next to it on a network—except it will be a bit slower, of course.

NOTE **A Dial-Up Networking connection differs from a full network connection in one significant way. While browsing the Network Neighborhood you will not always see the other computer when you're connected remotely. But if you don't see it, use Tools > Find > Computer from the Explorer to find it.**

Troubleshooting Your Connection

While Windows 98 will correctly set up your Dial-Up connection most of the time, every once in a while it'll mess up—or you'll want it to do something just a bit different from the usual. Here are some quick tips on what to look out for, and settings you might need or want to change.

- Check all your modem settings.

- Check that the server type is set correctly.
- If you're in a different location from your usual one, add a new location description and settings.
- Turn on the modem's speaker to listen for the connection tone when you dial.
- Set your modem's properties to open a terminal window after dialing to see if your server is asking a question you didn't expect.
- Choose a different network protocol to do the connection.

See the next section and the modem section in Chapter 11 for more information.

Setting the Server Type

The default server type for Windows 98 is PPP: Internet, Windows NT Server, Windows 98. If this is not the kind of machine you are connecting to, right-click on the icon for the connection in the Dial-Up Networking folder (not on a shortcut to it) and select Properties. This will open the property sheet for the connection, shown in Figure 10.5.

FIGURE 10.5: Each Dial-Up Networking connection has its own properties sheet.

Click on the Server Types tab as shown in Figure 10.6. From here you can set a variety of options including the network protocols to use, the server type, and logon options. You may need to contact the operator of the server to obtain this information.

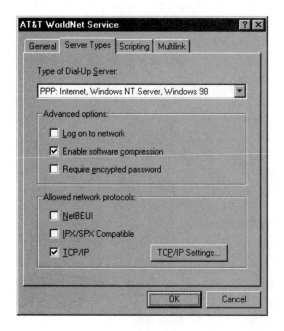

FIGURE 10.6:
Use this page of the connection property sheet to choose your remote server type and connection options.

Type of Dial-Up Server   Here you choose the type of server. The default is for a standard PPP connection, or choose NRN for connecting to a Netware Network. Choose Windows for Workgroups type for connecting to older Windows for Workgroups or Windows NT 3.1 networks. (If you have installed SLIP networking you will have a choice for it, and you may find other options, as well.)

Log on to network   This option automatically logs you on to the network you are connecting to using your current Windows user name and password. This logon and password may well be different from the dial-up password you entered in the Connect To dialog.

Enable software compression   This tells Windows 98 to compress data sent over the link automatically, increasing the speed of the connection. This option must be available on the remote system in a compatible form.

Allowed network protocols   Select the networking protocols to use with this connection. The default is to select all three, but if you know what your remote server is using you can de-select the ones you don't need.

TCP/IP Settings   This button opens the dialog in Figure 10.7. Specify your IP address for this connection, or let the server automatically assign one, whichever is appropriate. Leave the rest of the settings alone unless you know what they mean and why you need to change them. They should be correct for the vast majority of connections.

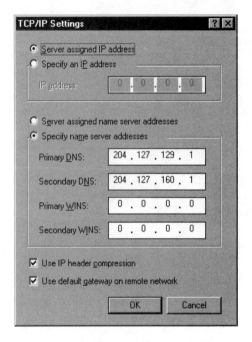

FIGURE 10.7:
Here's where you set the TCP/IP properties for your Dial-Up connection.

Adding New Locations

When you use your portable computer to log on to a remote network—whether it's the Internet by way of your Internet service provider, your company network, or just your machine at home if you have it set up as a Dial-Up Server—you are likely to have to do it from different locations.

Here's how to add these additional locations:

1. Double-click on a connection icon to open the Connect To dialog box shown in Figure 10.4.

2. Click the Dial Properties button and you'll get the Dialing Properties dialog shown in Figure 10.8.
3. To add a location, click on New and type in a name for your location, in place of the default New Location. This might be something like "Office," or the name of the city, or a hotel.

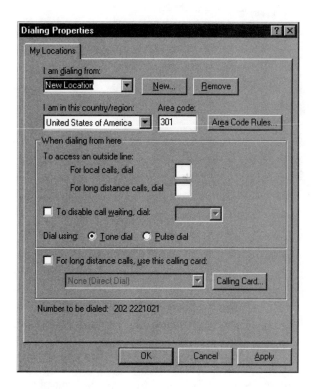

FIGURE 10.8:
Adding a new location is done in the Dialing Properties dialog.

4. Enter the Area Code and other details about how you dial out from this location. Click Area Code Rules to enter such details as ten-digit dialing or other local peculiarities.
5. If you need to use a calling card from this location, check the box at the bottom and click the Calling Card button. Enter your calling card details in the dialog box shown in Figure 10.9. If the card you use, or the local phone system, requires a more complex series of steps than just dialing the access number, phone number, and PIN number, click one of the Calling Card Sequence buttons to enter all the details.
6. OK all the dialogs. Now, whenever you need to dial from this location, you can just select it and Windows 98 will remember your settings.

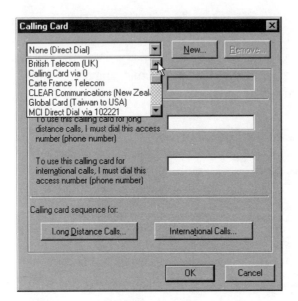

FIGURE 10.9:
Windows 98 is ready for a great variety of calling cards.

Creating a Dial-Up Server

Maybe you'd like to be able to call your own computer at home when you're traveling. You would use a Dial-Up Networking connection on your portable computer, but you also need to set up your home machine so it can take a call and respond correctly.

All you need is the Windows 98 Dial-Up Server. (In Windows 95 this was a Plus! Pack add-on called Remote Access Server.) This is a much more limited server than that included in Windows NT. It allows only a single client to connect to your machine at any one time.

The Dial-Up Server isn't installed by default. Here's how to install it:

1. Go to the Start menu and choose Settings ➤ Control Panel.
2. Open Add/Remove Programs and click the Windows Setup tab.
3. Select Communications and click the Details button.
4. Put a check in the Dial-Up Server box, then click OK twice and Windows 98 will install it.

To enable the service, open up the Dial-Up Networking folder and select Dial-Up Server from the Connections menu. The dialog box is shown in Figure 10.10.

FIGURE 10.10:
Setting up your
Dial-Up Server
is simple.

Select "Allow caller access" so your modem will answer incoming calls, then click the Change Password button and set a password for access to your computer. Passwords are a nuisance, we know, but it just doesn't make sense to not have a password when you are potentially allowing others to connect to your computer. After all, this limited server neither knows nor cares who is calling or from where. It also provides access to everything available on your machine without regard to the sharing properties you may have set up if you are on a LAN—so add a password!

WARNING   We don't suggest using the Windows 98 Dial-Up Server on a permanent basis or to allow access to your machine by anyone other than yourself. The password protection it offers is easily penetrated by any beginning hacker. It may be OK to use when you take an occasional trip, but be sure to switch back to "No caller access" when you return home. If you need dial-up access to your computer on a regular basis, or want to give others access to it, consider installing Windows NT Server, which offers far superior security.

Next click the Server Type button to open the dialog in Figure 10.11. The settings here need to match those in the dial-up connection that you will use to connect to this computer. For example, look in the dial-up connection that you will use for calling this computer (refer back to Figure 10.6). The Type of Dial-Up Server must be set the same here as it is there. Also be sure the other options match, then OK both dialogs.

FIGURE 10.11:
The settings here should match those you will be using to call in.

There's only one more step to setting up remote access to your home computer: test the setup from a nearby location before you count on using it from 3000 miles away.

The Briefcase

The Briefcase is a special folder designed to keep files on two different computers in sync. If you travel with a laptop, you probably have a set of files that relate in some way to another set of files on your home or office computer. The Briefcase will keep copies of the files coordinated, so you're always working with the latest version.

> **NOTE**   If you don't have Briefcase installed, use Add/Remove Programs in the Control Panel to add it. It's in Windows Setup, under Accessories.

Setting It Up with a Network

If your portable and desktop computers are connected over a network, setting up the Briefcase is easy. On your portable computer, open the Briefcase icon. Also open the Network Neighborhood or Windows Explorer on the portable to locate shared folders on your desktop machine. Drag files from these shared folders to the Briefcase.

> **NOTE**   To share a folder, right-click on it, select Properties, and then select the Sharing tab.

That's all you need to get things started. You can work on the original files as usual, or you can open the Briefcase and work on the versions stored there. After you've worked on the files on either computer (but not both) and want to coordinate the versions, reconnect the computers and follow these steps:

1. Click on the Briefcase icon to open it.

 2. Click the Update All button on the toolbar, or select Update All from the Briefcase menu. You'll see a window that looks like the one in Figure 10.12. (On the left is a list of files in the Briefcase, and on the right are the corresponding files on the other computer. The middle shows the suggested action.)

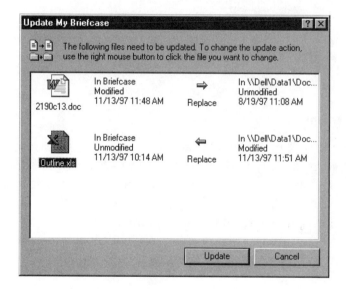

FIGURE 10.12:
This Briefcase shows files that need to be updated.

3. You can change the action for any pair of files by right-clicking on the action. You'll get a menu of choices as shown in Figure 10.13.

4. Click on Update when you're finished and all the files will be updated as you specified.

NOTE Another way to limit the update action is to select only those files in the Briefcase that you want to consider updating. Then click the Update Selection button. The Update My Briefcase window will then list only the files you selected for possible updating.

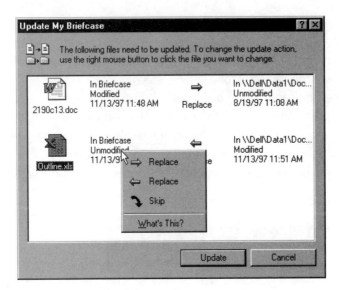

FIGURE 10.13:
You don't have to accept Briefcase's suggestions.

Using It on a Floppy

If your portable and your main computer aren't connected by a network, you can use Briefcase on a floppy disk to keep files synchronized by following these steps:

1. Open the Briefcase on your desktop and drag in the files or folders you want to keep synchronized.
2. Move the Briefcase to a disk in your floppy drive.
3. Take the floppy and put it in the disk drive on your portable machine. You can now work with the files in the Briefcase.

NOTE   **Remember, you can also work with the original files on your main machine, but don't update both copies of the same file. (More on this later.)**

---

4. When you're ready to synchronize the files between your two machines, take the floppy from the portable and put it into the disk drive on the main machine.
5. Double-click the diskette drive to open it. Right-click My Briefcase and choose Update All. You'll be presented with the dialog box shown in Figure 10.12.

NOTE It's important not to edit (or update) both copies of a file because all Briefcase can do is show you the most recent copy and suggest it as the one you want to copy over the older one. If the older copy contains changes that were never carried over to the newer one (because files weren't synchronized before the newer file was created), then the changes in the older file will be lost.

Multiple Briefcases

You can make a Briefcase anywhere. Just right-click in a folder and select New and then Briefcase. You can use this new Briefcase folder to keep any files on your computer or on a network synchronized. Just make sure that the folders in question are Shared (right-click and select Properties and then Sharing).

What's Next

Now that you're ready to go on the road with Windows 98, we'll move on to the Control Panel. It includes some new functions in Windows 98, and a great deal that will be new to users of Windows 3.1.

THE CONTROL PANEL

The control panel is a central location for most of the hardware and system settings, many of which can also be arrived at by other means. (For example, you can right-click on the desktop to get the same property sheet you get by clicking the Display icon.) If you check the Control Panel first, however, you don't have to remember the other places.

This chapter covers the common Control Panel items in alphabetical order. Some of them aren't installed by default, so if you see one here you'd like to add, check out the Add/Remove Programs section in this chapter.

If you have software or hardware that causes Control Panel items to be installed that aren't covered here, use the Help system and your software or hardware documentation to find your way. Such items might include ODBC for databases, and the Find Fast feature of Microsoft Office.

Opening It Up

The most direct way to open the Control Panel is to click the Start button, move the pointer to Settings, and then click Control Panel to open it (see Figure 11.1).

FIGURE 11.1: Here it is: a typical Control Panel.

Via Shortcut

If you'd like a shortcut to the Control Panel on your desktop (or in a folder), follow these steps:

1. Open My Computer (click or double-click the icon, depending on your set-up).
2. With the right mouse button, drag the Control Panel icon to the desktop or any other folder.
3. Select Create Shortcut Here.

From the Keyboard

Want to be able to open the Control Panel from the keyboard? You can add keyboard combinations to any desktop shortcut using these steps:

1. Right-click on the Shortcut icon and select Properties.
2. Select the Shortcut tab.
3. Click with the mouse in the text box next to Shortcut Key.
4. Choose a letter (such as "C" for Control Panel) and type the letter.
5. The keyboard combination of Ctrl+Alt plus the letter you selected will show in the text box and will open this shortcut in the future. Click OK when you're done.

NOTE   **While Windows 98 will let you make an entry in the Shortcut Key field of any shortcut, the resulting keyboard combination will only work for shortcuts located on the desktop.**

Accessibility Options

Accessibility
Options

The Accessibility Options are not installed by default. If they're not on your system, use Add/Remove Programs to add them (Add/Remove Programs is covered a little later in this chapter). Behind this icon, you'll find options for adding visual cues to the usual sound cues and making the keyboard and mouse easier to use for those of us with dexterity problems.

Not all the settings are obvious, so when you come across one that's unclear, right-click on the text and then click on the What's This? button for more information.

TIP   **The ToggleKeys option on the Keyboard page of Accessibility Options is of great help if you often hit the Caps Lock key inadvertently and look up to find your text looking like: cALL mR. jAMES IN cAPE vERDE. With Toggle Keys on, you'll hear a quiet but distinct warning beep when Caps Lock is switched on or off.**

After you've made your settings, don't leave until you click the General tab and check the Automatic Reset section.

- Check "Turn off accessibility features after idle for" if you want the options to be turned off if they're not used for the period specified in the minutes box.
- Clear the check box if you want to make your selections permanent.

TIP   **Besides adding the Control Panel item, installing Accessibility Options adds two more useful features: a wizard that will step you through the many possible Accessibility settings, and a screen magnifier. Find them on the Start menu under Programs ➤ Accessories ➤ Accessibility.**

Add New Hardware

If you are upgrading from Windows 3.1, you'll probably notice that your computer takes longer to start up in the morning than it used to. One reason for the computer's relative slowness is that Windows 98 checks all your hardware to make sure that: (a) it hasn't changed, and (b) that it's still working as expected.

So when you add a sound card or change your video card, Windows 98 detects the change and does what's necessary to make the new hardware work seamlessly with the rest of your system. If all hardware were new and designed for Plug and Play, and it always worked right, this would happen predictably.

While progress has been made since the appearance of Windows 95, this utopia does not yet exist. Sometimes it seems as if every guy who owns a soldering iron is making video cards in his garage. This makes for a certain amount of non-standardization. Also, a lot of hardware is still around that's more than two years old. Hence the need for the Add New Hardware Wizard.

Add New
Hardware

If you add a new component to your system and Windows 98 doesn't appear to recognize it, click this icon.

You can let Windows 98 detect your hardware or do your own specifying. Try automatic detection first; if that doesn't work, try specifying the exact equipment yourself. If all else fails, go to Chapter 16 for information on the hardware troubleshooting functions built into Windows 98.

Add/Remove Programs

Add/Remove
Programs

Windows 98 provides a good deal of aid and comfort when it comes to adding or removing programs from your system. Click this icon in the Control Panel.

The Add/Remove function has three parts, one on each tab:

- Installing or uninstalling software applications
- Installing or removing portions of Windows 98
- Creating a Startup Disk to boot from in case of trouble

Install/Uninstall

This is an easy-to-use tool for installing new programs. Just put the program's CD or the first floppy disk in the appropriate drive and click the Install/Uninstall tab. Click the Install button.

The program searches for an install routine first in drive A:, then drive B: (if it exists), and finally in the CD drive. Figure 11.2 shows the result of one search. Click Finish to continue.

FIGURE 11.2:
The Installation program finds the Install or Setup file and proceeds to install the program.

After this point, the install routine of the program being installed takes over.

Software producers who want the right to put a Windows logo on their product have to make sure the program can uninstall itself completely. So the days of trying to get rid of Windows programs that left errant files all over our systems are slowly being left behind. Unfortunately, many programs still lack this uninstall capability.

Programs that have an uninstall capability can be selected from the list. Click the Add/Remove button, and one of two things will happen:

- The program's uninstaller will start, and will uninstall the program after you confirm, or after you select components to be uninstalled.
- The program's installation routine will start and will offer removal of components as one of its options.

Windows Setup

Click the Windows Setup tab to remove or add a component of Windows 98. The various parts are organized by type (see Figure 11.3). As you click on each item, a description of its function appears at the bottom of the page. The rules are simple.

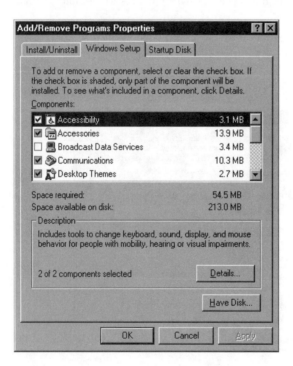

FIGURE 11.3:
Here's where you can install or uninstall various parts of Windows 98.

- If an item shows a check mark in a white box, it's fully installed. Remove the check mark and it'll be removed.

- If an item is checked and the box is gray, some parts of that group are installed. Click the Details button to see the individual items and install or remove any of them.
- If an item is not checked, it's not currently installed on your system. Put a check mark next to it, and it'll be installed.

Click OK once or twice until the window closes. If you installed from a CD, you'll have to return the Windows 98 compact disk to the CD drive.

Startup Disk

You probably made a Startup disk when you installed Windows 98. Of course, you may have since lost the disk or made major changes to your system, in which case it's wise to make a new one. Simply click on this tab and select Create Disk. You'll be prompted for a floppy and the new Startup disk will be made.

If, for some strange reason, your system fails to boot on its own, a startup disk will be necessary to save the day.

Date/Time

Windows 98 uses the system time and date from your computer's internal
Date/Time clock, and it even keeps track of Daylight Saving Time. However, if you're zipping around the world with your laptop, you'll probably want to operate on local time. To make changes to the time or date, click on this icon in the Control Panel.

The Date/Time properties are on two pages. The first one sets the day, month, and year, as well as the exact time. Contrary to what you might expect, this is where you make any change to local time by adjusting the hour (and, if necessary, the date or minutes).

The second page sets the time zone. There are only twenty-four hours in a day, but Windows 98 knows about at least 63 time zones and sub-zones around the world. Find yours on the drop-down list. Changing the time zone does *not* change your system's clock. Setting the correct time zone is important when making network connections and to make sure the correct rules are used for going on and off daylight savings time. The name of the zone and its variation from Greenwich Mean Time are shown at the top of the window. Click the OK button when you've made your changes.

Desktop Themes

Do you find the Windows desktop boring? Of course, you can customize the wallpaper or pattern, and change the color scheme, fonts, and so on if you wish. But for a quick fix that you may find more interesting anyway, check out Windows 98's Desktop Themes. (In Windows 95 these were part of the add-on Plus! Pack.) Go to Windows Setup in Add/Remove Programs. Choose Desktop Themes and click Details to see what's available. Once they're installed, the icon at left will appear in the Control Panel.

Desktop Themes

When you open it, you'll find a Theme drop-down list where you can choose between the themes you installed. There's a preview window to give you an idea of what it will look like. You can also choose which elements of a theme to use, and which you'd rather leave alone. You can also preview the screen saver and the mouse pointers, sounds, and icons that are part of the theme.

Display

 Back in Chapter 4, we talked about the property sheets that appear when you right-click on the desktop and select Properties. These same property sheets can be found by clicking on the Display icon.

Display

Check Chapter 4 for information about these property settings, including setting up active HTML content on your desktop.

Fonts

TrueType fonts are managed in Windows 98 in a completely transparent way. To see the list of installed fonts, click on this icon.

Fonts

Selecting and Viewing Fonts

The Fonts folder is a little different from the usual run of folders. In the View menu shown in Figure 11.4, you'll find, in addition to the choices for viewing icons and lists, an option called List Fonts by Similarity. The toolbar also has a button for each view.

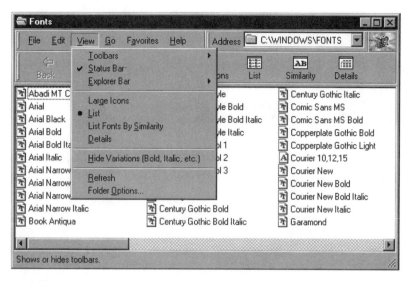

FIGURE 11.4: The view menu is a little different in the Fonts folder.

TIP **If your font list is very long and unwieldy, select View and then Hide Variations. That will hide font variations such as italic and bold and make the list easier to look through.**

If you click List Fonts by Similarity or the Similarity button, a drop-down box appears below the toolbars. Select a font in the drop-down box and the other fonts will line up in terms of their degree of similarity (see Figure 11.5). Before you make a commitment, you can right-click on any of the font names and select Open (or just double-click). A window will open with a complete view of the font in question.

For Windows 3.1 Users

TrueType fonts that you may have located elsewhere should be moved into the Fonts folder. Just drag-and-drop or cut and paste.

A Fonts that are identified with an icon like this are not TrueType fonts. They're not scaleable, which means that at large point sizes they tend to look quite crummy (see Figure 11.6). Some of these fonts can be used only in certain, limited point sizes.

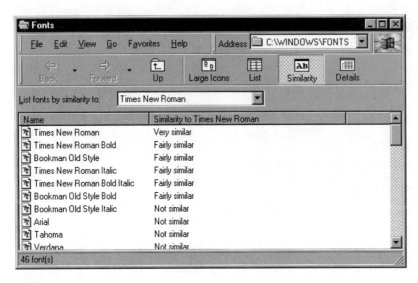

FIGURE 11.5: Fonts can be viewed in terms of their resemblance to one another.

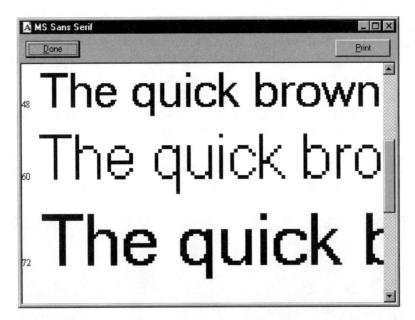

FIGURE 11.6: The non-True Type fonts are not much to look at in the larger sizes.

In the Fonts folder, View ➤ Folder Options has a special tab labeled TrueType. On it, you can select an option to show only TrueType fonts in your applications.

Installing New Fonts

Installing new fonts is a pretty easy project. Just open the Fonts icon in the Control Panel and select Install New Font from the File menu. In the Add Fonts window (Figure 11.7), you can tell the system the drive and directory where the font(s) reside. If there are TrueType fonts at the location you specify, they'll show up in the List of Fonts window.

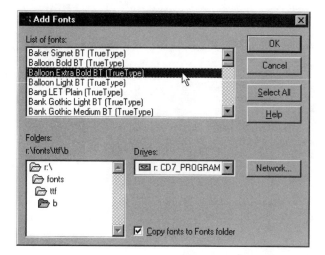

FIGURE 11.7:
Here's where you add fonts to the Fonts folder.

Highlight the font or fonts you want installed and click OK.

TIP
Other types of fonts, such as those installed by the Adobe Type Manager, will reside elsewhere on your hard drive, depending on the location you selected. You won't be allowed to put them in the Fonts folder and you won't be able to view them by double-clicking on them. However, numerous applications can display fonts and many font packages have their own viewers.

Game Controllers

Game Controllers

The Joystick icon in Windows 95 has been replaced by the more comprehensive Game Controllers. Open it and use the Add button to install your controller. As you can see in Figure 11.8, there's a controller type for all occasions. If you have a device that's not on the list but came with a driver disk, click Add Other, then Have Disk to install the manufacturer's drivers.

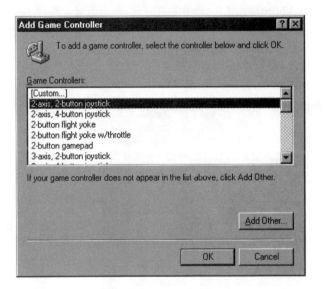

FIGURE 11.8:
Over twenty varieties of game devices are listed; you can also choose Custom and configure your own.

The Properties button on the General page of Game Controllers allows you to test and calibrate your controller. On the Advanced page you can assign ID's to multiple controllers and otherwise customize your setup.

NOTE **If you are unable to add your game controller, it's possible that your gameport is not properly installed. Open the System item in Control Panel, click the Device Manager tab, and click the + sign beside Sound, Video, and Game Controllers. If Gameport Joystick is not listed, use the Add New Hardware function in the Control Panel.**

Internet

Internet

This icon gives you access to a wide variety of settings for Internet Explorer and your Internet connection. It's the same as View ➤ Internet Options in Internet Explorer. Refer to Chapter 7 for a discussion of these settings.

Keyboard

Keyboard

To find settings for the keyboard, click this icon in the Control Panel. The Keyboard property sheet has two tabs, Speed and Language.

TIP **Changing your keyboard type is now done by adding the new keyboard with Add New Hardware.**

Keyboard Speed

Click on the Speed tab to adjust keyboard rates. These are similar to the settings available in previous versions of Windows.

Repeat delay determines how long a key has to be held down before it starts repeating. The difference between the Long and Short setting is only about a second.

Repeat rate determines how fast a key repeats. Fast means if you hold down a key, you almost instantly get vvvvvvvvvvvvery long streams of letters. (Click on the practice area to test this and the delay setting.)

Cursor blink rate makes the cursor blink faster or slower. The blinking cursor on the left demonstrates the setting.

Keyboard Languages

If you need multiple language support for your keyboard, click the Language tab. Click the Add button to select languages from Afrikaans to Ukranian—including fifteen varieties of Spanish. Once you have more than one language selected, the settings on the Language tab let you choose a keyboard combination to switch between languages (see Figure 11.9).

Check "Enable indicator on taskbar" and an icon will appear on your taskbar. Right-click on it and you can instantly switch between languages.

FIGURE 11.9:
Set your keyboard up for more than one language.

Keyboard Shortcuts

If your keyboard was made in the last two or three years, it probably has a couple of special Windows keys. The Windows key has the Windows logo on it, and the Menu key shows a menu and mouse pointer. These keys offer a lot of quick ways to move around in Windows 98. Here are some shortcuts that use the special Windows keys:

Minimize all Windows	Windows+M
Undo minimize all	Shift+Windows+M
Open the Run dialog box	Windows+R
File Find	Windows+F
Explorer	Windows+E
Start menu	Windows key
Windows Help	Windows+F1
System Properties	Windows+Break
Pop-up menu	Menu key

Mail and Fax

We aren't going to say much about the Mail and Fax item in the Control Panel because it's not part of Windows 98. If you installed Windows 98 as an upgrade over Windows 95 with Exchange installed, then Exchange is still on your system. You can use it as you did under Windows 95, using Mail and Fax to set its options.

The other reason you might encounter this icon in your Control Panel is that you have installed Microsoft Outlook (part of the Office 97 package) or are on a network that uses the Windows Messaging system. Refer to your Outlook documentation or your system administrator for information on how to set the correct options in Mail and Fax.

NOTE **Windows 98's Outlook Express does not make use of Mail and Fax settings.**

Modems

The Modems icon in the Control Panel gives you access to all the settings for the modem (or modems) on your system. To install a modem or change the settings, you need merely click on this icon to open the Modems property sheet.

The Modems property sheet opens to the General page. If you already have a modem installed, there will also be a Diagnostics page. From the General page, you can install or delete a modem, look up a modem's settings, and select Dialing Properties—specifications on how your calls are dialed. First, we'll cover the settings on the General page.

Installing a Modem

Installing and configuring a modem in Windows 98 is much simpler than it used to be (and almost as simple as it should be).

1. Open the Modems icon in the Control Panel. Select Add to start the Install New Modem Wizard.

2. You can let Windows 98 search for the modem or you can select your modem directly (see Figure 11.10). As a rule, let Windows try first—it's the easiest way. If Windows 98 has difficulty, you can always specify your particular modem on a second go-round.

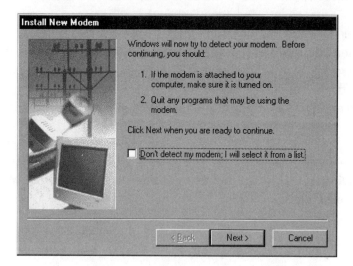

FIGURE 11.10: Another Windows 98 Wizard steps you through the process of installing a modem.

3. Windows will search around your communications ports and try to find a modem. If it finds one, you'll see the verify window shown in Figure 11.11. If the found modem isn't correct, or the designation seems too generic, click the Change button and continue with the next step.

4. If Windows 98 fails to find the modem (or if you click Change in the Verify dialog), you'll be asked to get specific. Figure 11.12 shows the window where you select a manufacturer in the left box and the particular model in the right box. If your modem isn't listed, but you have a driver diskette that came with it, click Have Disk.

Keep clicking OK, Next, or Finish until the installation is complete.

Deleting a Modem

If you change modems (or install the wrong one), it's easy to correct the situation.

1. Open the Modems icon in the Control Panel.

2. On the General page, highlight the modem name.

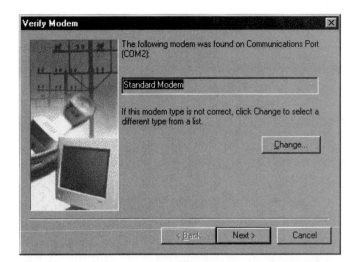

FIGURE 11.11:
Windows 98 has detected a modem. It's up to you to agree or disagree with the finding.

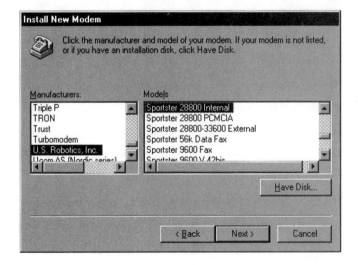

FIGURE 11.12:
If Windows 98 doesn't find your modem, you can install a modem by selecting a particular manufacturer and model.

3. Click the Remove button, and it's gone!

4. Go back to the Installing a Modem section to re-install.

Modem Settings

To find the hardware-type settings for your modem, open the Modems icon in the Control Panel. Highlight your modem (if it isn't already) and select Properties. What opens is the property sheet for this particular modem (see Figure 11.13).

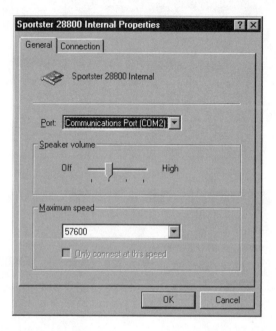

FIGURE 11.13:
This is the place to check up on the settings for your modem.

On the General page, you will find:
- The full name of the modem
- The port it's connected to
- A slider for setting the volume of the modem speaker
- A drop-down box for setting the maximum speed

TIP

These settings (except for volume, which is strictly a matter of preference) rarely need to be fooled with. That's because they come from what Windows 98 knows about your specific modem. Only change the settings when you've had some difficulty with your modem being recognized and you're sure a particular setting is wrong.

For Windows 3.1 Users

What's TAPI?

TAPI is still another in the long series of unbearable computer acronyms. It stands for Telephony Applications Programming Interface. What that means (short version) is that communications programs can adopt the settings you've already made on your system: modem type, port, and that sort of stuff. Up until now, you've had to tell each communications program what kind of modem you have, where it is on your computer, and sometimes even the dread initialization string. And if you buy a new modem, you have to do all that stuff all over again for every program.

TAPI puts a stop to that nonsense. All programs written to the TAPI standard can detect the settings of your modem. If you change modems, you just go to the Modem icon in the Control Panel and delete the old modem and install your new one. Another aspect of TAPI is that you can set up various locations you're calling from, and when you select one, any TAPI application can use that information to properly dial the number—whether it's a local call, a long distance call, or a call charged to a particular credit card.

The bad news is that applications designed for Windows 3.1 won't be able to take full advantage of all the TAPI features. But any new programs you buy should be written to the TAPI standard.

The Connection Page

On the Connection page are more of the hardware settings. Again, unless you have a good reason for changing the Connection preferences, leave them alone. The Call preferences can be changed if you find the default ones unsuitable.

Advanced Settings

If you click the Advanced button, you'll see the window in Figure 11.14. These settings are rarely anything to be concerned about. They're just here for those odd and infrequent times when it might be necessary to force error correction or use software for error control. The one thing on this page that might be used more often is the log file. If you're troubleshooting a bad connection, click View Log to open a text file containing a log of the last connection or attempt. (This file resides in your main Windows directory and has a .log extension.) Normally, this file is overwritten with the new log each time you connect. If you want to keep an ongoing log, check the "Append to log" box.

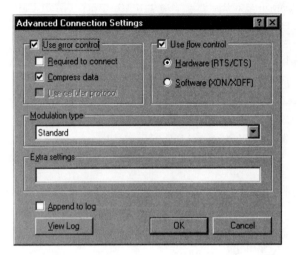

FIGURE 11.14: You might try these Advanced settings with a connection that's otherwise difficult.

Dialing Properties

In addition to centralizing the modem's hardware and software settings, you also want to enter information about how you're dialing and where you're dialing from. Windows 98 allows for the configuring of multiple dialing locations, so if you travel with your computer, you can make calls from your branch office (or the villa in Spain where you take your vacations) without making complex changes.

Click Dialing Properties on the Modems property sheet's General page (not the General page of your specific modem) and fill out the information for your location. Click the Add button to supply additional locations. When you change physical locations, you need only tell Windows 98 where you are (see Figure 11.15) and all your necessary dialing information will be loaded.

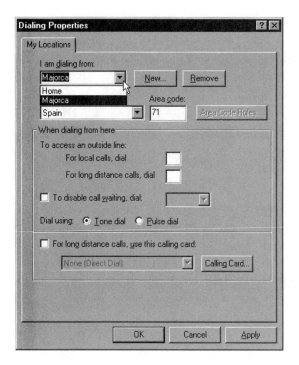

FIGURE 11.15:
If you travel with your computer, you don't have to redo your communications settings when you change locations.

Troubleshooting

As a general rule, when your modem is uncooperative, it's for obvious reasons:
- It's not plugged into a phone line.
- The modem's turned off or it's not plugged into an active electrical socket (external modems).
- One or more programs have confused the settings.

After you check the first two items, click on the Modems icon in the Control Panel. On the Diagnostics page, highlight the port your modem is connected to and click More Info. The resulting page (see Figure 11.16) tells you that the system recognizes the modem and describes it in terms of speed, interrupt, memory address, and the modem's response to various internal commands.

If your modem isn't recognized, go back to the main Modem property sheet and select the Remove button. After the modem's removed, close everything and reboot your system. Then go back to the Modems icon and add your modem back.

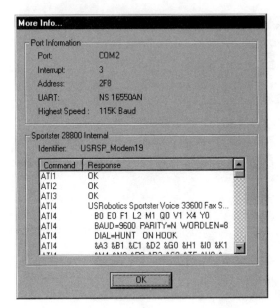

FIGURE 11.16:
Here's where you verify that the system knows where your modem is and that it's functional.

Mouse

Mouse

The role of the mouse took a big step forward with Windows 95, and it takes on a few more functions in Windows 98. To change your mouse settings, click on the Mouse icon.

The settings are mostly like those in earlier versions of Windows—you can adjust the pointer speed and double-click speed and add mouse trails.

A Page Full of Pointers

The biggest mouse difference in Windows 98 can be found on the Pointers page. Here you can choose from several pre-installed schemes or make up your own. There's a substantial cottage industry in animated cursors. If you have access to an on-line service or a BBS, go to the Windows sections and browse for files with the extension .ani for animated horses, basketball players, and dinosaurs (among others). Ani files should be moved to the Cursors sub-folder inside your main Windows folder.

Another source of alternate mouse pointers is the Desktop Themes supplied with Windows 98. If you don't like the whole theme, you can install only its mouse pointers. And if you don't like all of them, you can change individual ones as described in the next section.

Changing Cursors

To change a cursor assignment, follow these steps:

1. Open the Mouse icon in the Control Panel. Select Pointers.
2. Highlight the pointer you want to change. Click on Browse.
3. In the Cursors folder, select the cursor you want to use. Files with the .cur extension are pointers of various kinds, while ani files are animated. Click the Open button.
4. Click OK when you're done.

If you want more than one set of cursors, arrange one set, click the Save As button, and provide a name in the Save Scheme box. Repeat for subsequent sets.

TIP   **For a better look at your cursors, open the Windows\Cursors folder and choose Large Icon view.**

Multimedia

Multimedia

The multimedia settings in Windows 98 are pretty impressive, though they're available only to the extent that you have hardware to use them.

Audio Settings

The first tab on the Multimedia property sheet is for Audio, as shown in Figure 11.17. This is your gateway to playback and recording settings. The speaker and microphone are buttons. Click them for access to play and record volume controls for various sound sources. The Advanced Properties buttons allow you to tell Windows 98 what type of speakers you have, and to make settings that affect the quality of sound playback and recording.

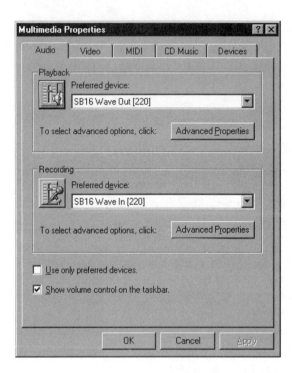

FIGURE 11.17:
Here's the
property sheet
for setting your
audio preferences.

Video

If you want to play back video clips, here's where you can set the size of the video window relative to your monitor. If you choose Full Screen, pressing any key will stop the video and return you to the desktop.

Understand that your monitor is still not the equal of the local cinema multiplex. The larger the image on your screen, the more blocky or grainy it will appear. Your ability to play video clips on your screen will be affected by:

- The speed, acceleration features, and memory on your video card
- The type of bus or port the video card is plugged into: AGP, PCI, VESA, or ISA
- The power of your CPU

MIDI

The MIDI page on the Multimedia property sheet lets you set output devices for MIDI files. If you have a sound card that can process MIDI files or an attached MIDI instrument, the page will be available for you to adjust settings or add a different instrument.

CD Music

The page for CD music includes only a place to indicate which CD-ROM drive you want to use for playing audio CDs and a slider for volume control. This control is in addition to the CD Audio slider on the playback volume control reached from the Audio page. For information on the CD player applet, see Chapter 14, where the multimedia applications are described.

Devices

On the Devices page you will find a tree layout of all the numerous multimedia software devices installed on your system. You can use it to set properties for some devices, but in many cases the only thing you can do is tell the system not to use the device. This would be useful mainly for troubleshooting problems.

Network

Click on the Network icon in the Control Panel to add or change network settings. The Network dialog box is the place to go if you are having trouble communicating over your local area network. It also plays a role in your Internet access. Some items may have been added in already when you installed Windows 98 or a new network card. If you didn't get all you need or want, this is where you can add in the rest.

The Network dialog lets you add client protocols, hardware adapters, networking "stacks" or protocols, and networking services to your Windows 98 configuration.

NOTE **In the following sections, we'll just cover how to add the most basic of protocols and the minimum services for a small network based on Windows 98's built-in networking capacities.**

Client Choices

Network clients let you use the services being provided by another machine on your network. The default network configuration includes the client for Microsoft Networks. A client for Novell Netware networks is also included with Windows 98.

If you are connecting to other networks, such as Banyan VINES or Sun's PC-NFS, you will need to add them in here. For these, however, you will need disks (and instructions) from the manufacturer. We'll stick to just adding in the Microsoft Networking Client.

Open the Network dialog and be sure you are looking at the Configuration page as shown in Figure 11.18. If you don't see the Client for Microsoft Networks in the list at the top, click the Add button, select Client, and then click Add again.

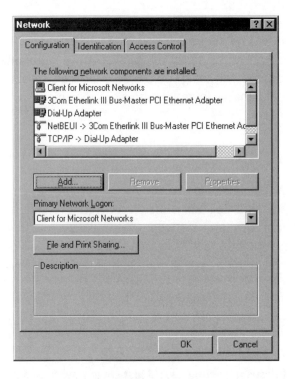

FIGURE 11.18:
Your starting point for adjusting network components and properties

This opens the Select Network Client dialog box shown in Figure 11.19. Highlight Microsoft, select Client for Microsoft Networks, and then click OK.

Adapters and Protocols

Adapters are your modem, network card, and other hardware that allow your computer to communicate with others. They should have been detected when you installed Windows 98, and so should already be listed in the Network Components list on the Configuration page, as shown in Figure 11.20.

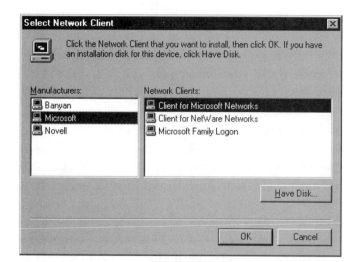

FIGURE 11.19:
Adding the Microsoft client for a Microsoft network is easy.

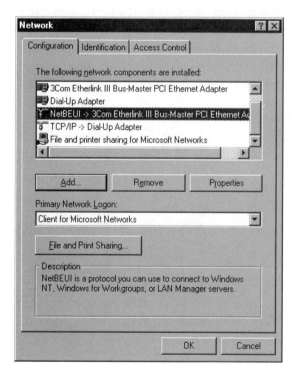

FIGURE 11.20:
Here you can check on your network adapters and the protocols that are installed.

Protocols tell the various machines on a network how to communicate. The TCP/IP protocol may have been installed by default when Windows 98 Setup detected either a modem or a network card. TCP/IP is used on the Internet and company intranets, but if you are connected to a Microsoft-based local area network, it is likely to use either the IPX/SPX-compatible protocol or the older NetBEUI. You need to use whatever the rest of the network uses.

Protocols are the items indicated by this icon, as shown in Figure 11.20. If one you need isn't listed, install it just as described above for clients. Click Add, double-click Protocol, then select the provider and the specific protocol you need. Notice that the Network Components list also tells you which protocols are set up for use by which network adapters.

TIP   It's a good idea to remove any protocols you're sure you don't need. While the memory hit is hidden better now than in Windows 3.1, there's still no such thing as a free lunch. Remove each protocol-adapter combination that you won't be using.

Service Choices

The default installation doesn't install any services at all, which is fine if you never want anyone else to be able to use the resources of your computer. If your local network has one main machine everyone else shares—the one with the fax modem, the big hard drive, the printer, and such—then you can leave this choice alone. But if others need access to the resources on your computer, you will need to add services to share your files and printer (if you have one).

Click Add, then select Services from the Select Network Component Type dialog and click Add again. Highlight Microsoft in the resulting Select Network Service dialog box, as shown in Figure 11.21, select "File and Printer Sharing for Microsoft Networks," and click OK. This will add the necessary network services to allow you to let others on the network use your documents and folders as well as any printers or fax modems attached to your computer.

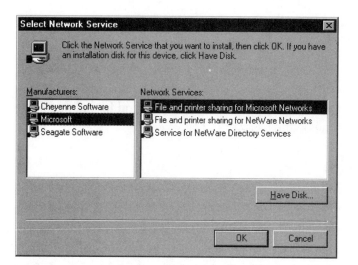

FIGURE 11.21:
Adding file and printer sharing allows others to use the resources on your computer.

This should be enough to solve any basic problems of connecting to your network. You may need to reboot your machine when you get done adding the necessary components.

TIP   If you have a notebook computer with PCMCIA card support, once you have done the initial installation of the network components, you can insert or remove the network PCMCIA card and Windows 98 will detect the change without rebooting.

More Network Settings

The Identification tab of the Network dialog is where you can set a name to identify your computer on the network and determine what network workgroup it belongs to. On the Access Control tab, you can determine whether access to resources on your computer is to be granted to anyone with the necessary password, or whether access is granted only to users you specify.

Passwords

You can set several different kinds of passwords on a Windows 98 computer. If you're on a network, there's the usual network sign-on password, as well as passwords for others to access your machine and for individual user profiles. Set them up by clicking on the Passwords icon.

Setting Them Up

If you want to establish a password for your computer to prevent unauthorized access, select the Passwords icon in the Control Panel. On the first page of the property sheet, click Change Windows Password. In the box that opens (see Figure 11.22), you'll be asked for your old password. If you haven't established one, just leave this field blank. Type in the new password and then type it again to confirm. Click OK when you're done and you'll see a message confirming that a password has been established.

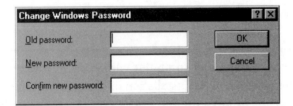

FIGURE 11.22: In the Change Windows Password box, you need to supply your old password if you've designated one previously.

For Multiple Users

If more than one person uses a computer, there's bound to be the occasional disagreement about wallpaper and sound schemes, much less desktop arrangements. These problems can be mitigated by setting up individual user profiles. Basic settings can be made on the User Profiles tab, but the best way to set up multiple users is to use the wizard found by opening the Users icon in the Control Panel. It's discussed later in this chapter.

Allowing Remote Access

Remote access is a step up from merely sharing your drives or files. Someone with remote access can run your computer as if they were you. In other words, they can turn sharing on or off, turn passwords on or off, and otherwise use every facility. To allow remote access, follow these steps:

1. Open the Passwords property sheet by clicking on the Passwords icon in the Control Panel. Select the Remote Administration tab.
2. Select "Enable remote administration of this server."
3. Type in a password that the remote administrator must use to get access to your machine. Confirm the password by entering it a second time.
4. Click OK when you're finished.

WARNING   **Be very cautious about allowing remote administration of a machine set up with the Windows 98 Dial-up Server. The security level is very low.**

PC Card (PCMCIA)

PC Card (PCMCIA)

Though it was only for laptops in Windows 95, power management has come to all machines in Windows 98.

The dialog box behind this icon tells you what is currently in each PC Card slot and allows you to select a device and stop it, so you can safely remove it from its slot. It also has an option (on by default) to add an icon to the system tray so you can stop and remove PC Cards without having to go to the Control Panel.

Power Management

Power Management

Though it was only for laptops in Windows 95, power management has come to all machines in Windows 98.

The pages present in Power Management depend on the type of machine you are using. On the Power Schemes tab you can set the amount of idle time before your monitor shuts off and the idle time until your computer goes to low-power standby. Standby mode only works on machines that have the necessary power management hardware. Computer and monitor both come back to life when you move the mouse or press a key, or to perform scheduled tasks. On a laptop, the Power Schemes tab will have separate settings for battery power or plugged-in operation, and for turning off the hard drive before the full standby time.

Power Management is complex because it depends on interactions between Windows 98 and your computer hardware. Some desktop machines and many laptops offer a feature that Windows 98 calls "hibernate." The entire contents of memory are saved to disk, then the machine shuts off completely. Scheduled tasks will not be performed while the computer is hibernating. When you turn it back on, all your work and programs are restored exactly as you left them.

TIP   **Power management terms are somewhat confusing, and many laptops use "standby" to mean the same thing as Windows 98's "hibernate." For more details on power management, look up "OnNow" in the Windows 98 Help index.**

The Advanced tab allows you to show a battery meter on the taskbar. You can also require that your password be entered when the machine comes off standby. A laptop will also have pages for more details about the state of the batteries and for setting low-battery alarms.

Printers

Printing is generally a lot easier in Windows 98 than in any previous system. As in earlier versions of Windows, printers are set up to use a common set of drivers so you don't have to configure each program independently for printing. Adding or removing a printer is as easy as point and click, and sharing printers over a network is painless.

Printers are accessible through the Printers folder inside My Computer, off the Start menu under Settings, or in the Printers folder in the Control Panel. And, of course, you can drag a shortcut to the folder (or any of the printers in it), to your desktop, or to any folder where you'd like it.

Adding One

You probably installed a printer when you installed Windows 98, but if you didn't or you want to add another or a network printer, it's very easy to do.

Adding Locally

For a printer that's connected directly to your computer, open the Printers folder and follow these steps (clicking the Next button after each entry):

   1.   Select Add Printer.

2. When the Add Printer Wizard starts, click Next, and check the Local printer entry.

3. Highlight the name of the printer's manufacturer and the model name.

4. Select the port you want to use. Unless you know of some special circumstances, choose LPT1.

5. Type in the name you want the printer to be known by and indicate whether this is to be the default printer for all your Windows programs. If this is the printer you plan to use practically all the time, select Yes. Otherwise say no— you'll still be able to select the printer when you want to use it. In the Printers folder, the default printer will have a check mark by it.

6. Print a test page to verify all is well. Then click Finish.

Adding a Network Printer

 A network printer (indicated by this icon) is plugged into someone else's computer—a computer to which you have access via a network.

To install a network printer so you can use it, open the Printers folder and follow these steps (clicking Next after each entry):

1. Open Add Printer. When the Add Printer Wizard starts, click Next, and then select Network printer.

2. You'll need to tell the system the address of the printer. Click on the Browse button to look for available printers. Highlight the printer (as shown in Figure 11.23) and click OK.

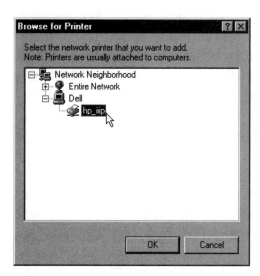

FIGURE 11.23:
Here's where you select a printer on the network.

3. If you expect to print from DOS programs, click Yes so the system can add the necessary information to the printer setup.

4. Enter the name you want to call the printer and check whether you want this printer to be the default printer. Only check Yes if you expect to be using the network printer for the majority of your printing.

5. Print a test page to make sure everything's running properly and click Finish.

NOTE **To be able to use a printer set up this way, the printer and the computer it's connected to must both be switched on.**

Uninstalling One

Sometimes you may need to uninstall a printer, which is quite easily done. Just right-click on the printer's icon in the Printers folder and select Delete. You'll be asked to confirm the deletion. You may also be asked if you want to delete files that are associated with this printer that won't be necessary if the printer is gone. If you're getting rid of the printer permanently, select Yes. If you're planning on reinstalling the same printer soon, select No.

Printer Settings

To get at the settings for a printer, you need to right-click on the printer's icon and select Properties. On the property sheet that opens, you can set details as to fonts, paper, how the printer treats graphics, and so on.

Most of these settings are made by the printer driver that Windows 98 installed to run the printer. Change ones that you need to change but avoid changing settings if you're not clear what the setting does. You can inadvertently disable your printer. If this happens, you can usually cure it by uninstalling the printer (see the previous section) and then installing it again.

Troubleshooting

If you're not having any success getting your printer to print, or there appears to be something wrong with the printer, Windows 98 comes with excellent tools for troubleshooting the problem.

Select Help from the Start menu. On the Contents page, open Troubleshooting. Then open Windows 98 Troubleshooters and select Print. The guide is interactive in that you select the problem you're having, and then you will be stepped through the process of finding a solution.

Regional Settings

Regional Settings

The Regional Settings icon in the Control Panel is where you set the variations in how numbers, time, and dates are formatted in different parts of the world. For example, if you're producing materials for an audience in Europe or Asia, the currency symbols as well as how time and dates are displayed will be different from how they are shown in the US. To change these settings, open the Regional Settings icon.

First select the language and geographic variant you want, then confirm or change the individual settings. Your system will have to be rebooted for the settings to take effect system-wide.

Scanners and Cameras

Scanners and Cameras

If you have a scanner connected to your computer and Windows 98 detects it, this icon will be added to the Control Panel.

Opening Scanners and Cameras Properties will give you a list of installed devices. In many cases you will not see devices that were not turned on when you started the computer. Turn the device on, then restart Windows 98. Selecting a device and clicking Properties will allow you to perform simple troubleshooting tests. If you want to add a device that Windows 98 did not detect, click the Add button.

Of course, if no scanner or camera has been detected, you won't have this icon to begin with. To manually install what you have, open Add New Hardware. After the Plug-and-Play detection step, choose "No, the device isn't on the list" (assuming it isn't), and click Next. You can try letting Windows search for the hardware, or select your hardware from the list under the category Imaging Device. Once it's installed, the Scanners and Cameras item will be in the Control Panel.

TIP

While Windows 98's built-in drivers offer basic functionality for a variety of scanners and cameras, you should try installing the software supplied with the device. In many cases, it will offer better control over the device than Windows 98 can provide on its own.

Sounds

Sounds

What with Windows 98's emphasis on multimedia, it's no surprise that using sound with your computer is easier than ever. Double-click on the Sounds icon in the Control Panel to set and change sound schemes.

A Sheet Full of Sounds

The Sounds property sheet is shown in Figure 11.24. The Events window lists everything on your system that can be associated with a sound. Most are Windows events. For example, opening a program can cause a sound, as can maximizing or minimizing a window. Many other actions cause sounds as well.

FIGURE 11.24:
Use the Sounds property sheet to associate a sound with an event.

If there's a Speaker icon next to the event, a sound is associated with it. Highlight the event—the name of the sound file will appear in the Name window—and click the Play button next to the Preview window to hear its sound. Several sound schemes are included with Windows 98 and you can choose one of them from the drop-down list.

> **NOTE**   If sound schemes don't appear in the Schemes drop-down list, you'll need to install them. Go to the Add/Remove Programs icon in the Control Panel. Under the Windows Setup, select Multimedia and click Details. Put a check in front of Multimedia Sound Schemes, then click OK twice.

Customizing a Sound Scheme

All the sound schemes that come with Windows are nice enough but none of them is perfect. They either have too many sounds, not enough, the wrong sounds attached to various events, or whatever. Fortunately, there's a way to make as many customized sound schemes as you like. Here's how:

1. Open the Sounds icon in the Control Panel.
2. If there's a sound scheme that's close to the one you want, select it from the Schemes drop-down list. Otherwise select Windows default.
3. Starting at the top of the Events list, select an item that you want a sound associated with.
4. Select a file from the Name drop-down list. To make sure it's the one you want, click the Preview button to hear it.
5. Select (None) in the Name list for events that you want to make silent.
6. Repeat steps 3-5 until you've completed the list.
7. Select Save As to save this particular assortment of sounds under a specific name. (The new scheme will appear in the Schemes drop-down list.)

> **NOTE**   Windows 98 stores all its sound files in the Windows\Media folder. You'll probably want to move any additional sound files you acquire to that folder because a single location makes setting up and changing sound schemes much easier. Also, since the .wav files for a sound scheme may total a megabyte or more, you might want to delete files you're not using if disk space is tight.

System

The property sheet that opens when you double-click on the System icon in the Control Panel can also be reached by right-clicking on My Computer and choosing Properties. Most of the settings are of little interest as long as your computer is working properly. It's only when things go awry that you need to be changing anything here.

General

The General page only tells you the version of Windows 98, the registered owner, and a little bit about the type of computer. The main computer information starts on the next page.

Device Manager

The Device Manager page is where you can see what your system thinks is going on. Usually this is a reflection of reality, but when something is wrong with your computer, this is often where you'll see it first.

The plus signs to the left of items indicate there's more to see under those entries. To get the details of the setup for each item, highlight it, and click Properties. A list of hardware interrupts, I/O addresses, DMA assignments, and memory addresses can be found by highlighting Computer and selecting Properties.

Devices that Windows 98 finds are not working properly will be highlighted with an exclamation point. Don't automatically assume, however, that these are problems with your setup.

For example, Figure 11.25 shows a Device Manager listing with exclamation marks on the IDE controller and two PS/2 mouse entries. This is normal and proper for this machine because it uses SCSI hard drives and CD drive, so the IDE controller for such devices has been disabled in the BIOS. Also, the PS/2 mouse has been disconnected and a serial mouse device used instead.

Hardware Profiles

Hardware profiles are something you may need if you're using a portable computer with a docking station. In a limited number of circumstances, you may need to configure alternate setups when the hardware on your system changes.

If you think this might be your situation, consult the Windows 98 help files for instructions. Look under Hardware Profiles in the index.

Performance

The Performance tab is used almost exclusively for troubleshooting. For example, Windows 98 is pretty good at figuring out what will work best on your system, but it's not always perfect. Because of the mixture of 16-bit applications in a 32-bit system, there may come a time when you want to check that your system is running optimally.

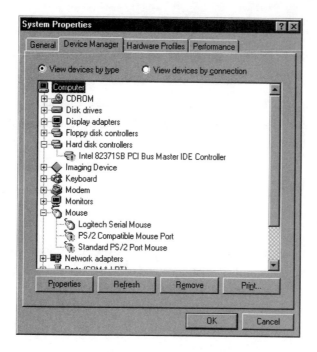

FIGURE 11.25: Exclamation marks indicate possible problems, but not always.

Behind the File System button on the Performance tab is a File System Properties dialog with pages for changing some important operations (see Figure 11.26). It has a page for each kind of storage device on your machine and a general troubleshooting tab. If you have a disk drive that refuses to run properly under Windows 98, you may be able to isolate the problem by changing one or more options here. In any case, all the Performance entries are for solving problems. If you don't have problems, leave them alone.

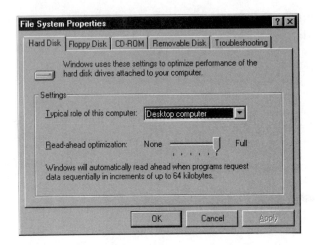

FIGURE 11.26:
Here are some disk-drive trouble-shooting options.

NOTE   **You can learn much more about hardware troubleshooting in Chapter 16.**

Telephony

Telephony

This icon provides access to a property sheet for drivers and services related to telephone features such as voice modems. There is also a duplicate of the Locations page found under the modems icon.

Users

Users

The Users icon starts a Wizard to help you set up individual profiles for different users of the computer. The features that can be different in each profile include the desktop, Start menu, Favorites, My Documents, and Internet-related files. You can even set up user profiles with different views in the Network Neighborhood. Just follow these steps:

1. Open Users in the Control Panel.
2. Read the introductory information, then click Next and enter the name you want to use to start Windows 98 with your preferred setup.

3.   Enter and confirm the password you want to use.

4.   In the next dialog, select which features you want to be able to customize, and whether or not you want to start with them set up as they currently are.

5.   Click Next when you're done. Read the final information before clicking Finish.

Once you make these settings, every user (including you) will be prompted for a password at sign-on. New users can run the Users Wizard to set up their own profile with their preferences. Individual profiles are stored in a folder called Profiles under the main Windows folder.

What's Next

Windows 98 runs DOS programs at least as well as DOS and many times better than Windows 3.1. The next chapter tells you how DOS programs execute in Windows 98 and what you can do to fine-tune those that need a bit of help (like some of the more aggressive games).

WHITHER DOS?

So, you're basically a DOS kinda guy or gal. You've struggled with Windows, but when you really need to get something done, you fall back on the old, reliable DOS applications. Maybe you have a favorite game that won't run in Windows 3.1, and you worry about what will happen now that Windows 98 is your operating system, and DOS acts as just one more Windows program. Perhaps you, or your company, still use one or two DOS programs because they do what you need and you've never seen a reason to switch to a Windows version. This might be especially compelling in the case of custom applications.

Your ranks may be dwindling, but that's no reason to despair. This chapter shows you how to get those DOS applications up and running, and even gives you specific guidelines on troubleshooting them within Windows 98.

NOTE The DOS facilities offered by Windows 98 are essentially unchanged from Windows 95. If you already have your DOS programs running under Windows 95, you can probably skip this chapter.

You Don't Do Windows?

Maybe you used to say, "I don't do Windows," but here you are, loading up and running Windows 98. You went all this time, watching others struggle with Windows 3.1 or their Macs or UNIX XWindows with their cute little icons, their mice, and all that other GUI stuff, and you weren't tempted. So what's changed?

Well, maybe:

- Your boss said you had to.
- You've finally decided that you can't limp along running WordPerfect 5.1 and Lotus 2.01 any longer when the rest of the world is running WordPerfect 8 for Windows and Microsoft Excel 97.
- All your computer could really handle before was plain old DOS and now you've spent big bucks on a screamin' machine and you want to be able to have all those neat .bmps on your screen.

Doing It GUI

Probably the biggest difference about running any GUI (pronounced gooey) is the way it looks, which is why it's called a Graphical User Interface. But beyond the aesthetic differences, a GUI also works very differently from the way a text-based interface works. For some things, you're still going to wish you had your familiar old command line to get something done. But cheer up: you can still get a perfectly usable DOS command line, either in a window on your desktop or on a full screen, as shown in Figure 12.1.

All the Old and Unfamiliar Places

Almost all your familiar DOS commands are still there. Which is just as well, because it'll take a while to figure out how to do things with Windows 98. It's just not obvious, for example, that to format a floppy, you right-click on the drive's icon in Windows Explorer or My Computer (see Figure 12.2).

FIGURE 12.1: You can still run all your favorite DOS programs and even get a DOS command line in Windows 98.

FIGURE 12.2: Here's how you format a floppy in Windows 98.

And this is just one example of the new stuff you're facing.

NOTE Windows 98 even has some new twists for the hard-core DOS nerds in the crowd. Our favorite is the extension of the "dot-dot" syntax. Most DOS users with pretensions to nerddom know that the current directory is . and the parent directory is .. but now you can go even farther. If you find yourself down in the subdirectory structure with a prompt like: C:\Windows\Start Menu\Programs\Accessories\ Games> and you want to get back to the main Windows 98 directory, WINDOWS in this case, just type: cd ..... and you'll move up four directory levels to the WINDOWS directory.

Life's a Drag and Then You Drop

Want to move a file or files from one directory to another? In Explorer or another folder, highlight the file(s) with your mouse, then right-click and select Cut from the menu. Right-click where you want them to go, and select Paste from the menu. The file(s) will magically appear in the new destination.

Too much work? OK, then highlight the files with your mouse and drag them to where you want them to go. If you drag within the drive (perhaps to another folder), the file will move. A drag across drives—between drives on a network, for example, or from your hard drive to a floppy—produces a copy (unless the file is an executable, in which case you get a shortcut). Right-click with the mouse and drag, and you get a choice of Move, Copy, or Create Shortcut at the destination. Figure 12.3 shows a file called "Dental Insurance" being copied onto a floppy disk.

If this all sounds terribly confusing, don't worry. You'll get used to it quickly, and in the meantime you can always open up a DOS window if you're desperate.

What You Really Get

The new applications you'll be using, whether for word processing, spreadsheets, or whatever, will all show their documents on screen pretty much as they'll appear when printed out. This is one big advantage that comes with using GUIs. In addition, Windows 98 incorporates OLE2. With recent versions of most major programs being OLE-compatible, the distinction between a spreadsheet and word processor becomes even less important. In Windows 98, you'll be focusing on the document, not what application created it.

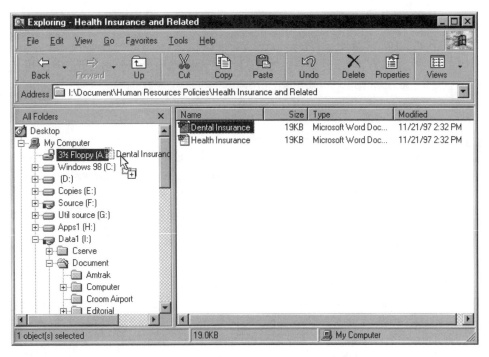

FIGURE 12.3: Copy an object by clicking it and dragging it to the destination.

For Windows 3.1 Users

One of the biggest differences between Windows 98 and DOS or even other GUIs is that Windows 98 is document-centric, not program-centric. At first, you may not think it's a big deal, but once you understand this difference, you'll find Windows 98 makes a lot of sense.

For example, how do you copy a section of text in your favorite word processor? You highlight or select it in some way, copy it to a clipboard, and later paste it where you want the copy to appear. Well, if you think of files and even whole drives or directories as simply documents, then you begin to get a handle on how Windows 98 deals with them. Want to move them? Cut them onto the clipboard and paste them back in exactly where you want them.

Or Doing It DOS

This graphical stuff is all well and good, but what about those tried and true DOS applications you've used and loved over the years? Windows 98 is much better at running these applications than any previous version of Windows, even letting you run many of them in a window on the desktop without having to go to a full screen.

NOTE   Communications programs actually do better in Windows 98 than in earlier versions of Windows because communications drivers are now substantially better than the stock versions that were part of Windows 3.1. Full support for 16550 UARTs (high-speed, buffered communications chips) is also built into Windows 98.

More (and Better) Memory

Another major plus for your DOS programs running in Windows 98 is the increase in available memory they'll see. Because Windows 98 will load most drivers into 32-bit flat memory, you can easily expect to see more than 550K, or even 600K, of free DOS memory available to your DOS programs, even when running in a window. (This is 550-600K for each program!) Open four DOS windows and you can have four DOS programs running—each with as much as 600K of memory available and each in blissful ignorance of the other programs' existence.

NOTE   A DOS program can even be kept ignorant of the existence of Windows 98, though this is rarely necessary. Right-click the .exe file in Windows Explorer and select Properties ≻ Program ≻ Advanced. Put a check in the box labeled "Prevent MS-DOS-based programs from detecting Windows."

The memory management is much better than one could hope for in Windows 3.1. Things like network drivers are implemented as VxD's (virtual device drivers). They're fully available to your DOS applications, and you don't have to pay a memory hit for them.

Opening More Windows

If you've ever tried it, you know that getting a second DOS window to even open in Windows 3.1 is a fruitless task. And forget trying to get two DOS programs to run at the same time.

Windows 98 does an outstanding job of isolating one DOS session from another. You can have a DOS window open with a high-speed communication program running at the same time you have another DOS window open copying files from floppy to hard drive. While you will get an occasional and slight slowdown on the communications program, the overall result is faster—yes, faster than that same program running in regular Windows 3.1 without a second DOS window open.

One thing about running DOS programs in Windows hasn't changed, however. You still aren't going to want to run a graphical DOS application in a Windows 98 window. In some cases, depending on the application, you could do it, but the results are pretty slow and quirky at best. So your graphical DOS applications will still need a full screen.

Keeping Your Favorite Things

If you are upgrading from DOS only, or from Windows 3.1, being able to keep your old DOS programs can really ease the transition to Windows 98. For one thing, you won't be faced with the daunting expense of upgrading all your applications at once (not to mention the learning curve involved).

There's no better time to re-examine your software than when moving from DOS to Windows, anyway. You won't necessarily want to buy the same vendor's Windows 95 version of your favorite DOS spreadsheet or word processor. Take a long hard look at what your options are and decide what you want your new software to be able to do.

Are My Utilities Still Useful?

The short answer is an emphatic no. Because of the many and far-reaching changes to the file system and its structure, using any of your DOS or Windows 3.1 file, directory, or hard drive utilities is a really bad idea. Because they were written before long file names and other file system changes were implemented, they will be thoroughly confused by Windows 98 and could cause serious damage if you tried to run them.

That's the bad news. The good news is that all the major manufacturers of utilities have come out with Windows 95 versions, most of which will work just fine in Windows 98 as well. Windows 98 also comes with a number of built-in utilities. A third-party unerase program, for example, isn't really necessary, since items deleted in Windows 98 go to the Recycle Bin first. But if you want even more powerful protection, then you may want to look at packages like Norton Utilities, which add an extra layer of security to the Recycle Bin.

NOTE   **If you intend to use the FAT32 file system (described in Chapter 15), be sure any new disk utilities you buy are compatible with it.**

Are My Games DOOMed?

Some older games require almost total control of all your computer's resources, including the screen, mouse, keyboard, everything. Games like this would not run under Windows 3.1 or OS/2, or in fact under anything at all except bare DOS. However, you can relax, your old favorites will run just fine with Windows 98.

> **NOTE** **Remember that most games now on the market are written for Windows 95, and will probably run even better under Windows 98.**

Many older games, including Dark Forces, Simcity 2000, DOOM, Descent, Master of Magic, Warcraft, Transport Tycoon, and Hardball IV will run perfectly in a full screen DOS session. When your boss creeps in, just press Alt+Tab and you're back to your regular Windows 98 screen.

> **TIP** **A word to the wise: If you have a sound card, you'll probably want to make sure the sound is turned down. It can be hard convincing your coworkers that all those shrieks are coming from your spreadsheet program.**

While most games run just fine in a Windows 98 full screen DOS session, there are some that don't. If your favorite game is one of these, don't despair: there's still a solution. Windows 98 has the ability to remove itself almost entirely from the picture, leaving only a tiny little stub around—just enough to load Windows 98 back into memory when the game program finishes. This is called DOS mode, and the only catch is that when you run a program in this mode, you can't have anything else running. Not too surprising, given that Windows 98 no longer controls the hard disk, the keyboard, the mouse, or the display.

In DOS mode, you can even create special AUTOEXEC.BAT and CONFIG.SYS files to launch the program and control which resources the DOS mode program has access to, including the hard disk and the network.

> **NOTE** **To assign a program to DOS mode, see the "Advanced Settings" section later in this chapter.**

Setting Some DOS Options

When you run a DOS program, whether from the desktop or off the Start menu, you can set a wide variety of properties for the program. Just as for any other program in Windows 98, you can get to those properties in a number of ways:

- Right-click the program's executable file in Windows Explorer.
- Right-click a desktop shortcut to the program.
- If the program is already running, click the little MS-DOS icon in the upper left corner of the window.

In all cases, you'll select Properties from the menu that opens. This will open up a property sheet for the DOS program like the one shown in Figure 12.4.

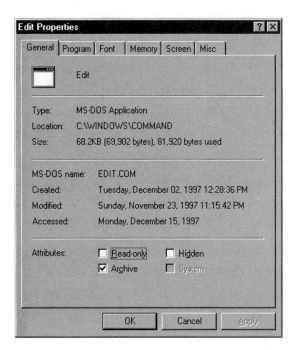

FIGURE 12.4:
Windows 98 lets you open a DOS program's property sheet.

The property sheet has six tabs—five if you got here by right-clicking in the upper left corner of a running program or DOS Window.

General shows information about the file and file attributes. You won't see this one if you examine the properties of a running program or DOS prompt.

Program sets command line options and sets the program's icon.

Font specifies the font to be used when the program is run in a window.

Memory sets how much and what kinds of memory are made available to the DOS program.

Screen changes whether the program runs full screen or in a window, and sets the characteristics of the window.

Misc sets stuff that doesn't fit in any other category.

The default settings are usually adequate for most programs, but if you need to fuss with one or more of these pages, the following sections contain some guidance.

General Properties

The General tab shows information about the program, and allows you to set the attributes of the underlying file. As you can see in Figure 12.4, this tab shows the type of program or file, its location and size, the DOS file name associated with it, and when the file was created, modified, and accessed last.

If you're looking at a shortcut, the information about the file size, location, and type will refer to the shortcut and not to the original object (the file itself). If you are looking at an open DOS Window or program, you won't see this tab.

NOTE   **Information about the dates a program was created or last accessed is stored by the long file name system used in Windows 95 and 98. The information will not be accurate for files created or last accessed before Windows 95 or 98 was installed.**

On this tab you can change the MS-DOS attributes of the program, including whether the archive bit is set, whether the file can be modified or not (read-only bit), and whether the file is a hidden or system file. Generally you won't want to change these bits except in very special circumstances, and then only if you're sure you know why you're making the change.

Program Properties

The Program tab of the property sheet (see Figure 12.5) lets you change the running parameters of the program as well as the name and the icon associated with it.

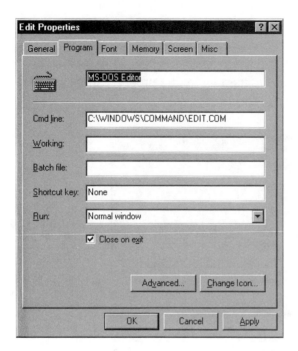

FIGURE 12.5:
The Program tab lets you control the command options of a DOS program.

Some Basic Settings

The Program tab will have the following items:

Cmd line This box shows the actual command line executed. Here you can add any command line parameters that you need. (If you want to be able to add parameters each time you run the program, add a question mark as the only command line option and Windows 98 will prompt you for parameters when you start the program.)

Working If your program has a favorite working directory, set that here.

Batch file If you want to run a batch file either before or as part of the program, place the name (and full path, if necessary) for that batch file in this box.

Shortcut key This tab lets you add a shortcut key. (DOS programs may not work well with this option.)

Run You can decide whether the program will run in a normal window, maximized, or minimized.

Close on exit You'll probably want to check this box, so the DOS window will close when the program exits.

Advanced Settings

Use the Advanced button only if you have an extremely ill-behaved or avaricious application—such as a game or other very specialized, hardware-dependent program. Click Advanced from the Program tab of the property sheet to open the Advanced Program Settings dialog box shown in Figure 12.6.

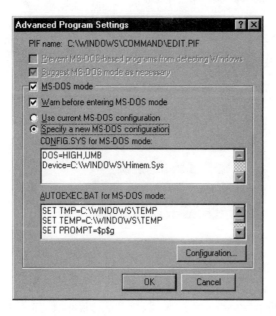

FIGURE 12.6: This program will not only run in DOS mode, it'll also have its own CONFIG.SYS. and AUTOEXEC.BAT to make sure it's happy.

You can use this setting to keep the program from knowing it's even running in Windows. If really drastic measures are required, you can set the program to run in MS-DOS mode. This closes all your applications, restarts your computer in DOS mode, and may reboot your computer.

NOTE **You don't need to guess whether your game needs DOS mode to run. Go ahead and run it. By default, the DOS property sheet is set up to suggest DOS mode when the program requires it. So, except in unusual situations, the system will let you know when a particular program needs DOS mode to run.**

In DOS mode you can only run a single program, and when you exit from it, the system re-starts Windows 98. Again, this may well mean a reboot, so don't be startled. If you need to set up a specialized configuration for the program, you can type in new CONFIG.SYS and AUTOEXEC.BAT files.

Running programs in DOS mode should be a last resort, primarily because you lose the multitasking advantages of Windows 98 and, since a reboot may be required, the whole process takes a substantial amount of time. Almost everything should run fine in a full-screen DOS session or a DOS window. Even old versions of DOOM and Flight Simulator run fine without DOS mode.

Change Icon

Click the Change Icon button on the Program tab to change the program's icon on the desktop. You can accept one of the icons offered or use the Browse button to look elsewhere.

Font Properties

The Font tab of the property sheet (see Figure 12.7) lets you set which fonts will be available when the program is running in a window on the desktop. You can select from either bitmapped fonts or TrueType fonts, or have both available.

FIGURE 12.7:
The Font tab of the property sheet lets you control what fonts are available for the DOS program when it's running in a window.

In general, bitmap fonts look better on high-resolution displays and are easier to read. The Window Preview shows how much of your screen will be occupied by the DOS window using the font size you have selected. If you want to be able to scale the window when it's open on your desktop, set Font Size to Auto, and the font will change as you resize the open window.

Memory Properties

The Memory tab of the property sheet (see Figure 12.8) lets you control how much and what kind of memory is available to DOS programs.

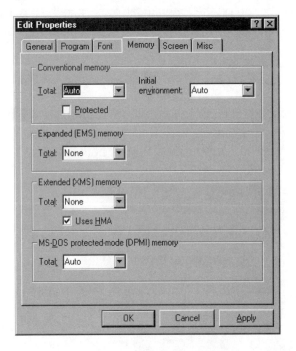

FIGURE 12.8: The Memory tab lets you fine-tune the memory accessible to your DOS programs.

On this tab you can make sure your program has a specific amount of conventional, expanded, and extended memory. You can also let Windows 98 automatically determine how much to make available. Generally, you'll want to leave the settings here on Auto, but if you know you have a program that requires a specific amount of expanded memory to run well, you can set that here.

If you have a program that has a habit of crashing occasionally, and you want to be sure it doesn't cause problems for the rest of the system, check the Protected box in the Conventional Memory section. This may slow down the program a little but will provide an additional layer of protection.

Some programs can have a problem with too much memory. Older versions of Paradox, for example, have difficulty coping with unlimited extended memory. If you leave the Expanded and Extended sections set to Auto, programs like this may get bogged down organizing memory they don't need. Try setting expanded and extended memory to some reasonable maximum number, such as 8192. This should be enough for most programs.

Screen Properties

The Screen tab of the property sheet (shown in Figure 12.9) lets you set parameters for your program's display. If you're running a graphical program, set it for full screen. Most text-based programs run better in a window. Unlike Windows 3.1, Windows 98 handles windowed DOS programs extremely well, and there is no real gain to running them full screen unless you need the extra visual real estate.

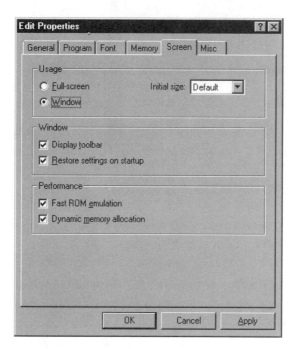

FIGURE 12.9:
The Screen tab lets you decide how your DOS programs are displayed.

WARNING The options on this page are best left alone unless you know why you're changing them. If you're sure you need to make a change, right-click an item and select What's This? If you understand what's in the box, you're hereby authorized to change it!

Miscellaneous Properties

The Misc tab of the property sheet (shown in Figure 12.10) lets you tweak several other characteristics of your DOS program that don't fit in any of the other categories.

FIGURE 12.10:
The Misc tab lets you set other characteristics of your DOS program's behavior.

The properties you can set here include the following:

Allow screen saver   When this box is checked, the Windows screen saver will come on even when the DOS program is in the foreground.

Quick Edit   This option allows you to use your mouse to select text for cut and copy operations. When this box is cleared, you must use the method specific to the program to mark text.

Exclusive mode   The mouse will be set to work exclusively with the program when this option is checked. This means that the mouse isn't available outside the program's window (when it's open).

Always suspend   When this box is checked, no system resources are allocated to this program while it's in the background (open, but not the active window). Don't check this box if this is a communications or other type of program that you want churning away in the background while you do something else.

Warn if still active   Some DOS programs are very fussy about being closed properly. When this box is checked, you'll get a warning message if you try to close the window without closing the program first.

Idle sensitivity   When this slider is set to high, the DOS program will release resources and processing time more quickly to other, foreground tasks. For communications programs, however, you will probably want to set this to the low side.

Fast pasting   Checking this option will allow a faster method of pasting, but if you have trouble with pasting correctly in this application, clear the box.

Windows shortcut keys   Clear these boxes if you want special keystrokes that would normally be reserved for Windows 98 passed on for use with your DOS program. Generally, though, you will want to leave these alone unless your DOS program absolutely needs to use one of these keystrokes.

Running Even Stubborn DOS Programs

If your favorite DOS application is having trouble running in Windows 98, there are a variety of ways to get it going. They are presented here in approximately the order you should try them, one at a time—from the relatively mild to the seriously serious. You should only try these if you have problems running a program after you have installed it.

NOTE   **The default settings in Windows 98 are excellent for the vast majority of DOS-based programs and should only be messed with if you're having problems.**

Run the program full screen.   You can do this by pressing Alt+Enter when the program is active, or from the program's property sheet. Select Full-screen from the Screen tab. This should be all that most graphical programs need, and with text-only programs, this step can usually be skipped.

Give the program only the kind of memory it absolutely needs.   From the Memory tab of the property sheet, select None for any memory types that you know the program doesn't need. Most DOS programs will not use Extended

(XMS) memory or DPMI memory, so those are good choices to try turning off first.

Give the program the exact amount of memory it needs.   If there's a minimum amount of memory that you know the program requires, set the conventional memory setting on the Memory tab of the property sheet to some figure slightly above that. This will ensure that the program will only attempt to run when there is sufficient memory available.

Protect the memory that the program uses.   From the Memory tab of the property sheet, check the Protected box in the Conventional Memory section.

Turn off dynamic memory allocation on the Screen tab.   If the program uses both text mode and graphics mode (an example would be Symantec's TimeLine), this will prevent Windows 98 from trying to change the amount of memory allocated when there's a mode change.

Turn off fast ROM emulation on the Screen tab.   This may make the program run a bit more slowly, especially in text mode, but if the program is having problems with writing text to the screen, this may help.

Turn off the Windows 98 screen saver.   Clear the checkbox on the Misc tab. Turn the idle sensitivity down to minimum by moving the slider on the Misc tab all the way to the left.

Prevent the program from recognizing Windows.   If your program refuses to run from within Windows, try lying to it. Click the Advanced button on the Program page, and check the Prevent MS-DOS-based programs from detecting Windows box. Only do this as a last resort before trying DOS mode.

Run the program in MS-DOS mode.   OK, everything else failed, so it's time to get serious. This is the last resort, for reasons we have already gone into. If nothing else works, this will. From the Advanced Program Settings dialog box of the Program tab of the program's property sheet, check the MS-DOS mode box. If the program needs special CONFIG.SYS and AUTOEXEC.BAT files, type them into the appropriate boxes, or use the current versions by checking the Use current MS-DOS configuration box.

WARNING   **This list of troubleshooting tips should help you get that recalcitrant DOS program to behave. But one word of warning: Never change more than one thing at a time! Try each suggestion then run the program. If it doesn't fix the problem, restore the setting and try the next suggestion.**

If you try something and it doesn't work, return it to the default setting and try the next item on the list. If you try to change too many things at once, you're likely to make the situation worse, and even if it does work, you won't be sure which setting was the important one.

What's Next

In this chapter we've seen that Windows 98 has a lot to offer the hard-core DOS user who has finally stopped resisting the move to Windows. With the vastly improved means of handling DOS programs in Windows 98, you can finally have the best of both worlds. You can keep your existing DOS programs, knowing they will work well in Windows 98, while taking advantage of the latest Windows programs.

In the next chapter we'll show you the programs that come with Windows 98. They can help you get an idea of how applications work in the GUI world.

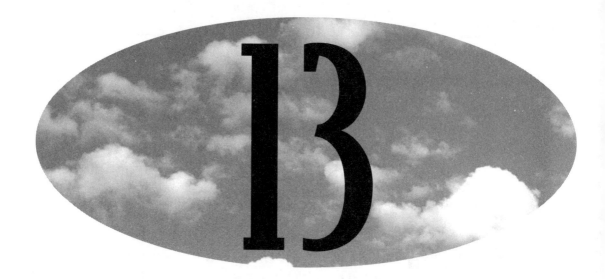

TOOLS, APPLETS, AND OTHER GOODIES

In this chapter we will briefly discuss some of the dozen or so mini-applications that come with Windows 98. We'll begin with the two designed for writing—or more likely, note-taking: WordPad and Notepad. Next come the image manipulation tools: Paint and Image. The Clipboard Viewer, Calculator, Character Map, and Phone Dialer applets round out the "serious" items. We'll finish the chapter with Windows 98's games.

Working with WordPad

WordPad is the successor to the Write program in Windows 3.1, and how you felt about Write may determine how you feel about WordPad. WordPad's an odd duck—it's more elaborate than Notepad but still falls way short of being a real word processing program. However, WordPad is fully enabled for Object Linking and Embedding, so we will use it as an example to explain OLE later in this section.

NOTE **WordPad will read Write and Word for Windows documents as well as text and Rich Text formats. Apart from the ability to read Word 97 documents, it's unchanged from the Windows 95 version.**

To open WordPad, click on the Start button and follow the cascading menus from Programs to Accessories. At the bottom of the Accessories menu you'll find WordPad.

Opening It Up

When you open WordPad (see Figure 13.1), it looks like most other editors, and on the menus you'll find the usual things one associates with text editors. Pull down the menus to see the various options.

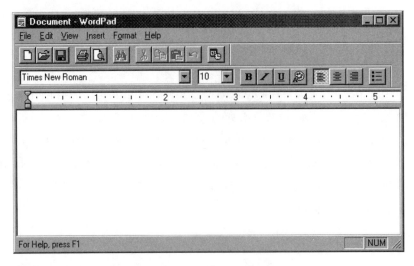

FIGURE 13.1: This is the opening screen for WordPad.

NOTE By modern standards, WordPad is a very basic word processor. It may be adequate if all you do is write short notes or letters. Though WordPad can open and create documents in Microsoft Word format, it ignores Word features that it does not support. For example, comments or footnotes in Word documents are invisible in WordPad because it lacks these features. Remember this if you use Word to create documents that others will view with WordPad.

Making and Formatting Documents

You can always click on a document and drag it into WordPad. WordPad can open documents created in Microsoft Word (.doc) or Windows Write (.wri, from Windows 3.1), as well as text (.txt) and Rich Text format (.rtf) documents. To create a document from scratch in WordPad, just open the program and start typing. WordPad can save your document in any of the formats it reads except .wri. Use File ➢ Save As to choose the format.

Formatting Tools

The toolbar (Figure 13.2) and format bar (Figure 13.3) are displayed by default. You can turn either of them off by deselecting it from the list under the View menu.

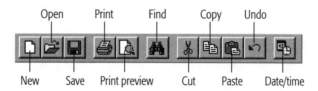

FIGURE 13.2: Here are the various functions on the WordPad toolbar.

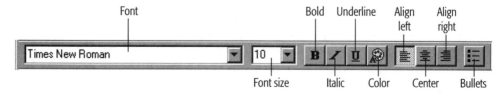

FIGURE 13.3: The WordPad format bar lets you manipulate text in all the basic ways.

Tabs are set using the ruler. Click the ruler at the spot where you want a tab. To remove a tab, just click on it and drag it off the ruler.

Other Options

Other formatting tools are under Options on the View menu. You can set measurement units here, as well as word wrap and toolbars for each of the different file types that WordPad recognizes.

Page Setup and Printing

The File menu has the usual Print command, but there's also a Page Setup item that you can use to set margins as well as paper size and orientation. Unlike its predecessor, WordPad can print envelopes as well as varying sizes of paper.

It may take some fooling around to get envelopes lined up correctly, but fortunately there's a Page Preview choice (also on the File menu). There you can see how the envelope or paper is lining up with your text. Adjust the margin in the Page Setup dialog box until you get it the way you want.

TIP   **To change printers, select Page Setup from the File menu. Click on the Printer button and you can select any printer currently available to you.**

Linking Documents

WordPad supports Object Linking and Embedding (OLE) so you can easily copy information from other documents as well as link or embed information.

Linking Information

Making a linked connection is easily done. Just follow these steps:

1. In the original document, highlight the information you want to link, and then select Copy from the Edit menu.
2. Go to the document where you want to place the information and click the spot where you want it to appear.
3. On the Edit menu, select Paste Special.
4. Select Paste Link, then click OK. The result should look like Figure 13.4.

For Windows 3.1 Users

Linking and Embedding—Simplified (We Promise!)

Object Linking and Embedding (OLE) is a technology that's been worked on for a while now. Early versions were part of some Windows 3.1 applications. Many programs now support it, and it generally works pretty well. WordPad, no matter how humble its appearance, is a full 32-bit application with support for OLE.

An embedded object (text, chart, graphic, or whatever) is a transplant from another application. Changes made to the transplant don't affect the original. If you double-click on the transplant, however, the toolbars and menus from the program that created the object will appear so you can make changes.

When an object is linked, your transplanted information is updated automatically if the information in the original document changes. If the original document is on your computer, this change to linked information works both ways: you change the transplanted object, and the linked information will change back in the original as well.

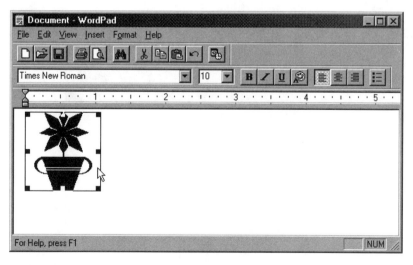

FIGURE 13.4: Click on a linked or embedded object and a frame will appear. Double-click to edit the object in place.

> **NOTE** If the program where the information was created doesn't support Linking for the selected information, the Paste Link choice will be dimmed in the Paste Special dialog. Programs that do not support OLE do not have a Paste Special choice on the Edit menu.

Embedding Information

Embedding information in WordPad (or any other application that supports embedding) is easy. Just follow these steps:

1. Select the information you want to embed by highlighting it, and then select Copy from the Edit menu.
2. Go to the document where you want the information to appear and click the location for it.
3. On the Edit menu, select Paste Special.
4. In the Paste Special dialog box, select Paste and choose the format you want to use. Then click OK.

If you want to check whether an imported object is linked or embedded, right-click on the object. As shown in Figure 13.5, the bottom of the pop-up menu will say "Linked ... Object" if it's linked. You can also use the pop-up menu to check detailed properties of the object, or to open or edit the object.

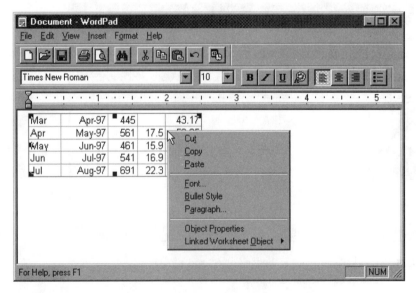

FIGURE 13.5: The pop-up menu indicates whether the object is linked.

> **TIP**   **Editing an embedded object affects only the embedded copy of the object. Editing a linked object changes the original and all linked copies, regardless of which linked copy you edit.**

Confidence and Security with OLE

When you include an embedded or linked object in a document, you want to be sure recipients of the document will have access to the information you want them to have, and to that information only. With embedded objects, there are two concerns:

- Be sure the embedded object includes only what you intend. When the document shown in Figure 13.5 was opened on another computer, the recipient could see the *entire* embedded spreadsheet—not just the portion that was deliberately pasted in.
- To edit the embedded object, the recipient needs to have the program that created the object.

When you send someone else a document containing a linked object, things are a bit more complex:

- Without access to the original linked file, the recipient will see only what you pasted in. If the recipient does have access to the original, say because it's on a shared network, he or she can do the same things with the link that you (the creator) could do, subject to the limitations imposed by his or her level of network privileges.
- As with embedded objects, opening or editing a linked object requires having the program that created the object.

Using Notepad

Notepad is a simple text editor with very few charms except speed. Double-click on any text file and it will immediately load into Notepad (unless it's bigger than 64K—in which case you'll be asked if you want to load it into WordPad instead).

What It's Got

Notepad has the bare minimum of facilities on its menus. You can:

- Search for characters or words.
- Use Page Setup to set margins, paper orientation, customize the header and footer, and select a printer.

- Copy, cut, and paste text.
- Insert the time and date into a document.

New for Windows 98

You may find Notepad easier on your eyes with the new ability to use a font other than Fixedsys on the screen. Go to Edit ➤ Set Font and choose any font installed on your system. Printing will still use your printer's default font.

Creating an Activity Log

Notepad retains the handy feature of being able to keep an activity log. Follow these steps to set one up:

1. Open Notepad. On the first line of the document, enter: **.LOG**—making sure you include a period before LOG and that all the letters are capitals.

2. Save the document under any name you choose.

Now, whenever you open this document, the time and date from your computer's clock will automatically be added (see Figure 13.6). To separate your entries with blank lines, be sure to hit Enter after you finish typing your information.

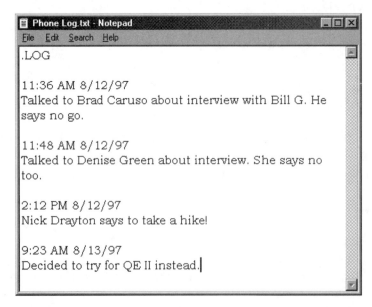

FIGURE 13.6: If you need to keep an activity log, Notepad makes it easy.

NOTE   For some unfathomable reason, word wrap is not on by default in Notepad. You have to select it from the Edit menu. Otherwise, your text stays on one line forever and ever, until you hit Enter.

The Paint Program

The Windows 98 version of Microsoft Paint is pretty much unchanged from the Windows 95 version, except for a slight rearrangement of some of the menus. As a drawing and painting program, Paint has its limitations. To find it, look under the Accessories menu. If you don't see it, use the Add/Remove Programs function in the Control Panel. (It's under Accessories on the Windows Setup page.)

When you open Paint (as shown in Figure 13.7), it'll look familiar.

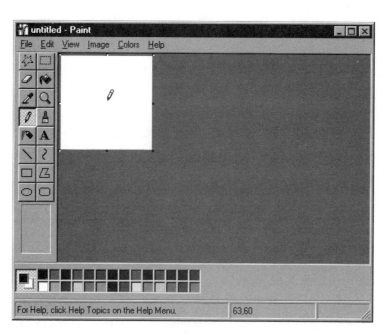

FIGURE 13.7:   This is the Paint program's opening screen.

TIP   For a really good painting program at a very reasonable price, check out the excellent shareware program Paint Shop Pro. It's available for download on the Internet and major online services.

For Windows 3.1 Users

If you use the Paintbrush program included with Windows 3.1, you'll find significant improvements in the Windows 98 version. Among the many new capabilities:

Zooming   Much better zooming capability—from 100 percent up to 800 percent.

Opaque drawing   With opaque drawing your additions cover the existing picture.

Transparent drawing   Transparent drawing lets the existing object show through your additions.

Manipulation options   The new Paint has more choices for stretching, skewing, flipping, and rotating objects.

Imaging

Imaging is a new addition to the Windows 98 package. You can find it under Programs ➢ Accessories on the Start menu. It's provided by Kodak and offers a very different set of functions from those found in Paint. One is its ability to open a wider variety of bitmapped image files, including fax files. Another is that Imaging can acquire images from a scanner. Figure 13.8 shows Imaging with a .bmp file open.

By way of a quick visual summary of Imaging's capabilities, the tools on its Scanning, Imaging, and Annotation toolbars are labeled in Figure 13.9. Together, they cover virtually all the image manipulation functions of the program.

Imaging's default file format is TIFF (.tif). The format allows for compression and for the creation of multi-page files. When combined with Imaging's ability to annotate TIFF files, the program seems ideally suited to creating electronic "albums" of photos or other scanned images. Annotations are saved on an overlay, so they can be hidden or removed. Annotations can also be made permanent, to ensure they will be visible in other programs that may not read the overlay.

Strangely, Imaging offers the ability to save images using an Internet standard color palette, but can't save files in the GIF and JPEG formats that are common on the Internet. (You can open those formats though.) The only formats available for saving a file are TIFF, fax format (.awd), and Windows bitmap (.bmp).

FIGURE 13.8: The newly added Imaging program

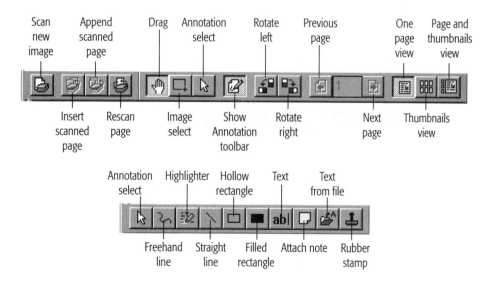

FIGURE 13.9: A quick summary of what you can do with Imaging

In the Tools ➤ General Options dialog box, you can set whether files registered to Imaging are opened in the full program or in Imaging Preview. Preview opens the file more quickly, but is only a viewer. It doesn't allow editing. By default, files with extensions .tif, .dcx, .awd, .pcx, wif, and .xif are registered to Imaging, and they open in Preview.

Clipboard Viewer

The Clipboard Viewer is not much different than the one shipped with Windows 3.1. When you copy or cut something, Windows needs to have a place to store it until you decide what to do with it. This storage place is called the clipboard.

Sometimes it's nice to see what's on the clipboard and to be able to save its contents, especially since it can hold only one thing at a time. Here's what the Clipboard Viewer can do for you.

Taking a Look

Let's take a look at the viewer. Here's how:

1. Click on the Start button in the Taskbar at the bottom of your Windows 98 desktop.
2. Slide your mouse through the sequence Programs ➤ Accessories ➤ System Tools.
3. Slide to Clipboard Viewer and click, and you should see the window shown in Figure 13.10.

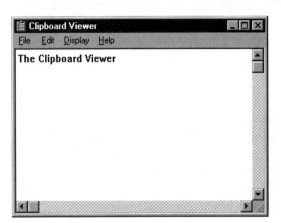

FIGURE 13.10:
The Clipboard Viewer looks like this.

NOTE Immediately before snapping the screen shot of the Clipboard Viewer, we selected and copied the text you see in the figure. If we had copied the screen by pressing PrintScreen (which captures the entire screen to the clipboard) or Alt+PrintScreen (which captures the active window to the clipboard), there would be an image of the Windows 98 screen in the figure. The Clipboard Viewer is dynamic: You can leave it open, and it will change automatically when the contents of the clipboard change.

Saving the Clipboard's Contents

If you want to save the current contents of the clipboard, pull down the File menu and select Save. You can save files under a proprietary format identified by the CLP extension. These files are (as far as we have been able to tell) only used by the Windows Clipboard Viewer.

Once you've saved the contents, you can use the clipboard to copy and paste other material, and later, you can reload what you saved by pulling down the File menu and selecting Open.

TIP Pull down the Display menu and you'll be able to see all your options for viewing the data on the clipboard.

The Calculator

You actually have two calculators in Windows 98—a standard calculator, the likes of which you could buy for $4.95 at any drugstore counter, and a scientific calculator.

Just the Basics

You can start the standard calculator by clicking the Start button and following through the menu sequence Programs ➢ Accessories ➢ Calculator. It's shown in Figure 13.11, and is unchanged from Windows 95 except for better labeling of some keys.

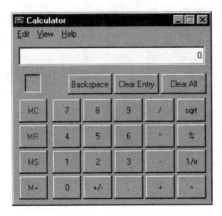

FIGURE 13.11:
The standard calculator is pretty basic.

Click on the numbers and functions just as if you were pressing the keys on a hand-held calculator.

TIP   You can also use the calculators with your numeric keypad. Just press the NumLock key to link them.

Or One Step Beyond

To open the scientific calculator, pull down the View menu and select Scientific. That displays the item in Figure 13.12.

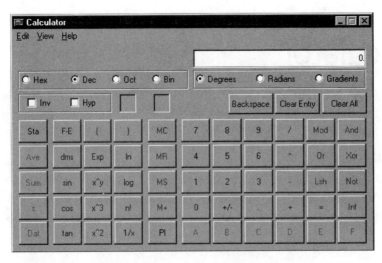

FIGURE 13.12:   The scientific calculator is a whole different animal.

The scientific calculator includes a variety of functions which we will not attempt to explain. If it's unfathomable, or just more fancy than you need, you can always pull down the View menu and select Standard, which will take you back to the standard calculator.

TIP

If you're unsure of the use for a function, right-click on its button. You'll see a rectangle containing the words "What's This?" Click on the text to see a short explanation of the function.

Getting Statistical

To enter a list of data for deriving statistical results:

1. Enter the first value in the series.
2. Click on the Sta button.
3. Click on the Dat button.
4. Enter the second value in the series.
5. Click Dat.
6. Repeat steps 4 and 5 until you have entered the last value in the series.
7. Click Sta.
8. Click on the function key that corresponds to the statistical command you want to enter, such as Ave, to find the Average.

Pasting in the Numbers

The calculators can be used in conjunction with the clipboard. Select a number in any application by dragging through it. Press Ctrl+C, the Windows shortcut for Copy. Press Alt+Tab until the calculator is selected (or click on it in the Taskbar) and press Ctrl+V (the shortcut for Paste). The number will appear in the number display of the calculator as if you had entered it from the calculator keypad.

Work your magic: adding, subtracting, multiplying, or deriving the inverse sine. Press Ctrl+C again, or pull down the Edit menu and select Copy, which places the contents of the display on the clipboard—ready for you to paste into your document.

Translating Number Systems

Probably most of us who do some programming will use the scientific calculator to translate numbers from one number system to another. This is easily done. Click on the number system (*Hex*adecimal, *Dec*imal, *Oct*al, or *Bin*ary) the number is currently in. Enter the number exactly as it appears (for hex numbers, use the A, B, C, D, E, and F keys to enter the numbers from 10 to 15 decimal), and then click on the number system into which you want to translate the value.

TIP   To make a shortcut to any of the applets (so you can, for example, have the calculator permanently available on the desktop), click the Start button and move through the menus till you find the program you want. Right-click on it and drag it to another location—selecting Create Shortcut Here when you arrive.

Character Map

There's a lot more to a font than numbers and letters. You have access to all kinds of symbols and accented letters that don't appear on the keyboard. How do you enter these characters? With the Character Map—another little applet you can't live without.

Starting It Up

Like the Clipboard Viewer, Character Map has been hidden one step further down on the Start menu structure from where it was in Windows 95. Open it with the sequence Start ➤ Programs ➤ Accessories ➤ System Tools ➤ Character Map. It will look like Figure 13.13.

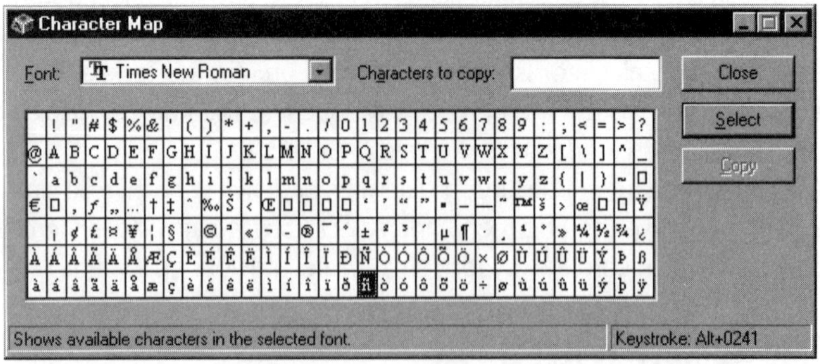

FIGURE 13.13:   The Character Map tells all.

Entering Characters

Select the font you want to use by clicking on the downward-pointing arrow at the right end of the Font list box. To enter a character (or string of characters), double-click on them in the window. They will appear in the text box at the top right of the window. When you have all the characters you want in the text box, click Copy. Then return to your application using the Taskbar or by pressing Alt+Tab until your application is selected.

NOTE As characters are selected in the Character Map, the key combination necessary to make the character appear on the screen is displayed in the lower-right corner of the window. This can be particularly useful for placing Wingdings and Webdings in your document since it's very hard to figure out which key gives you which symbol. For a better view of the symbols, drag your mouse over the Character Map with the left button pressed. The current symbol will be enlarged.

Phone Dialer

Have you ever had to make dozens of telephone calls in a single morning? Has your dialing finger ever felt as if it were going to fall off? If you have Windows 98 (and if you don't, what the heck are you doing reading this?), you can turn over the grief of dialing to its capable, if virtual, hands.

NOTE Essentially, Windows uses your installed modem to dial your telephone. In order for this scheme to work, your telephone and modem must be connected to the same phone line. Take a moment to make sure you have everything properly attached.

Find Phone Dialer on the Start menu under Programs ➤ Accessories ➤ Communications. It will open looking like Figure 13.14.

FIGURE 13.14:
The Phone Dialer window can help you put an end to the heartbreak of "Digititis."

The Phone Dialer gives you three simple ways to make phone calls using your computer.

Simple Dialing Enter the number in the Number To Dial box. You can type the number, click it out using your mouse on the keypad, or paste it from another application. After entering the number, click Dial.

Speed Dialing If you have a number you need in an emergency or one you call constantly, you can enter it in the Speed dial list.

The Telephone List Numbers entered in the Number To Dial box are added to the telephone list when you click Dial. Use numbers from the list by clicking on the downward-pointing arrow at the right end of the Number To Dial box, and selecting the number you want. Then click Dial.

Whatever method you use, a Dialing dialog box appears as the number is dialed. You should pick up your phone and click Hang Up in the dialog as soon as dialing is complete.

Speed Dialing

To set up your speed dial numbers, pull down the Edit menu and select Speed Dial. You will see the dialog box shown in Figure 13.15.

Here's how to set it up:

1. Click on the speed dial button you want to assign.
2. In the Name text box, type the name of the person or place that you will dial with that button.

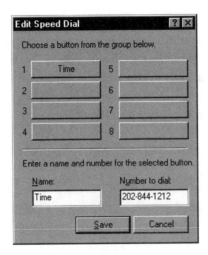

FIGURE 13.15:
The Edit Speed Dial dialog box puts you on the telephone fast track.

3. Type the number to dial in the Number To Dial text box.

4. Click on Save. (You'll be returned to the Phone Dialer dialog box and the name you entered in the Edit Speed Dial dialog box will appear on the speed dial button you selected.)

5. To speed dial the number, just click the button and lift your telephone receiver.

A word to the wise: If you have a spouse or significant other who is likely to see the list, make sure that person is assigned to speed dial button number 1.

TIP You can add a single number to Speed Dial by clicking any blank speed dial button. To change a button that's already assigned, return to the Edit ➢ Speed Dial dialog.

Games

Unenlightened bosses notwithstanding, games are not a waste of time. They allow you to escape for a few minutes from the linear thinking that leads to disaster (you can tell just by looking at them that the Edsel, the Hindenberg, and the Tower of Pisa were designed by workaholics). Stuck for an idea? Play a quick game (or maybe two), and odds are you will return to your work with a solution in mind.

TIP Games are also excellent training devices for someone intimidated by computers, Windows, or the mouse. A few minutes with Solitaire will clue any user in to the basics—starting programs, using menus, dragging, clicking, and double-clicking. All the games in Windows 98 are identical to the Windows 95 versions.

Solitaire

Solitaire hasn't changed a bit from Windows 3.1. It's as fun as ever. If you aren't familiar with it, we'll walk through starting it up and discuss how to play it.

NOTE Games are not automatically installed with Windows 98. To install them, start up Add/Remove Programs in the Control Panel, click on the Windows Setup tab, double-click on Accessories in the Components list, and then locate Games in the Accessories list.

Your Basic Game

To start up Solitaire and get your first deal, click the Start button and choose Programs ≻ Accessories ≻ Games ≻ Solitaire. This will open the window shown in Figure 13.16.

This is the standard Solitaire layout that most of us learned as kids. A lot of people have disparaged the notion of playing Solitaire on an expensive computer, and we have to admit that it is a little silly on the surface. But you know that every shuffle is truly random, you don't have to hide an entire layout of cards when the boss walks in (just click the Minimize button to hide Solitaire instantly), and it gives you something to do during those long downloads and database sorts.

The basic game is that you try to pile all of the cards on the four empty rectangles at the upper right, from the ace on the bottom to the king on the top, sorted by suit. To accomplish this:

- Pile cards in descending order (king on the bottom, deuce on the top) in alternating colors on the seven piles at the middle of the screen.
- Move a card by placing the mouse pointer on the card you want to move (if you want to move a pile, place it on the mostly hidden card at the bottom of the pile you want to move). Press the mouse button and drag the card to the new location. When you release the mouse button, the cards will be put in place. If your move is illegal, the cards will snap back to their original position.

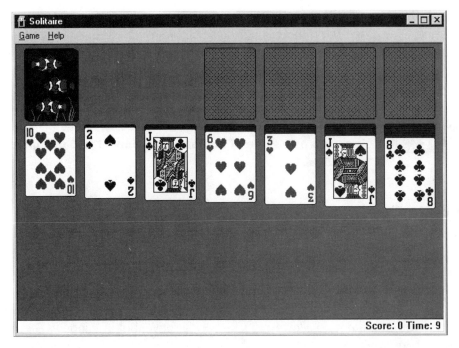

FIGURE 13.16: Here's your basic Solitaire window.

- Each time you clear a pile (so there are no cards face-up on the pile), you can turn over the top card by clicking on it.
- Each time you eliminate a pile (so there are no more cards face-up or face-down in the pile), you can drag a king, or a pile with a king at the bottom, to that position.
- To move a card to the piles at the top right, double-click on it.
- When you're through organizing the face-up cards in the window, click on the pile of cards at the upper left of the window and you will be given additional cards to play.
- When this pile is depleted, click on the rectangle where it was and the pile will return, face-down.

Options

If you want, you can change the design on the card backs by pulling down the Game menu and selecting Deck. In the dialog box, click on the deck you like. Some of the decks are animated, which adds a little extra fun to the game. The deck that looks like a sun shining down on a palm tree is particularly interesting. Periodically, the sun turns into a smiling face in sunglasses, which sticks its tongue out at you.

You also have several play options. Pull down the Game menu and select Options to select Draw One (which makes traditional Solitaire much easier to win), Vegas play (where you only go once through the deck and your score is based on how many cards you can get into the piles at the upper right), and some alternate screen, timing, and scoring options.

NOTE **To start a new game of Solitaire, pull down the Game menu and select Deal.**

How to Cheat

Windows 98 Solitaire allows you to cheat in two small ways:

- You're not supposed to remove a card from the piles at the upper right of the screen, but Windows 98 Solitaire allows you to drag these cards onto the seven piles at the middle of the screen.
- You have an Undo command on the Game menu. In a real game of Solitaire, you would not be allowed to take back a move, but in Windows 98 Solitaire, you can.

Of course, as in real Solitaire, you are basically on the honor system—no one is watching. If you cheat, unlike in the real world, no one will know except you.

FreeCell

This is the Windows 98 game that, in our opinion, has the greatest potential for destroying your productivity at work. If you're a prudent person, you'll remove it from your hard disk or never install it in the first place. It has a horrible way of turning perfectly rational people into FreeCell fiends.

The First One's Free

FreeCell looks deceptively like Solitaire, and even looks easier because all the cards are face-up, but it's much harder, and it requires great powers of logic to master. Start FreeCell by choosing it from the Start menu under Programs ➤ Accessories ➤ Games. Press F2 or choose Game ➤ New Game to begin.

Once again, the object of the game is to stack all the cards in ascending order from ace to king in the rectangles at the upper-right corner of the window, sorted by suit. To play:

- Move the cards from pile to pile and arrange them in descending order (king to two) in piles of alternating colors.

- Remove up to four cards from play by shifting them temporarily (or so you hope) into the four rectangles at the top left of the window.
- If you are moving stacks of cards from one pile to the next, however, you must move them through these four empty slots.

TIP   **Say you have a red five on top of one pile and the cards four through two on another. You want to move the stack of cards to the five. You click on the two (this is how you select either a single card or a stack of cards) and click on the five (this is how you move cards).**

- If there are at least two open slots at the upper left, FreeCell will automatically move the two and the three to them, move the four to the five, then return the three and the two to the four.
- If there is only one open slot, FreeCell will display a dialog box telling you how many cards can be moved (1) and how many cards you are asking it to move (2).

It's a simple game to play and a maddeningly difficult game to master—which is why it's so frustrating and so much fun. Figure 13.17 shows a game that has made a bit of progress but now seems to be stalled.

TIP   **If you make a stupid, bonehead move, pull down the Game menu and select Undo. This, of course, is cheating, and you should never, ever do that.**

A Few Alternatives

There are few options. You can pull down the Game menu and select New Game to let FreeCell pick a game at random (there are 32,000 games). If you have a favorite (the definition of a favorite is a game you've lost more than 23 times), choose Game ➢ Select Game. Simply type the number of your favorite game in the dialog box, click OK, and give it one more try.

Choose Game ➢ Options to change the settings for error messages, fast play, and double-clicking so you can move selected cards to free cells. If you are particularly masochistic, you can choose Game ➢ Statistics to see a record of your play.

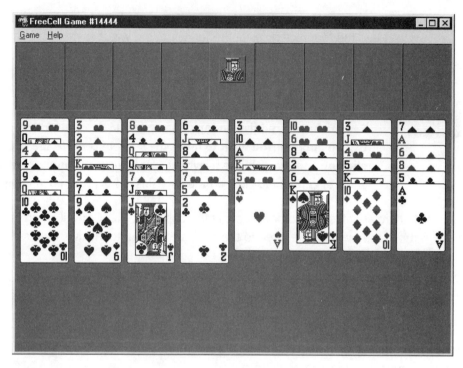

FIGURE 13.17: FreeCell leads you down the garden path.

WARNING   Don't play this game if your job is in any way important—if people depend on you to do specific things at specific times, to be specific places, to save lives, or whatever. (In other words, it's the perfect game for authors of computer books.)

Minesweeper

Minesweeper is a very, very simple and logical game that is identical to the version in Windows 3.1. After choosing it from the Start menu, you should see a game board like this one.

Mine Over Microsoft

To search for a mine, click on a block. One of three things will happen. You will either:

- Click on a mine and therefore die; or

- Click on a space so far from a mine that an entire clear area is uncovered; or
- Click on a space next to a mine, which will reveal a number indicating how many contiguous spaces contain mines.

That's it. Click away. The only strategy involved is when you have several squares uncovered and you have to figure out which of the other squares has a mine under it. One such square is indicated in Figure 13.18.

FIGURE 13.18:
The indicated square has a mine under it.

Some Nasty Twists and Turns

When you know for certain a square has a mine under it, right-click on that square to place a flag. The total number of mines is shown in the upper-left corner of the window at the beginning of play and counts down as you place flags. However, you don't get any warning if you place a flag in error—and the consequences can be devastating.

When you have correctly identified the location of all the mines, you've won the game. There's one other twist. A timer in the upper-right corner of the window challenges you to clear the field quickly. When you beat your previous time, your record performance is saved. You can try to beat that next time.

Other Levels of Play

Minesweeper has several levels of play. The minefields shown in here are beginner-level fields with 10 mines hidden under 100 squares. To select intermediate-level (40 mines under 256 squares) or expert-level (99 mines hidden under 480 squares), pull down the Game menu. You can also create custom fields of your own specification.

To see the best times, pull down the Game menu and select Best Times. It will display the record for each of the three levels.

NOTE   To start a new game after being blown to bits, click on the not-so-smiley face icon, press F2, or pull down the Game menu and select New.

Hearts

In Hearts the person with the lowest score wins. Game play is basically like Bridge with no trump: All 52 cards are dealt out in four hands of 13 each. For the first three games, you pass three cards to one of your opponents, first to the one on your left, then to the one on your right, then to the one across from you. The fourth game is played without passing.

Getting Started

The game is started when:

- The person who holds the two of clubs lays that card on the table.
- Each of the four players lays down a card in turn. Any card will take any lower card in the suit led.
- You must lay down a card of the suit led unless you are out of that suit, in which case, you can lay down any suit.
- You can't, however, lead with a heart until someone has played a heart because he or she has run out of cards in the suit led.
- You can't in any case play a heart or the queen of spades on the first trick, and any card of any suit other than the suit led is forfeited.
- Once you have played a heart ("broken hearts"), they can be played at will and laid down as forfeit cards.
- Each heart is worth a point, and the queen of spades is worth 13 points all by herself.

NOTE   Generally, you try to give away hearts and the queen of spades, but if one player manages to collect all of the hearts and the queen of spades (called "shooting the moon"), everyone else gets a penalty of 26 points.

- The person who wins a trick leads the next trick by laying down the first card.

Start Hearts on your computer by choosing it from the Start menu under Programs ➤ Accessories ➤ Games.

On the Network

Hearts is a network-aware game, so if you are on a network, you will have the option of initiating a game by clicking on "I want to be dealer" or joining a game by clicking on "I want to connect to another game." If you choose to connect to another game, you will then be asked for the dealer's name. Playing Hearts on the network gives you the dizzying ability to waste four times as much time as playing it against the computer.

Or All Alone

To play against the computer, click "I want to be dealer" and then press F2 to begin. The Hearts window will open and you will be asked for your name. Enter a name in the text box and click on OK to start the game. You will see the window shown in Figure 13.19.

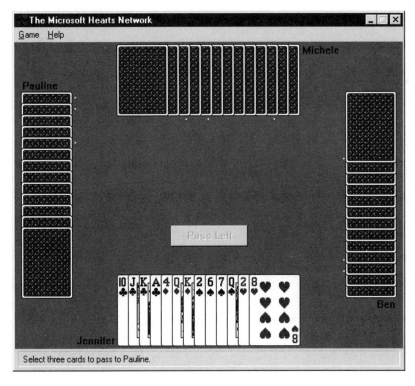

FIGURE 13.19: The Hearts window lets you play your computer.

At this point, you (Jennifer) should click on three cards that you want to send to your neighbor to the left (Pauline) and click on the button that says "Pass Left" in the middle of the window. When play begins, simply click on the card you want to play.

NOTE   **Use the Options command on the Game menu to change the speed of play and the names of your companions.**

What's Next

In the next chapter, we'll be discussing two more fun aspects of the Windows 98 environment: the CD player that is part of the operating system, and how to view and listen to multimedia files with the Media Player and the Sound Recorder.

THAT'S ENTERTAINMENT

Few people were more skeptical than we were when multimedia features began moving into computers. High-productivity people like writers, accountants, and computer consultants are not looking for more ways to get distracted but ways to remove distractions. Who needs moving pictures or music to get a book written?

Well, as usual, it was the wrong question. The fact is that publishing is different in the age of the computer, and so is accounting and data crunching. Books can be published online with animation, pictures, or music. Spreadsheets can include pictures of products or factories to make data more concrete. Databases can include pictures of clients and employees to make information seem more personal.

This chapter examines only a small part of multimedia—the CD Player, Multimedia Player, and Sound Recorder built into Windows 98. The first can be used for your private enjoyment or to accompany a presentation with a soundtrack. The second controls how movie files are played on your machine. The third can be used to display multimedia presentations, and the last allows you to create your own sound files.

CD Player

Let's begin our discussion of the CD Player by opening the Entertainment menu as follows:

1. Click on the Start button on the Taskbar.
2. Select Programs.
3. Select Accessories in the Program menu.
4. Select Entertainment in the Accessories menu to open the Entertainment menu.

Depending on the programs you selected when you installed Windows 98, you might have several applications on this menu.

NOTE **Depending on how you did your installation, there's an outside chance you might not have any multimedia applications installed. In that case, you won't have an Entertainment menu under Programs ➤ Accessories. On the Start menu, choose Settings ➤ Control Panel. Open Add/Remove Programs and go to the Windows Setup tab. Highlight Multimedia in the list box and click Details to select individual applications. Click OK twice, and the ones you selected will be installed.**

Starting It Up

To start the CD Player, click on it in the Entertainment menu. That will start the program. You will see the window shown in Figure 14.1.

All you have to do is supply a music CD. The player will play it through the speakers connected to your sound card or through the headphone jack on the front of your CD-ROM drive.

FIGURE 14.1:
The CD Player window works just like the real thing.

TIP

By default, the CD Player will start playing the minute you put a music CD in the drive. To overrule this automatic play feature for a particular CD, hold down the Shift key while you insert the CD. To turn the automatic play feature off completely (or back on), right-click on the My Computer icon and select Properties. On the Device Manager page, double-click on CD-ROM, highlight your CD-ROM drive's name, and click Properties. On the Settings page, click Auto Insert Notification. With a check in the box, music CDs will play automatically. Without the check, you need to open the CD Player applet yourself.

How It Works

Just for demonstration, we popped our favorite CD in the drive and clicked on the large triangle next to the digital read-out (the play button). The playing CD Player can be seen in Figure 14.2.

FIGURE 14.2:
Here's what the CD Player looks like while working.

Notice that several of the buttons that were gray and unavailable in Figure 14.1, when there was no CD in the drive, are now black and available in Figure 14.2. The controls are labeled just like a conventional CD player.

Play   At the top, the Play button is gray because the CD is playing. If you prefer keyboard control, it's Ctrl+P.

Pause   Click here to hold your playback while you answer the door or the phone. Ctrl+P while playing gives you Pause.

Stop   For when you're tired of listening or when the boss walks into your office. Ctrl+S to keep your hands on the keyboard.

Previous Track   The button at the left end of the second tier will move you first to the beginning of the current cut. A second click will take you back to the previous track on the CD.

Skip Back   The second button on the lower tier is Skip Back. Each time you click it, you will move back one second in the music.

Skip Forward   This will move you one second forward in the music.

Next Track   Second from the right on the lower tier is the Next Track button. It will take you instantly to the next cut.

Eject   The button at the right end of the second tier looks like an arrow pointing upward. It is the Eject button. It will cause your CD-ROM drive to stick its tongue out at you—which is what it looks like when your CD is ejected from most drives.

Setting Time and Play Options

Is that all there is? No way. If you're an information freak, click on the digital readout. The first time you click, the readout will tell you the current track number and the time remaining on the track. The second time you click, you will see the time remaining for the CD. The third time you click, you'll see the track number and the elapsed time for that track (shown in Figure 14.2).

If you want to set these without clicking on the digital display, pull down the View menu and select from:

- Track Time Elapsed
- Track Time Remaining
- Disc Time Remaining

The Options menu lets you opt for continuous play, random play, or intro play. Select the Preferences option. Here you can set whether CD play should stop when you close CD Player. There are a few other settings, including the font size for the digital readout and the length of intro play (10 seconds is the default).

Editing the Play List

As if all those things weren't cool enough, there's an entire layer of the CD Player we haven't even touched yet. Here's how to access it.

1. Pull down the Disc menu.
2. Select Edit Play List. You will see the dialog box shown in Figure 14.3.

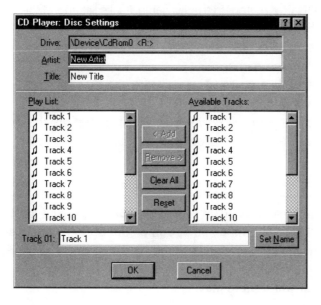

FIGURE 14.3:
The Disc Settings dialog box lets you program a play list.

Using this dialog box, you can do things that CD player owners often never get the hang of—programming your player to play specific songs in a specific order.

By Track Number

Let's set up the CD-ROM to play Tracks 5, 12, and 3. Here's how:

1. Click the Clear All button to clear all the entries on the Play List.
2. Double-click on Track 5 in the Available Tracks list box. It will appear in the Play List.
3. Double-click on Track 12, and then double-click on Track 3 in the Available Tracks list box.
4. When you click OK, CD Player will be ready to play the tracks you selected, in the order you chose.

This is so simple we can't wait to have this kind of control over our car CD player.

By Track Name

If you would rather deal with track names than track numbers, you can insert names for each of the tracks (or just the ones you care about) as follows:

1. Click on a track—for this example, we'll click on Track 3 in the Available Tracks list.
2. Click the text box next to the Set Name button.
3. Refer to your CD packaging to get the name of the third song on the CD.
4. Type the name in the text box. (You can type it next to Track 3, or delete the track and type the name instead.)
5. Click the Set Name button. In the Available Tracks list and in the Play List, Track 3 will be replaced with the name you entered.
6. Just for the sake of completeness, click on the text box marked Artist and type the performer's name.
7. Highlight the text box marked Title and enter the CD's title.
8. Click on the OK button.

Once you've supplied your CD Player with this information, the program will remember it, recognize the CD, and follow your programmed instructions every time you play it.

TIP   If you have a CD-ROM player capable of playing multiple disks, Multidisc Play will be an option on the Option menu. Select it, and when you click on the downward-pointing arrow at the right end of the Artist box, you will see each of the CDs available to you. Select the CD you want to play.

Media Player

These days the word "media" conjures up more talk show blather about how everything's the fault of the media. Not this media. The media in this section is fun—never trouble.

Let's begin by starting the program. Click the Start button and move your mouse through the menu sequence Programs ➤ Accessories ➤ Entertainment ➤ Media Player. Click when you get there. You should see something similar to the window shown in Figure 14.4.

FIGURE 14.4:
The Media Player
looks like this.

The Media Player will play ActiveMovie files, Video for Windows animated files (.avi), sound files (.wav), MIDI files (.mid and .rmi), or your audio CD. It opens an additional window to play movie and video files.

Playing Files

Windows 98 comes with a wide variety of multimedia files. The simplest way to play a file is just to open it—click or double-click, depending on your Windows 98 settings. For more control, follow these steps:

1. Pull down the Media Player Device menu and select the type of file you want to play.
2. Locate the file you want to play and double-click it, or highlight it and select Open.
3. Click on the right-pointing arrow (the Play button).

You can select sections of animation or movies just like you select recorded music tracks (see the CD Player section of this chapter). Although the buttons are in different places than the ones on the CD Player, you should be able to identify them by their icons.

Copying and Pasting Files

You can copy and paste sound, animation, or movie files using the Select buttons, which look like tiny arrows pointing down (Start Selection) and up (End Selection) above a horizontal bar.

Selecting a Section

To select a section of a musical piece:

1. Listen until you reach the point where the section begins.
2. Click the Start Selection button.
3. Continue listening until you hear the end of the section.
4. Click the End Selection button.
5. Pull down the Edit menu and select Copy. The music you have selected will be placed on the Clipboard for pasting into any document that supports sound files.

| **TIP** | You can also drag the slider along the time scale to begin play at any point you wish, or to start the selection at that point by clicking the Start Selection button. You can set the end of your selection the same way. |

Clearing a Selection

To clear the selection, pull down the Edit menu and select Selection. Click None in the Selection dialog box.

Getting Looped

If you want a piece of music, film, or animation to repeat continuously, pull down the Edit menu and select Options. Click on the option marked Auto Repeat. Your media file will play over and over until the end of time, you turn off the media player, or you lose your mind and destroy your computer with a fire ax, whichever comes first.

Sound Recorder

If you have an audio input device on your computer (either a microphone or a CD-ROM player), you can use the Sound Recorder to make a .wav file that you can associate with a Windows event or send in a message.

Making .Wav Files

Here's how to make a .wav file with the sound recorder:

1. Open Sound Recorder from the Entertainment menu under Accessories.
2. Select New from the File Menu.
3. To begin recording, click the button with the dark red dot.
4. Start the CD or start speaking into the microphone.
5. Click the button with the black square to stop recording.
6. Select Save from the File menu to save the sound clip.

Figure 14.5 shows the Sound Recorder recording from a CD being played in the Media Player.

The Sound Recorder also lets you play other types of sound clips in the Media Player and record them as .wav files. The .wav files you make can be played back with the Sound Recorder or the Media Player.

FIGURE 14.5:
You can record a
.wav file from a
CD-ROM with the
Sound Recorder.

Special Effects and Editing

Use the Effects menu to change some of the sound's qualities—to add an echo or decrease the speed. The sound can also be edited, using the menu controls.

ActiveMovie Control

The ActiveMovie Control is the default player for .avi and .mpg movie files, and runs when you open such a file. (The Windows 98 CD includes some of these as samples.) If you open ActiveMovie Control from the Start menu under Programs ➤ Accessories ➤ Entertainment, all you see is a dialog box to choose the file you want to open. When you click Open, the file appears in a window that looks like Figure 14.6.

Click the Run button at the lower left to start the movie. The same button serves for Pause. The Stop button beside it resets the movie to the beginning. You can also grab the slider with your mouse and drag it back and forth to see still frames from any part of the movie.

If you right-click the window and select Frames from the menu, the time counter changes to a frame counter. Now, when paused, you can use the ← and → keys to step through the movie one frame at a time.

On the ActiveMovie Control property sheet (right-click the window and choose Properties), you can set several options including Auto Repeat and the default size of the display window.

FIGURE 14.6:
The ActiveMovie
window is the
height of simplicity.

ActiveMovie Control supports quite a few different movie file formats. If you simply open a movie file (from a folder or Windows Explorer), the movie opens, plays through, and the window closes without any further action on your part. If you click one of the controls while the movie is playing, you gain full control over the movie, and it will not exit until you close the window.

Volume Control

The Volume Control panel not only lets you adjust the sound level but individually tune the stereo balance for different types of files. The easiest way to reach the Volume Control panel is to right-click on the small speaker icon at the end of the Taskbar and select Volume Controls. You can also open it from the Multimedia menu under Accessories (Figure 14.7).

For tone controls (bass and treble), select Advanced from the Options menu, then click the Advanced button that appears at the lower left. To adjust recording volume, select Properties from the Options Menu.

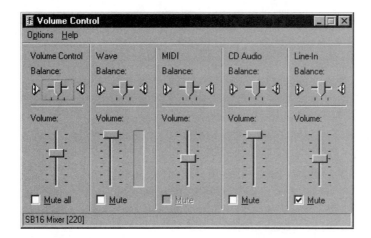

FIGURE 14.7:
The Volume Control panel lets you adjust your sound files.

What's Next

Chapter 15 is about system tools—all the things Windows 98 provides for keeping your system operating smoothly like Backup, Disk Defragmenter, ScanDisk, and System File Checker.

RUNNING YOUR SYSTEM SMOOTHLY

Windows 98 comes with several indispensable system maintenance tools, which we'll be discussing in this chapter. Unless you've bought a satisfactory Windows 98-compatible substitute, you should be using these tools at regular intervals. Windows 98 even has a Task Scheduler so you can automate most maintenance.

All the tools can be found by clicking on the Start button, then cascading through Program to Accessories to System Tools (see Figure 15.1).

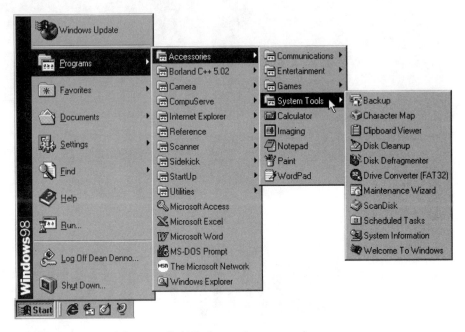

FIGURE 15.1:   Here's how you find Windows 98's system tools.

Backing Things Up

Backing up your computer or data files means making a copy that can be kept in a safe place and used to restore your computer or (at least) the important information you keep on your computer. It provides protection against everything from a hard drive failure to a fire in your office—if you keep the backup somewhere else. Windows 98 has a very good backup program.

Remember, there are only two kinds of computer users:

- Those whose hard drives have crashed
- Those whose hard drives haven't crashed—yet

No matter how sure you are of your hardware, it's a good idea to back up your files regularly. Listen: This is the voice of bitter experience speaking.

Getting Started

To start Microsoft Backup, glide through the Start menu as shown in Figure 15.1 and select Backup. The Backup window will open with the dialog box shown in Figure 15.2 on top of it. For your first use of Backup, choose Create a New Backup Job, and click OK.

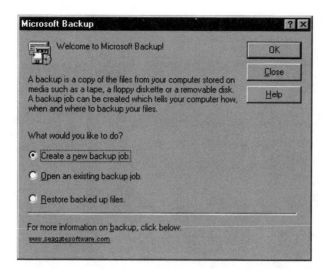

FIGURE 15.2:
The Welcome to Microsoft Backup dialog box gets you started.

NOTE The first time you run Backup you may see a message saying that the program did not find any backup devices. It asks if you want to run the Add New Hardware Wizard. Click Yes if you have specific backup hardware, such as a tape drive, that may not yet have been properly installed in Windows 98. Otherwise, click No and continue. Backup can use lots of devices that aren't specifically recognized as "backup devices."

Next you will see the Backup Wizard, shown in Figure 15.3. Here you choose whether to back up everything on your computer, or whether you want to designate particular drives, folders, or files to be backed up.

Full System Backups

If you choose "Back up My Computer," Backup will prepare to back up your entire system. This will require considerable capacity on your backup device. For example, your Windows 98 installation alone is likely to exceed 250 megabytes, without even considering your applications and data.

The most common devices that offer enough removable capacity for a full system backup are tape drives. Other likely candidates are Jaz or similar removable hard-disk type devices with at least several hundred megabytes capacity. Before you buy a device to use for backup, you should be sure it is supported by Microsoft Backup or by whatever other backup software you choose to use.

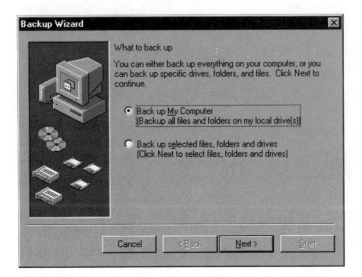

FIGURE 15.3:
Back up every-
thing, or just
some things?

When your hard disk suddenly sounds like it's full of little pebbles, there's nothing more comforting than having a Full System Backup on your shelf. If you have a tape drive or other suitable device, you should make a Full System Backup after you first install Windows 98, when you install new applications, and occasionally thereafter.

After you choose Back up My Computer and click Next, there are several more options to be selected. They are the same as if you choose to back up only selected drives or folders, so we will discuss them a bit further on. If you want to actually create a full system backup now, skip to step 7 in the section, "Backing Up a Single Folder."

Regular Backups

Regular backups involve less than your entire computer and will probably depend on how valuable certain of your files are, how difficult they would be to re-create, and how often they change. This is the type of backup you should create on a regular basis, even if you do not have a tape drive or other device suitable for making full system backups.

To begin your first regular backup, choose "Back up selected files, folders and drives" in the first dialog of the Backup Wizard (Figure 15.3).

Creating a Backup

Let's create a regular backup to see how it's done. Once you choose "Back up selected files, folders and drives" and click Next, you should see the window shown in Figure 15.4.

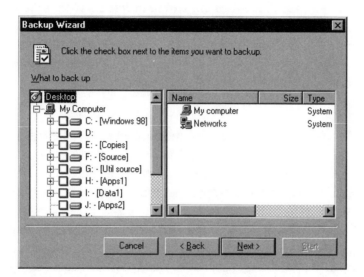

FIGURE 15.4:
The Backup window lets you choose what you want to back up.

By clicking on the objects in this dialog box, you will indicate to Backup which device, folders, or individual files you want to back up.

NOTE   Each of the drives shown in the Backup window has a tiny check box next to it. If you want to back up the entire drive—every file and directory from the root to the farthest branch—click on this box to automatically select everything.

Backing Up a Single Folder

For the sake of this example, let's back up one folder to save time. So far, you've spent a fair amount of time creating lots of shortcuts and several folders on your desktop. To avoid possibly losing your customizations, let's back up the \Windows\Desktop folder.

WARNING Even if you use the My Documents folder created by Windows 98 to store your word processing and spreadsheet files, don't make the mistake of assuming that all your valuable information is in that folder. For example, if you use Outlook Express for your e-mail and newsgroups, those files are stored in folders within the Program Files\Outlook Express folder. Your Windows Address Book may be stored in the Windows\Application Data\Microsoft folder. For backup purposes, you need to think about the location of files created by every application in which you enter data.

Here's how:

1. In the left pane of the dialog box, click the drive letter (not the check box) of the hard disk where the folder is located. In this example, it's drive C:. All of the top-level folders on that drive will appear in the right pane, along with any files located in the root folder of the drive. You may need to use the scroll bars to see everything.

2. Search through the list of folders in the right pane to find your Windows folder. If you wanted to back up every file and folder in Windows, you would click on the box to the left of the folder name. Here's how to select a single folder within Windows to back up.

3. Double-click on the Windows folder icon or name (not the check box). You'll see something like the window shown in Figure 15.5. Notice that the Windows folder, and the other top-level folders on the C: drive, are now listed in the left pane, and the contents of the Windows folder are listed on the right.

4. In the right pane, scroll through the contents of the Windows folder until you locate the folder called Desktop.

NOTE If the folders and files are not in alphabetical order, you can click on the Name block at the top of the list to list them alphabetically. Or you might want to click on another column header to sort the list another way.

5. When you locate the folder, click its check box.

6. To back up additional folders or drives, or individual files, repeat steps 1–5 until you have checked everything you want included in this backup.

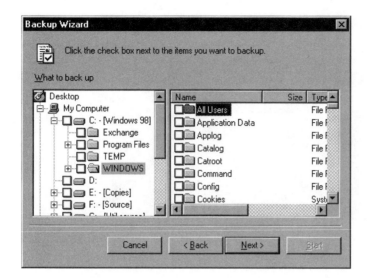

FIGURE 15.5:
Here's the list of
folders and files
in the Windows
folder.

7. Click the Next button at the bottom of the Backup Wizard dialog. Now you
    must tell the Wizard whether to back up all the files you have designated, or
    only those that are new or changed since your last backup. Because this is
    the first backup, choose All Selected Files.

TIP If you are backing up a large quantity of data, you can save time
and storage space by backing up only what has changed. But
remember: if you do this, you will need the full series of backups to
successfully restore your data.

---

8. Click Next again to bring up the dialog in Figure 15.6. Here you tell Backup
    where to create the backup file. Generally, this will by your tape drive (if you
    have one) or some other removable storage device such as a Zip drive or
    even your diskette drive.
9. Click the folder button to the right of the lower text box to open a standard
    browse window. Navigate to the device you want to use for backup, and enter
    a file name that will identify this backup for you. We called this one Desktop.
    You might use a more general name such as Weekly. Then click Open.
10. Click Next again to tell the Wizard whether you want your backup verified
    and whether it should be compressed. Accept the defaults of Yes for both
    options.

FIGURE 15.6:
Tell the Wizard
where to create
your backup.

11. Click Next for the last time and verify all the choices you've made. If necessary, click Back to change an option. Also, choose a job name under which this set of options will be saved for future use. Label the tape or disk with the same name, along with the date. See Figure 15.7.

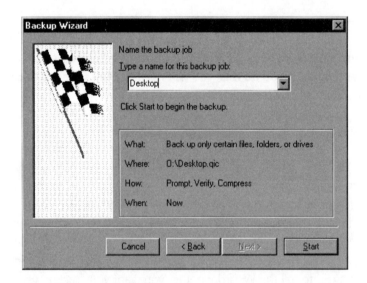

FIGURE 15.7:
The last step
of the Backup
Wizard.

12. Click Start and the backup will be created. As the backup proceeds, you will see the dialog box shown in Figure 15.8.
13. If you like, you can click the Report button to see a text file describing the details of the backup process just completed. The final step is to click OK.

> **NOTE**
>
> What is a backup job? Backup is based on the idea that you have a large hard disk with perhaps thousands of individual files in hundreds of folders. You don't often want to back up everything on the disk. Usually you will want to back up a select few folders—the folders containing your Corel drawings, your Photoshop paintings, your Ami Pro documents, your appointment book, customer database, and so on. Therefore, you need to tell Backup which folders need to be backed up every day or every week. The job tells Backup which directories to back up. In previous versions, backup jobs were called file sets.

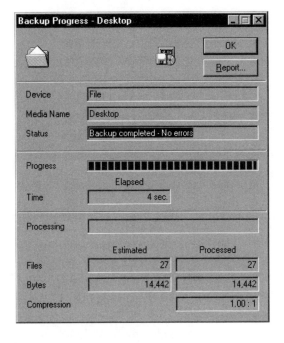

FIGURE 15.8:
This dialog box lets you know how it's going and when it's finished.

Backing Up an Existing Job

Let's do a backup of an existing job. Since you just created it, use the Desktop job. Here's what to do:

1. Begin by shutting down Backup. Click the X icon in the upper right corner of the Backup window.
2. Start Backup by following the instructions near the beginning of this chapter.

3. In the Welcome to Microsoft Backup dialog (Figure 15.2), choose "Open an existing backup job," then click OK.

4. In the Open Backup Job dialog box, double-click on the name Desktop (or whatever you used as the name of the job you just created). The backup job will open in the Backup main window, shown in Figure 15.9.

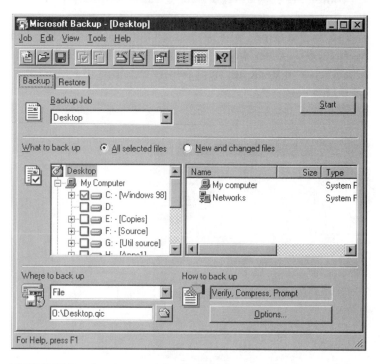

FIGURE 15.9: Running an existing Backup job

5. If you have put a new disk or tape in your backup device, you can just click Start and your backup will be created in the same place, under the same name, and according to the same rules as before.

6. If you want to create the backup on the same disk or tape as before, you have two choices: You can change the file name in the lower left corner of the Backup window, or, after clicking Start, you can choose to overwrite the old backup.

You can also modify the backup options before clicking Start. For example, with the same disk or tape in place, you might choose to back up only New and Changed Files and change the file name to Desktop1. The two backups taken together would then be up-to-date.

TIP   You might want to create several jobs for backups of different extent. Back up really important directories at the end of every work day (or at lunch) and less important ones at the end of major projects.

Choosing Backup Options

To use Backup's other options, click the Job Options button on the toolbar or the Options button in the lower right corner of the window. This will display a dialog box where you can set more details of how the current backup job should be carried out. Additional options include:

- Degree of compression to use
- Whether to automatically overwrite a backup of the same name on the same media (disk or tape)
- Password encryption
- Whether to use differential or incremental backup when you choose to back up New and Changed Files only
- File types you want to exclude from backups
- What details to include in backup reports
- Whether to back up the Windows registry (this makes sense only with a full system backup)

NOTE   A *differential* backup backs up all selected files that have changed since your last All Selected Files backup. To restore, you need the All Selected Files backup plus your most recent differential backup. An *incremental* backup backs up only selected files that have changed since the last backup of any kind. To restore, you need your last All Selected Files backup plus *all* backups made since then.

Any time you make changes to backup options, those changes relate only to the current Backup Job named in the box at the upper left of the Backup window. When you exit Backup, you will be asked whether you want your changes to be made a permanent part of that backup job.

Restoring Them Later

Restore is useful for more than recovering from disaster. It's a good way to move large files off your hard disk when they aren't immediately needed, and then restore them at a later date.

How to Do It

Let's use Restore to restore the Desktop folder you backed up earlier.

1. Start Backup.
2. In the Welcome to Microsoft Backup dialog, choose "Restore backed up files" and click OK.
3. The Restore Wizard will start with a dialog like Figure 15.6, asking you to choose the device (drive) that contains the backup files you want to restore. Click the folder icon to open a browse window and select the drive. The browse window will list the backup files on that drive.
4. Select the backup file from which you want to restore, and click Open.
5. Click Next. The Select Backup Sets dialog will list the backup job(s) contained in the file you selected. Be sure check marks appear only beside the job(s) you want to restore, and click OK.

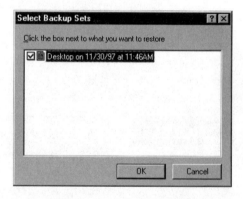

6. The next dialog of the Restore Wizard is similar to Figure 15.4, but lists only folders and files included in the backup job you selected to restore.
7. Navigate through the folder structure as necessary and put a check beside the folders or specific files you want restored. Checking the top-level box (for drive C: in Figure 15.10) will restore all backed-up files in the backup job you selected. Click Next.
8. Now you choose where to restore the files. Generally this would be Original Location. Choose Alternate Location if you are using Backup and Restore to move files from one machine to another, or if you want to compare the backed-up versions to current versions of the same files. If you choose Alternate Location, a folder icon will appear. Click it to browse for the location where you want the files restored. Click Next.

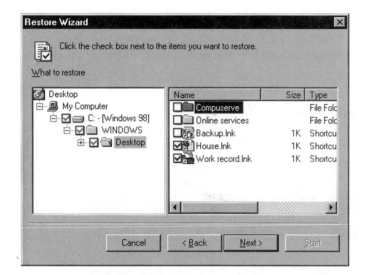

FIGURE 15.10:
Restoring just some of the files that were backed up in the chosen job

9. Consider carefully which option to choose in the next dialog, shown in Figure 15.11. It tells Restore what to do if it finds files of the same name in the same place as those you are restoring. The recommended option is to leave the files on your computer undisturbed. The second option is to keep whichever version of the file is more recent. If the files on your computer are corrupted, you would want to choose the last option, to restore from the backup regardless of file dates. When you are ready, click Start.

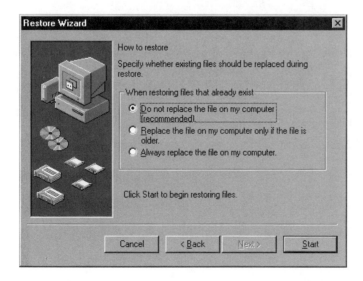

FIGURE 15.11:
Think carefully about what you want done if Restore encounters files of the same name.

10. Finally, Restore will name the backup file required to complete your restore. Be sure the tape or disk containing that file is in the appropriate drive and click OK. The files will be restored as you have specified. When the operation is complete, you can examine a report if you wish.

Options for Restoring

Once the Restore wizard has finished its work, you will see the Restore page of the main Backup window, as shown in Figure 15.12.

FIGURE 15.12: The basic approach to Restore

If you click the Job Options button on the toolbar or the Options button at the lower left of Backup's Restore page, the Restore Options dialog will open. There are only two options we haven't already discussed:

- What details to include in Restore reports
- Whether to restore the Windows registry

You can run the Backup or Restore Wizards any time by choosing them from the Tools menu. Once you are comfortable with using Backup, you can bypass the Wizards, if you wish. Just click Close in the Welcome dialog when you start Backup. If you don't want to see the Welcome dialog any more, choose Tools ➤ Preferences to set this and a couple of other options.

TIP   **Remind yourself to back up regularly by putting a shortcut to Backup on your desktop. Just drag it from the Start menu, using the right mouse button. Then it will always be staring you in the face.**

Routine Maintenance

Like any other kind of machine, a personal computer needs a certain amount of basic care to continue functioning at peak effectiveness. Windows 98 includes the necessary tools for regular maintenance of your computer, and can automate the essential tasks so that you don't even have to think about them.

First we will discuss the individual tools used for routine maintenance, so you understand when and how to use each one. Then we'll go through the use of the Windows Maintenance Wizard to set up an automated maintenance schedule.

Defragmenting Your Disk

Windows 98 is much like its Windows and DOS predecessors in that when it writes a file to your disk, it puts it anywhere it finds room. As you delete and create files, over time files start to be a piece here, a piece there, another piece somewhere else.

This isn't a problem for Windows 98—it always knows where these pieces are. But it will tend to slow down file access time because the system has to go to several locations to pick up one file. When a file is spread over multiple places, it's said to be fragmented. The more fragmented files you have, the slower your hard drive will run.

The new Disk Defragmenter in Windows 98 doesn't just address this problem, which has traditionally been the role of deframenter programs. It also uses information on what software you start most often to rearrange the files on your hard disk for improved program startup.

NOTE If you are upgrading from Windows 95, you will notice that Disk Defragmenter no longer reports the fragmentation percentage of a drive. This was done partly to improve performance, and partly because some specific fragmentation of program files may be desirable for better performance. This would make correct interpretation of the percentage difficult.

As a matter of good housekeeping then, Disk Defragmenter should probably be run at least once a month. Here's how it's done:

1. Select Disk Defragmenter from the System Tools menu.
2. Use the drop-down list shown in Figure 15.13 to choose the drive you want to defragment.

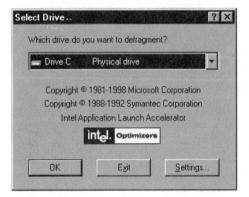

FIGURE 15.13:
Select the drive you want to defragment. Last on the drop-down list is All Hard Drives.

3. Click OK to start Disk Defragmenter. You can click on Show Details to get a cluster-by-cluster view of the program's progress. Or you can just minimize Disk Defragmenter and do something else. If what you do writes to the hard drive, Disk Defragmenter will start over—but in the background and without bothering you.

TIP You should avoid doing work that involves a great deal of writing to the disk while Disk Defragmenter is running. Starting over occasionally is no big deal for Defragmenter, but if it has to do so too often it won't get its work done. One thing you may need to do, if you have Microsoft Office 95 or 97 installed, is to pause Find Fast while Disk Defragmenter runs. Do this by opening Find Fast in the Control Panel and clicking Find Fast Index ➢ Pause Indexing.

If you want to check out Disk Defragmenter options, click the Settings button rather than OK. The dialog is shown in Figure 15.14. Here's what the options mean:

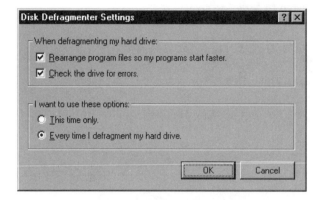

FIGURE 15.14:
The Disk Defragmenter has a few options, which are shown here.

Rearrange program files so my programs start faster   Windows 98 keeps track of how often you start each program on your machine and what files are required. Disk Defragmenter can use this information to optimize the location of program files for faster startup. In the process, it deliberately fragments some program files, so you should not use a third-party disk defragmenter (such as Norton Utilities) if you use this option.

Check the drive for errors   If this is selected, Disk Defragmenter checks the drive before defragmenting. If it finds errors, you'll be advised of this fact and Defragmenter won't continue.

Select one of the last two choices to determine whether these options are for this session only or should be saved for future sessions.

When Disk Defragmenter finds an error on your disk, run ScanDisk (described next) to repair the problem, and then run Defragmenter again.

Repairing Your Drive with ScanDisk

A computer constitutes a very complex system. There's lots of stuff going on all the time that you never know about. Like most complex systems, errors are made, and if not corrected, they tend to pile up into serious problems.

ScanDisk is protection against the accumulation of serious problems on your hard drive. It's a direct descendant of the CHKDSK utility in DOS with added features like those in the justly famous Norton Disk Doctor.

You may have seen ScanDisk when you installed Windows 98, because part of the installation routine is to do a quick check of the hard drive to look for errors.

Running ScanDisk

To run ScanDisk, follow these steps:

1. Select ScanDisk from the System Tools menu under Accessories. This will open the window shown in Figure 15.15.

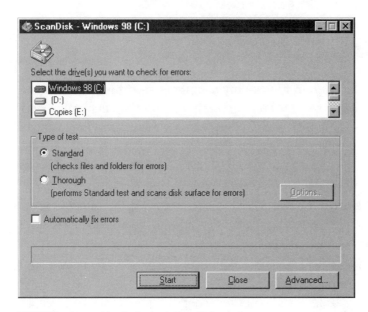

FIGURE 15.15: Here's the basic ScanDisk window.

2. Highlight the drive you want tested.
3. Select the type of test and whether you want ScanDisk to automatically fix all errors or to prompt you.
4. Click Start to run.

If the Automatically Fix Errors box is checked, ScanDisk will repair most errors without consulting you again. Such corrections are made based on the settings you can review by clicking the Advanced button.

Changing ScanDisk Settings

Click the Advanced button to see (and change) the settings that ScanDisk uses.

Display summary   This setting controls when you see the summary of ScanDisk's findings after a check (see Figure 15.16).

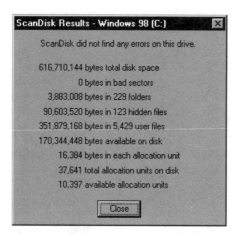

ScanDisk Results - Windows 98 (C:)

ScanDisk did not find any errors on this drive.

616,710,144 bytes total disk space
0 bytes in bad sectors
3,883,008 bytes in 229 folders
90,603,520 bytes in 123 hidden files
351,879,168 bytes in 5,429 user files
170,344,448 bytes available on disk

16,384 bytes in each allocation unit
37,641 total allocation units on disk
10,397 available allocation units

Close

FIGURE 15.16:
This is ScanDisk's summary report on the drive just scanned.

Log file   By default, ScanDisk creates a new log detailing its activities every time it's run. If you want one long continuous log or no log at all, change the setting.

Cross-linked files   A cross-link occurs when more than one file tries to use the same area (cluster) on the hard drive. Whatever information is in the cluster is probably correct only for one file (though it might not be correct for either of them). The default setting attempts to salvage order out of the mess by copying the information in the cluster to both files contending for the space. This is the best of the three settings—it may not save any of your data but the other two options definitely won't.

Lost file fragments   File fragments are a fact of computer life. You can leave the default setting to convert them to files. (They'll be given names like FILE0001 and FILE0002 and will be deposited in your root directory.) The odds are very high that these fragments aren't anything useful, and they do take up valuable disk space. We've changed our default setting to Free, but you can be extra cautious and leave it at Convert to Files. (Just remember to go look at these files periodically and delete the junk.)

Check files for   The default is to look just for invalid names, though you can add dates and times if you want. It will slow down ScanDisk's progress but not dramatically.

Check host drive first If you have a compressed drive, errors are sometimes caused by errors on the host drive. Leave this box checked so the host drive will be examined first.

You should run ScanDisk frequently. Daily is not too often. And at least once a month you should run its Thorough testing procedure, so the hard disk surface is checked for problems in addition to the standard checking of files and folders.

Disk Cleanup

Disk Cleanup is a new tool included in the Windows 98 package. It helps you free up disk space and keep your system tidy by checking the hard drive for several types of files that you may not need to keep.

Start Disk Cleanup by finding it on the Start menu under Programs ➣ Accessories ➣ System Tools. Select the drive you want to clean up, then click OK. After a few seconds of disk activity, you will see the dialog box in Figure 15.17. Click on a file type in the list box to see a description of the files and why you may not need to keep them. Put a check in the check box if you want Disk Cleanup to remove these files. For some file types you can click View Files to open the appropriate folder and see the list of files suggested for deletion. For an explanation of the item "Old ScanDisk files in the root directory," look back to the Lost File Fragments option under ScanDisk.

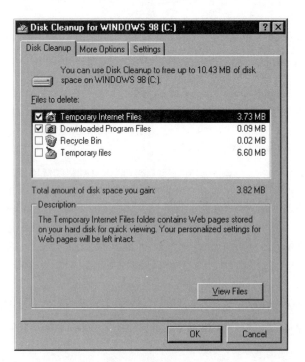

FIGURE 15.17:
The new Disk Cleanup helps keep your hard drive from being overwhelmed with junk, er…stuff.

A couple of things could be confusing here. The description for the Recycle Bin says these files are not removed until you empty the Recycle Bin. But Disk Cleanup will remove them if you check the box; that is, it will empty the Recycle Bin.

The Temporary files category refers to temporary files in the Windows\Temp folder. Checking the box will cause Disk Cleanup to remove temporary files in the folder that have not been accessed in at least a week. It will not remove ordinary (non-temporary) files that may have found their way into that folder, so you may want to check the folder yourself after running Disk Cleanup.

> **TIP** If you return to some Web sites frequently, you shouldn't delete temporary Internet files very often. When you do, performance will suffer the next time you return to each Web site. But if you never delete the files, you will gradually accumulate an enormous load of junk.

The More Options tab offers direct access to Add/Remove Programs so you can uninstall programs or Windows components you don't use. It also gives quick access to the FAT32 Drive Converter, if appropriate. (FAT32 Drive Converter is discussed later in this chapter.)

On the Settings tab you can tell Disk Cleanup to run automatically if space gets low on this drive. If you set this option, you will get a low space warning with the suggestion to run Disk Cleanup before you completely run out of space on the drive.

Windows Maintenance

The Windows Maintenance Wizard helps you set up a schedule to run Disk Defragmenter, ScanDisk, and Disk Cleanup regularly and automatically. You can start it from System Tools on the Start menu or from the Welcome to Windows dialog box that opens when you start Windows 98 for the first time.

The Maintenance Wizard's first dialog offers you the choice of Express or Custom setup. We will describe the Express setup first.

1. After selecting Express and clicking Next, you can choose between three daily time slots for the maintenance process. The easiest, if you don't mind leaving your machine on all the time, is Nights. If it's an older machine that can't go to standby mode to conserve power, you may want to choose a different schedule. The time slots are three hours long, but after the first time the process should finish much faster than that.

2. Click Next, and the Wizard lists the three tasks it will perform, as shown in Figure 15.18:

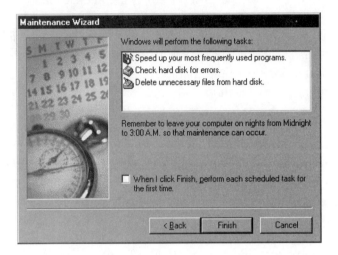

- Speed up your most frequently used programs: Disk Defragmenter will run weekly, processing all your hard drives with the option to "Rearrange program files so my programs start faster."
- Check hard disk for errors: ScanDisk will run weekly with its default settings, checking all your hard drives.
- Delete unnecessary files from hard disk: Disk Cleanup will run at the beginning of each month. It will remove temporary Internet files, downloaded program files, old ScanDisk files in the root directory, and temporary files.

3. Click the check box at the bottom of the dialog if you want all the maintenance operations to run immediately.

4. Click Finish. You're done. Remember to leave the computer on at the appropriate times so that the maintenance programs can run.

WARNING **Windows Maintenance may also offer to convert your hard drives to FAT32. We urge you to read the FAT32 section later in this chapter before allowing it to do so.**

The Custom setup is only slightly more complex. The schedule options include Custom, which will retain any custom schedule you may have set up the last time you ran the Wizard. After clicking Next, you work through three dialog boxes, one for each task that Windows Maintenance runs. For each task you can change the schedule and the settings, based on your knowledge of the three tools as discussed in this chapter. You can also choose not to run the task. When you get to the final dialog, the Maintenance Wizard shows the schedule for each task to be performed.

Scheduling Tasks

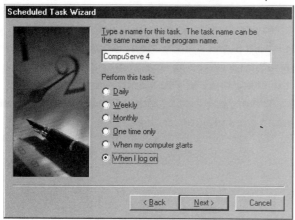 The Task Scheduler icon appears in the System Tray at the lower left corner of your Windows 98 desktop. Double-click it to open the Scheduled Tasks system folder. If you have run the Windows Maintenance Wizard, you will find several scheduled tasks already in the folder. That's what the Maintenance Wizard really does: it helps you create Scheduled Tasks items for three important system maintenance tools.

By clicking the Add Scheduled Task item, you can run the Scheduled Task Wizard to start any program on your computer according to a schedule you decide. The Wizard is simple and straightforward. You choose from a list of all the programs on your computer, then set the schedule. Schedule options include "When my computer starts" and "When I log on," so you can use Task Scheduler to start programs that you always want running when you work. Once a task is set up, you can change its schedule or other characteristics at any time. Right-click on it in the Scheduled Tasks folder and choose Properties.

Making Room on Your Drive

What with Windows 98 taking hundreds of megabytes of hard disk space and some applications nearly reaching that scale, space, on even a large hard drive, can soon be at a premium. Windows 98 includes two features that can effectively expand your hard drive by using it more efficiently.

- FAT32, which makes more efficient use of drives and partitions over 512MB by reducing wasted space
- DriveSpace 3, which compresses files so they take up less space

The two systems are unrelated but mutually exclusive: You can't use DriveSpace on a FAT32 hard drive. FAT32 is generally more useful on newer computers, which tend to have hard drives over one gigabyte (1000 megabytes), often in the two to three gigabyte range. DriveSpace is more useful on machines with hard drives of about a gigabyte or less. It is essentially the same in Windows 98 as it was in Windows 95, except that it includes features that were part of the Plus! Pack for Windows 95.

NOTE   **A partition is a section of a hard drive. When a hard drive is new, or if you are willing to wipe it clean, it can be divided into multiple partitions. Windows 98, like other operating systems, sees these partitions as separate drives, even though they are located on the same physical hard drive. The drive sizes referred to in discussing FAT32 and DriveSpace actually refer to the size of individual partitions, not the whole physical drive. However, most computer manufacturers format hard drives as one giant partition, so it usually amounts to the same thing. If you want to divide an existing hard drive into two or more partitions (without losing everything stored on it), you should get a program such as Partition Magic.**

FAT32

FAT is an acronym for File Allocation Table. From their beginnings, MS-DOS and Windows have used the FAT system for keeping track of the contents of hard drives. Basically, the directory (or folder) tells the operating system where to look in the FAT, and the FAT stores the list of hard drive clusters, or allocation units, where the file is located.

The system used by DOS in the 1990s, and by the original version of Windows 95, is now called FAT16. It could divide a hard drive into at most 65,536 allocation units, which meant that as hard drives got bigger, allocation units also had to get bigger, and large allocation units waste space.

The FAT32 system allows for a much larger file allocation table, which means smaller allocation units and much less wasted space. On a drive in the one to two gigabyte size range, containing about 7,500 files (which is typical for a Windows 98 machine), the saved space amounts to about 100 megabytes.

To Use or Not to Use

Microsoft introduced FAT32 in 1996 as an interim improvement to Windows 95, but made it available only to computer manufacturers, to be installed on new machines. So although you couldn't buy the FAT32 version of Windows 95 in a store, the system has now been installed on millions of computers and is known to be reliable.

There are several limitations on the use of FAT32. The first is that it is not designed for use on hard drives smaller then 512MB, or about 537 million bytes, the units by which hard drive sizes are stated by the manufacturers.

The second important limitation has to do with the use of operating systems other than Windows 98. No other operating system (OS) can read a hard drive formatted with FAT32. This means that if you run other OSs on your computer (such as Windows NT, Windows 95, DOS, or Unix), they will have no access to drives that you have converted to FAT32. It also means that you cannot dual-boot Windows 98 and any other OS if your C: drive is FAT32.

About the only way to make effective use of FAT32 on a machine that needs to run multiple operating systems is to use a third-party utility such as System Commander to choose the OS at start-up time. In that case, you can use FAT32 on the drive where Windows 98 is installed, as long as you don't store any files on that drive that you need to get to when running another OS. You will need System Commander version 3.09 or higher for use with a FAT32 partition, and you will have to temporarily uninstall System Commander before running the conversion.

Many "suspend" or "hibernate" utilities intended for use on laptop computers will not function with FAT32. Also, remember not to convert removable hard drives to FAT32 if they need to be used on other machines that don't have Windows 98 installed.

NOTE   If your computer is connected to a network, other machines on the network that run other versions of Windows will still have access to hard drives that you choose to make accessible, regardless of whether the drives use FAT32. This is because network access is provided by your machine, so it doesn't matter what operating system the other computers on the network use.

Another thing to think about before converting to FAT32 is third-party disk utilities. Most have now been upgraded to work with FAT32, but if you have older versions you will not be able to use them.

Briefly put, if your hard drive is larger than 512MB and you plan to run only Windows 98, you should convert to FAT32. Use only Windows 98's own disk utilities, or others that specify they are compatible with FAT32.

Converting to FAT32

If you install Windows 98 over Windows 95, FAT32 will only be used if Windows 95 was installed that way. To find out, open My Computer and right-click on the drive. Choose Properties. On the General page you will see File System; it will show either FAT (meaning FAT16) or FAT32. When installing over Windows 3.1, FAT32 will not be used. After Windows 98 is installed and running, you can convert your hard drive to FAT32 by using the Drive Converter program.

1. Start Drive Converter by selecting it from the Start menu under Programs ➢ Accessories ➢ System Tools. In the first dialog of the Wizard, you can click the Details button to see what Windows Help has to say about converting to FAT32. You should do this to once again review the pros and cons.

2. Click Next to see the dialog shown in Figure 15.19. On many machines, this dialog will show only drive C:. Make your choice and click Next.

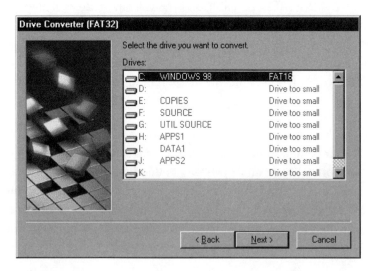

FIGURE 15.19: Choose the drive you want to convert to FAT32.

3. You may see a warning that other operating systems will not be able to read a FAT32 drive. Click OK. Windows 98 will then check your system for anti-virus programs and disk utilities that are not compatible with FAT32. Once this is resolved, you can click Next.
4. The Wizard will now offer to start Backup so that you can back up your files before converting the drive.
5. After creating the backup, click Next again to see the last dialog before actual conversion of your drive. Be sure you have closed all running programs, then click Next.
6. Your machine will reboot to MS-DOS mode and run the conversion. Windows 98 will then restart and run Disk Defragmenter.

WARNING   Even though converting a drive to FAT32 is considered a safe operation, you should always back up important data before starting any task that tampers with your hard drive.

TIP   Although the dialog in step 5 says the process might take a few hours, the basic conversion to FAT32 actually takes only a few minutes. Running Disk Defragmenter may take several hours. You can interrupt the defragmentation process if you wish. However, performance of the FAT32 drive will probably be poor until you run Disk Defragmenter and allow it to completely defragment the drive.

Going Back to FAT16

Windows 98 does not include a converter for going from FAT32 to FAT16. If you find you need to do this, you have two options:

- Back up all your data files on the FAT32 drive. Run FDISK on the partition and choose No to the option to enable large disk support. Then format the drive and re-install Windows 98 and any applications that were on the drive. For more details, see the installation appendices.
- Get a program such as Partition Magic, which can convert FAT32 to FAT16 without losing its contents. There has to be enough unused space on the drive to allow for the extra space the files will occupy using FAT16. If not, you can first use Partition Magic to change the partition size.

DriveSpace 3

Windows 98 comes with DriveSpace 3. It will let you:

- Compress and uncompress a hard drive partition or a diskette.
- Upgrade a DoubleSpace or DriveSpace compressed drive to DriveSpace 3.
- Use your free space to create a new, empty compressed partition.

Compressing an Existing Drive

To compress a drive, you need only follow these steps:

1. Click on DriveSpace in the System Tools menu under Accessories.
2. Highlight the drive you want to compress and select Compress from the Drive menu.
3. The next screen (shown in Figure 15.20) will give you the before and after picture for the selected drive.

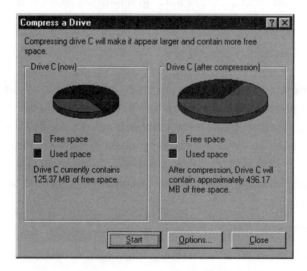

FIGURE 15.20: This shows a drive before a compress and how it will look after.

4. Click Start. You'll see a dialog asking whether you have an updated Windows 98 Startup disk. If you didn't create such a disk when you installed Windows 98 (or if you can't find it), you should do so now.
5. If you haven't backed up the files on the drive you want to compress, click the Back Up Files button and follow the instructions.
6. Click Compress Now.
7. The drive will be checked for errors, and then, if it's your C: drive that's compressing, you'll be advised that your computer needs to restart. Once

you click Yes here, there's no stopping, so be sure you've done all the preparatory steps correctly, and you have something else to do during the time the compression is going on. This is one process that can't be run in the background.

WARNING **If you're running more than one operating system, be sure the reboot is into Windows 98. This applies equally to reboots that are part of other DriveSpace conversion operations, such as uncompressing, creating a new partition, and adjusting free space.**

The compression can take quite a while, especially on the older machines that are most likely to need it due to limited hard disk space. For example, we compressed the C: drive on a 75MHz 486 laptop with 16MB RAM. The drive size was 375MB, with about 230MB of files. The process took about ninety minutes. At the end of the compression cycle (an on-screen progress bar is displayed), you get a before and after report showing the previous space on the disk and new statistics on free space and used space.

How Compression Works

When you compress a drive—let's say your C drive—the whole thing ends up as one big file on a "new" drive called H (by default—though you can give it any letter after H in the alphabet). The "new" drive H is called a host drive.

When you boot your machine, a DriveSpace command is loaded first. This tells the system to look for this big file and load it so it looks all the world like a regular boot into the C: drive. Any other compressed drives that are present when you boot your machine are also recognized and interpreted.

On the property sheet for the host drive, there's an option to hide this drive from view. This is a good option to take because there's nothing you can do in a host drive. There's a little bit of free space, but the rest is taken up by this big compressed file that you can't read and mustn't fool with.

DriveSpace 3 Settings

In DriveSpace, choose Advanced ➤ Settings to open the dialog box shown in Figure 15.21. Here you can set the degree of compression to be used when saving new files, or limit the circumstances where compression is used. For a more complete description of each option, click the ? button in the top right corner, then click the item for which you want more information.

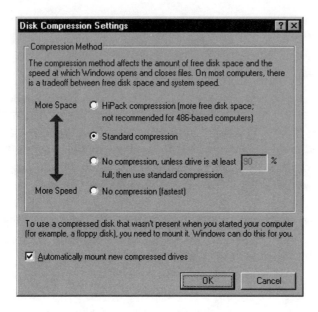

FIGURE 15.21:
Choose your
compression
options.

TIP   **To see the current status of compression on a drive, right-click the drive in My Computer. Choose Properties, then look at the information on the Compression page.**

You should also be sure that the option to "Automatically mount new compressed drives" is checked. If it is, you can usually avoid the steps described in the next section.

Mounting a Compressed Diskette

Unlike earlier versions, Windows 98 will usually recognize (mount) a compressed diskette even if compression has never been used on that machine. If it doesn't, you will see only two files on the diskette: one called Drvspace.000 (or Dblspace.000) and one called Readthis.txt. To properly read this floppy, you'll have to go through a simple mounting procedure. Here's what to do:

1. Insert the floppy in a disk drive and then open DriveSpace.
2. Highlight the drive in the list shown.
3. Select Mount from the Advanced menu.

Uncompressing a Drive

Providing you have room for the data once it's all uncompressed, you can get rid of the compression on a drive at any time. Just follow these steps:

1. Open DriveSpace and highlight the drive you want to uncompress.
2. Select Uncompress from the Drive menu.
3. You'll see a window showing the drive as it is now and as it will be after uncompression. Click Start to proceed.
4. You'll see a warning about backing up your files. If you haven't backed up the files on the compressed drive, click the Back Up Files button and follow the instructions.
5. Click Uncompress Now.
6. After a while, if this is the only compressed drive on your system, you'll be asked if you want to remove the compression driver at the end of the procedure.

   No—if you're still going to be reading compressed removable media (that is floppies or removable hard drives)

   Yes—if you're through using any compressed drives for the foreseeable future

The drive will be checked for errors, and then the computer will restart. Uncompression will be completed, and the computer will have to restart yet again (if drive C: is involved).

NOTE   **Uncompressing takes even longer than compressing. So it's not a task to undertake when you're in a big hurry.**

Creating a New Partition

DriveSpace can take the free space on your drive and make it into a new partition. This partition will be compressed and will provide more storage space than the amount of space it uses.

To make a new drive in this way, follow these steps:

1. Open DriveSpace.
2. Highlight the drive that contains the free space you want to use, and select Create Empty from the Advanced menu. This will open a window like the one shown in Figure 15.22.

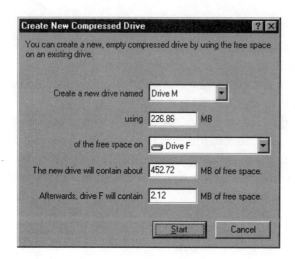

FIGURE 15.22:
This is how you
can create a "new"
drive out of avail-
able free space.

3.   Accept the suggested settings or make changes as you wish.
4.   When you're finished, click Start.

Compression Agent

Compression Agent works with DriveSpace 3 to control and change the degree of compression used on your files. For example, you could improve performance on file save operations by telling DriveSpace to use No Compression, as described earlier under DriveSpace 3 Settings. Then you can have Compression Agent compress these files when your computer is not in use.

Open Compression Agent from the System Tools menu. Click Settings to choose the compression options you want. The Overview button in Compression Agent takes you to the DriveSpace Help file, which offers explanations of all the options.

Changing the compression method used on files can take a substantial amount of time, so Compression Agent is best run on a regular basis by making use of the Task Scheduler, as described earlier in this chapter.

Checking Up on Your System

Another item on the System Tools menu is System Information. This utility offers a wide variety of information about your system and your Windows 98 installation. Though much of this information is beyond the scope of this book, some of it can be very useful. For example, the hardware resources information (Figure 15.23) might help you resolve a hardware conflict problem.

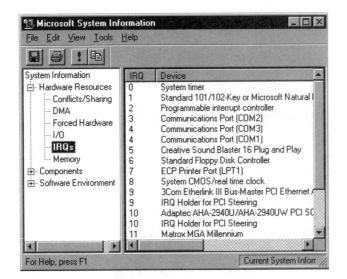

FIGURE 15.23:
An example
of System
Information's
usefulness

In addition, the Tools menu of System Information gives access to several more advanced system utilities. Among these are:

- Windows Report Tool helps you report details of a problem to Microsoft technical support.
- System File Checker checks on the integrity of a vast array of system files. It can also be used to extract a single file from the Windows 98 installation disk.
- Dr. Watson helps you gather information on software crashes.
- System Configuration Utility helps you check on and edit your system configuration files and allows you to do a diagnostic startup to help isolate hardware and software problems.

Windows Update

Windows Update is Microsoft's attempt to resolve the problem of keeping your system up-to-date with the latest Windows bug fixes and other program patches, as well as current drivers for your hardware. The plan is that as hardware manufacturers update their drivers, they will make them available as part of Windows Update.

When you click Windows Update on the Start menu, Internet Explorer starts and connects to the Windows Update Web site. To check for updated drivers or system files, click the Update Wizard link. At the beginning of the Wizard click Update, then follow the instructions that appear on your screen.

The Update Wizard includes active components that must be downloaded and run by Internet Explorer on your system. At some point, you will see one or more security messages similar to Figure 15.24. You must click Yes to allow the download to proceed and the active components to function on your system.

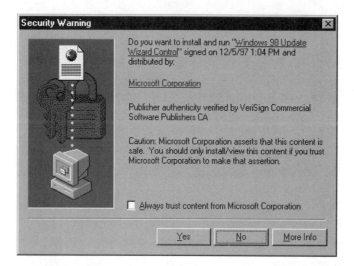

FIGURE 15.24:
Security warnings allow you to stop active components, but without them the Update Wizard can't function.

After the necessary components are downloaded, you will see a message that your system is being scanned to see what files need to be updated. When the scan is complete the Update Wizard will display a list of available updates for your system. To install an update, click it and then click the Install button.

The Update Wizard also offers a restore function to allow you to return to your previous version of a file you updated. You might need to do this if the update causes unexpected problems on your system.

What's Next

With this chapter, we've covered all the tools and applets supplied with Windows 98. In the next chapter, we'll discuss how to get your hardware to behave nicely, whether it's of the newer Plug-and-Play persuasion or something older.

IT PLUGS
(BUT WILL IT PLAY?)

Plug and Play is the hardware specification first supported in Windows 95 that promised to make adding new hardware to your computer much simpler than it had ever been before. Three years' experience has taught us that while it generally works, it's not perfect. Fortunately, Windows 98 gives you some powerful tools to make resolving any hardware problems you have a lot easier.

The Promise of Plug and Play

The Plug-and-Play specification has five formally stated goals:

- Easy, and in most cases automatic, installation and configuration of new devices
- Dynamic configuration changes
- Independent of operating system and hardware
- Compatibility with legacy (non-Plug-and-Play) hardware
- Increased flexibility without increased complexity

Meeting all these goals requires the cooperation of hardware manufacturers, BIOS vendors, and operating system designers. The potential paybacks for users and manufacturers, however, are very big and provide an enormous incentive to make it happen.

While any operating system can support Plug and Play, the first to offer full support was Windows 95. Not only did new devices install easier, but Windows 95 was a whole lot easier to install than previous versions of Windows, OS/2, or (shudder) UNIX. And Windows 98 is easier still.

In the vast majority of cases, Windows 98 will correctly sense all your hardware and configure it to work without conflict. And, when you add new hardware, or change your existing hardware, Windows 98 will find a place for it that doesn't step all over your existing stuff.

What to Do When It Won't

No matter how much Windows 98 does to let you simply plug in your new hardware and let you play with it immediately, sooner or later you're going to have problems with either a new piece of hardware or an existing one. Sometimes the source of the problem is a subtle conflict between two (or more) pieces of hardware, but much more often the root cause is something fairly simple and straightforward.

Windows 98 provides an outstanding set of tools for resolving problems and getting stuff working. They're called troubleshooters, and they are part of the Help system.

To get to the troubleshooters, follow these steps:

1. Click the Start button and select Help.
2. In the Help Topics window click the Contents tab.
3. Open Troubleshooting. Click Using Windows 98 troubleshooters and read it for some helpful tips.
4. Open Windows 98 Troubleshooters as shown in Figure 16.1. Click a likely looking troubleshooter to see whether it can help resolve your problem.

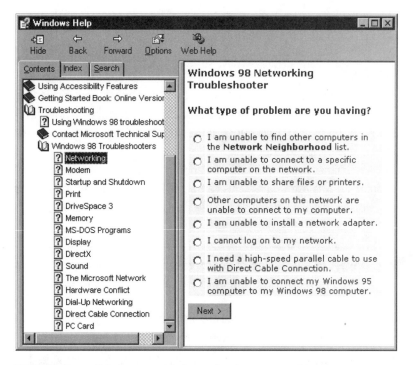

FIGURE 16.1: Help has a troubleshooter for almost any problem.

We can't walk you through the troubleshooters; there are quite a few of them, and most can branch in several directions depending on how you respond to the questions. What we will do is go over some of the more obvious places where you can have hardware problems and point out some things to check.

General Device Problems

Suppose your problem is a sort of general "It doesn't work" where "it" is some device. The following sections give you a few things to look for and think about.

External Devices

If the thing that isn't working is attached to your computer, as opposed to something inside the box, here are a few things to check:

Power   Check that the power is on to the device. Even if it is, try turning the power off and back on. This single step will clear up to 90 percent of all hardware problems.

Cable connections   Make sure that the cable that connects it is solidly attached at both ends with all the screws that lock the connectors screwed in.

Cable integrity   Check the cable, and make sure your cat hasn't decided it looked like a tasty supplement to the usual kibble.

Internal Devices

If the problem is with something inside the computer box, it gets trickier. First, shut down Windows 98 completely and turn the power off. Carefully remove the screws that hold your computer's box together (put them somewhere safe) and remove the cover. Here are a few things to check:

Dirt   Over time, the amount of dust and dirt that builds up inside your computer's box is astounding. This can actually degrade performance or cause a device to stop working, because the dirt can provide a conductive path.

TIP   **Invest in a little can of compressed air to blow dust off surfaces, or if you're really tidy, one of those mini-vacuums to suck it up.**

Cables   Check that all the cables are firmly attached and that there is no obvious physical evidence of problems (a worn spot or burn mark).

Cards   Make sure that all the cards are firmly seated. A poorly seated card can work loose over time, creating an intermittent failure.

When you think you've checked everything, before you put the cover back on, try to power the computer back up to see if you've corrected the problem. Some machines have cover interlocks that will prevent you from doing this.

Device Conflicts

If the previous checks aren't sufficient, you still have a few things to look for. Open the System Properties dialog (either from Properties of My Computer or System from the Control Panel) and click on the Device Manager tab. Click on the type of device you are having trouble with and see if there are any conflicts shown. If there are, then you'll probably want to run the Hardware Conflict troubleshooter from the Windows 98 Help system.

This little gem (see Figure 16.2) can resolve the vast majority of the hardware problems you have. Just follow the directions carefully and click the buttons as required. We're not going through every step, because there are just too many directions it can branch in—depending on what it finds and how you respond to its questions.

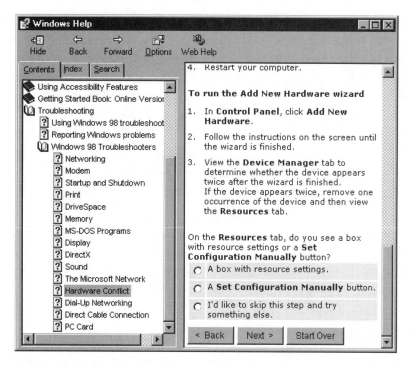

FIGURE 16.2: The Hardware Conflict Troubleshooter helps you resolve hardware problems.

Printing Problems

Probably the single biggest source of problems is printers. Besides the usual paper jam problems that we all hate, you can easily run into subtle conflicts between your application program and the printer drivers, as well as downright bugs in either. Here are some things to try:

Printer Online   This is the single biggest cause of problems, especially if the printer's not right next to you where you can see it. Make sure the Online light is on. If the printer doesn't have such a light, check its manual to find out how to be sure it's ready to work.

Power   Turn the power off and back on. This does two things. It forces you to check that the power is actually on, and more to the point, it causes the printer to do a complete reset getting back to the known starting point that Windows 98 expects to find it in.

Cable   Check the cable connections on both ends.

Switches, "Buffalo Boxes", Spoolers, etc.   There are all sorts of ways to share a printer that are left over from the bad old DOS days. With networking built in since Windows 95, these have started to go the way of the Dodo bird. But if you still have one, temporarily connect the printer directly to your computer with nothing in between except the actual cable—and make the cable a short one. Now try printing. If you can print now, you know where the problem is don't you?

Network Print Servers   Like the previous technique, try connecting your computer directly to the printer without the intervening network connection.

Test File   Try printing a simple test file from Notepad. If the basic stuff will print from within Windows 98, but you are having problems with the more complicated stuff from your application, chances are you have a driver problem or a problem with the application itself. Check Windows Update (described in Chapter 15) to see if there's a newer driver. Check with the publisher of your software to see if there is an updated version of the program.

Modem Problems

Modems have always been a pain—with their arcane configuration settings and completely incomprehensible command language. Although Windows 98 is remarkably good at finding, setting up, and controlling your modem, if you have problems, here are a few things to try:

Com Port   Make sure you have the correct com port selected.

Power   If the modem is an external modem, turn off the power to it, and then turn it back on. This will force the modem to re-initialize and return to a default condition. This will fix many modem problems.

Single Program   Make sure only one program that uses the com port is running. In Windows 98 you can frequently let different programs share a single modem—but not always. When you're troubleshooting, keep things simple until you find the source of the problem. Even if you don't think any other program is using the modem, try restarting the computer to make sure.

Older Communications Programs   Some pre-Windows 95 communications programs don't fully release the modem when you close the program. You may have to restart your system to allow another program to use the modem.

DOS Programs   If your modem is used by both DOS and Windows programs, or by multiple Windows applications, try adding the following line to the [386Enhanced] section of your system.ini file: **ComXAutoAssign=2** where the "X" is replaced by the com port number you have your modem connected to.

Network Problems

We could write a whole book about networks and their problems (and many already have), but here are some basic things to check:

Cables   Buy good quality cables in the first place, protect them from physical or environmental abuse, and they should never cause you a problem. Skimp on the quality, leave them where they can get cut, bent, stepped on, or otherwise abused, and you'll have nothing but trouble.

Connectors   Again, buy good quality connectors. This is another place where cheap is not inexpensive. Check all your connections to make sure they're tight, locked in place, and you don't have an open connector shorting out the network.

Termination   Make sure your network is properly terminated. If someone decides to stick another section of cable in and forgets about the termination, it'll bring your whole network down in a flash. Also, buy quality terminating resistors. The cheap ones can be a problem.

Network Card   This is the first place most people look, but it's usually not the problem. Once it's set up and properly configured, it usually stays that way. If it's a new card, and you're setting it up for the first time, make sure it's configured correctly for the type of network cabling you're using. Plug and Play should set its IRQ and memory addresses so they don't conflict with existing hardware. To check this, open the System applet in the Control Panel, and go to the Device Manager page. Click the + beside Network Adapters, then select the one with a problem. Click Properties and look on the Resources page for any possible conflicts. See Figure 16.3.

Network Hub   If your network has a hub, be sure its power is on.

Addressing and Protocols   Make sure you don't have any conflicting addresses or machine IDs on your network and all the machines are using the same protocols—especially the same default protocol. Leave room for any "sometime" machines like laptops and remote access users, so they won't conflict when they're attached to the network.

TIP

If you're still having problems after doing some conscientious trouble-shooting, run the Networking Troubleshooter. If that doesn't work, break down and call an expert. Between the lists in this chapter and the Troubleshooter, you have a very good chance of solving most of your problems.

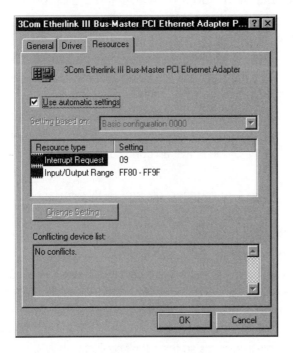

FIGURE 16.3:
Check the Device Manager for possible resource conflicts.

Video Problems

Most video difficulties can be traced to a driver problem and are therefore out of your scope of control, but here are a few things you can look at:

Refresh rate   If your screen has intermittent problems or seems to be otherwise flakey, you may be running on the raw edge of the maximum refresh rate your monitor and card can support. Try reducing it slightly. Right-click on your desktop and choose Properties. Go to Settings ➤ Advanced ➤ Adapter and use the drop-down list to change the refresh rate.

Distortion   If your picture is highly distorted, especially along one edge, you may be suffering from interference with other equipment (such as unshielded speakers) or monitors in the area. Check where your cables are running, and try moving them to see if that helps. If not, you may need to figure out what piece of equipment is causing the interference and move either it or the computer.

Setting defaults   Your (older) video card needs to have its options set from DOS and won't respond to Windows 98 settings or let you run the utilities in a DOS window from inside Windows 98? Well, in the first place, shame on the card! But to get around this problem: shut down Windows 98 and select "Restart the computer in MS-DOS mode." Once you've run the utility, you can exit out and reboot into Windows 98 again.

What's Next

In this chapter we've covered Plug and Play, how it usually makes life much easier for Windows 98 users, and some basic troubleshooting techniques if you do have problems. Remember, if what we've told you here doesn't quite get the job done, use the Windows 98 Help system, including troubleshooters and Web Help, to track down the problem.

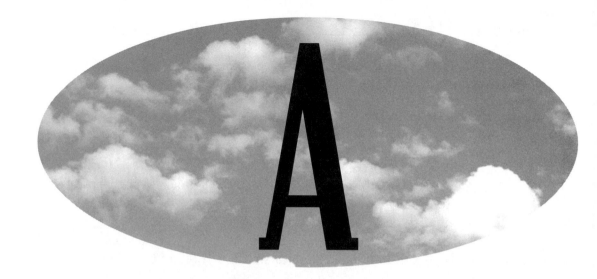

INSTALLING FOR WINDOWS 95 USERS

The designers of Windows 98 have worked hard to make the installation process for Windows 98 as simple and trouble-free as possible. If you use only Windows 95 and you are satisfied with the way it's working for you, the preliminaries are minimal and the upgrade will probably proceed without problems.

On the other hand, if the performance of Windows 95 on your machine has you twiddling your thumbs, you may want to consider hardware improvements. Running multiple operating systems can also complicate matters, but there are easier solutions available now than in the past.

Hardware

One of the design goals for Windows 98 was to improve performance, and in some respects this has been achieved. Windows 98 starts a bit faster than Windows 95, and application start-up is also a bit quicker. However, Windows 98 can't do much to reduce the demands made on hardware by ever more complex applications. In fact, new applications and technologies have raised hardware requirements substantially since the introduction of Windows 95.

The minimum hardware required to run Windows 98 is supposed to be a 486DX2-66 processor (or non-Intel equivalent) and 16MB of RAM. Our experience with installing on such a machine is that it doesn't always work. Installation does seem to work reliably on a 486-75, and Windows 98 will run reasonably well at this level if you don't expect it to handle the most demanding technologies, such as streaming video from the Internet. You also need about 200MB of free space on your hard drive.

The upshot is that Windows 98 itself is not likely to demand much in the way of hardware improvements for most users. If you are happy with the way your applications run under Windows 95, you should be just as satisfied with their performance under Windows 98. If you intend to take advantage of Windows 98's support for advanced technologies that place heavy demands on the processor, your hardware decisions should be based on those uses, rather than on Windows 98.

Multiple Operating Systems

If you currently run multiple operating systems and simply want to upgrade your Windows 95 installation to Windows 98, you can just run the Windows 98 installation from Windows 95. To be on the safe side, set your boot menu to default to Windows 95 before you begin. When you are done, you will probably find that the installation process has disabled your boot manager or System Commander. You will need to re-install or re-activate it by following the instructions that came with it.

If you want to keep your current Windows 95 installation in working order, things are a bit more complex. Basically, you need a separate primary partition on your hard drive for your Windows 98 installation. If the partition doesn't already exist, you will need to create it. Because doing so with Fdisk would delete everything on your hard drive, you'll probably want to invest in a program such as Partition Magic, which can repartition a hard disk without losing its contents. Set the partition where you will install Windows 98 to be active, then proceed through the instructions in the rest of this appendix. You will be doing a fresh (or clean) installation of Windows 98, not an upgrade installation.

Preliminaries

You need to do several things before installing Windows 98. Some depend on whether you want to install as an upgrade over Windows 95 or do a fresh installation. We will begin with the things everyone should do.

Back Up Your Data

We've all heard how important it is to do backups, and we've all ignored those warnings (at times). That doesn't change our obligation to warn you yet again!

The importance of first backing up your system cannot be stressed enough. While the installation program of Windows 98 is remarkably good, and the number of systems that fail is small, you should never, never make changes to your operating system without doing a backup.

Choosing a Backup Program

If you haven't invested in a third-party program, the backup program included with Windows 95 is adequate. It's safe, easy to use, and reasonably fast. If you have another backup program you prefer and are more comfortable with, by all means use it.

What to Back Up

If you have a tape drive or other high-capacity backup system, you can do a full system backup and be secure in the knowledge that everything is safe. You could even use it to return to your current Windows 95 setup, if necessary. If your backup device has a more limited capacity, you will probably only want to back up your data files. Even though it would take time, everything else could be re-created from the original disks. Make sure you have the original disks for all the software you use.

Take your time and review all the directories and even subdirectories on your hard drive. Besides all the places that you have knowingly created files, check the directories of programs that save data without a specific command from you. These would include personal information managers, e-mail programs, and navigation programs for online services, among others. If you have any doubts about whether you should back up a particular file or group of files, it's best to err on the side of caution.

Disable Anti-Virus Software

You should temporarily disable any anti-virus software installed on your machine. One of the things anti-virus software does is prevent changes to the boot sector of your hard drive. However, Windows 98 Setup needs to make such changes. Disable your anti-virus software according to the instructions that came with it. Don't forget to re-activate it after installation is complete.

Upgrade or Make a Fresh Start?

One of the most important decisions you need to make is whether to install Windows 98 as an upgrade over Windows 95 or to do a clean installation from scratch. Generally speaking, an upgrade installation is satisfactory if Windows 95 and your applications are running well. If most of the programs you have ever installed are ones you still use, or if you can remove unused programs with Windows 95's Add/Remove Programs, upgrading should be fine. The same is true if you can remove unused programs using uninstall routines that came with them, or if you use a good third-party uninstaller. The advantages of installing Windows 98 as an upgrade are that it's faster and you won't have to re-install your applications.

If Windows 95 or your application programs have not been running smoothly you may be well advised to get a fresh start by doing a clean installation of Windows 98. The same is true if you suspect your hard drive of carrying a heavy load of application-related files you no longer use. Another reason to do a clean install is if you have already done an upgrade installation of Windows 98 and are experiencing problems. The advantage of a clean installation is that you get rid of anything old that might be causing trouble. The main disadvantages are the additional preparation required, and the fact that you will have to re-install all of your Windows 95 applications. Also, you will lose Windows 95's built-in fax capability, because Windows 98 has no fax feature.

If you decide on an upgrade installation, you should read the following three sections on faxing, additional housecleaning, and defragmenting your hard drive. Then skip to the Step by Step section. If you will be doing a clean install, you should work through everything.

Fax

Windows 95 includes a program called Exchange, which can transmit faxes via your fax modem. Exchange is not a part of Windows 98, which includes no other fax capability. If you use Exchange to send faxes from your computer under Windows 95, you have several choices:

- If you install Windows 98 as an upgrade, Exchange will be retained and you can continue to use it. If it has been working reliably for you, this is probably the best option. Just remember that if it fails you will not be able to re-install it as you could when you were running Windows 95.

- Exchange is also part of Microsoft Office 95, and similar capabilities are included in Office 97. After installing Windows 98, you may be able to install Exchange or other Windows Messaging components from one of these sources, if you have them.
- You can purchase and install third-party fax software.

If Exchange is installed on your machine but you don't use it, you should remove it before upgrading Windows 95 to Windows 98.

1. Open the Control Panel, under Settings on the Start menu.
2. Open Add/Remove Programs.
3. Click the Windows Setup tab.
4. Remove the check mark in front of Microsoft Exchange.
5. Click OK.

More Housecleaning

Now's the perfect time to ponder which programs on your system are really needed and to clean up some of the clutter and detritus that build up on your hard drive. Windows 98 is going to need substantially more hard disk space than Windows 95, so this is an even better reason to clean house.

The first step is to take a look at installed programs you haven't used in the last year or two. It's time to get rid of them. If they're DOS programs, just delete them. If they're Windows programs, you have to delete them and find all the files they've stuck in your Windows directories without telling you.

Your best bet here is to get one of the ingenious programs designed to remove all traces of ill-behaved Windows applications. One of the best is CleanSweep 3.0, from Quarterdeck.

TIP If you have any doubts about removing a program from your hard drive, just save any data files off to a floppy. You can always reinstall the program from the original disks if you suddenly need it.

Defragment Your Hard Drive

Once you have all the extraneous files cleaned off your hard drive, you should do a complete disk defragmentation. This will consolidate your existing files on the disk, creating the maximum possible room for Windows 98 Setup to do its thing.

1. On the Windows 95 Start menu, go to Programs ➤ Accessories ➤ System Tools ➤ Disk Defragmenter.

2. The default drive to defragment is C:, so just click OK and let it do its thing.

If you will be installing Windows 98 as an upgrade over your existing Windows 95, skip down to the Step by Step section.

Create a Boot Disk

This is only necessary if you will be doing a clean installation of Windows 98. In Windows 95, open Add/Remove Programs in the Control Panel. Click the Startup Disk tab and follow the instructions. After you have created the disk, put it in the floppy drive and restart your machine. After your machine boots to an A: prompt, do this:

1. Type **c:** and press Enter.

2. When you see the C: prompt, type **dir** and press enter.

You should see a listing of the contents of the root directory on your C: drive. If neither of these steps produces an error message, your boot disk is giving proper access to your hard drive.

Now for the more demanding part: depending on how you plan to install Windows 98, you may need the boot disk to provide access either to your CD-ROM drive or to your local area network. Neither capability is part of the Windows 95 boot disk you just created; you will have to add the one you need.

Get out the instructions and driver disk that came with your CD-ROM drive or network card. Follow the instructions that tell you how to set up the device under DOS. This will generally involve creating CONFIG.SYS and AUTOEXEC.BAT files on your boot disk. You will also have to copy any required files to the boot disk. Driver files can be copied from the disk supplied by the device manufacturer. DOS files can be found in the \Command subdirectory of your current Windows directory.

When you have finished, be sure to test the boot disk. Restart your machine with the disk in the floppy drive, and be sure you have access to the Windows 98 CD-ROM, whether it's in a drive on your machine or connected via the network.

WARNING Remember that the version of Windows 98 commonly sold in stores will be an upgrade version, meaning it will expect to find an older version of Windows already installed on the computer. To do a clean install, you will either need to buy the full version of Windows 98, or be prepared to insert various disks from Windows 3.1 or Windows 95 when requested by Setup. The Windows 95 CD should also work if your boot disk gives access to your CD-ROM drive.

TIP   There are a couple of shortcuts and alternatives to these instructions. If you currently have CD-ROM or network access in a DOS
window under Windows 95, the lines that load the necessary drivers
should be present in your current CONFIG.SYS and AUTOEXEC.BAT
files. You can copy them from there. If you have a DOS boot disk
that provides access to the necessary resource, you can use it rather
than create a Windows 95 boot disk. Finally, if you have plenty of
hard drive space, you can just copy the entire contents of the Win98
folder on the CD to a folder or partition on your hard drive before
proceeding any further. When the time comes, you can install from
there. This is probably the simplest option, if you can spare the
nearly 200MB of hard drive space required.

FAT32

While it is theoretically possible to create a FAT32 partition and install Windows 98
to it, the road blocks are many. Not least is that you must first create a FAT32-aware
boot disk, including FAT32 versions of Fdisk and Format, something that can only be
done with Windows 98 itself (or some later versions of Windows 95). Explaining how
to get around all the difficulties would be long-winded and probably only benefit users
who already know enough to figure it out for themselves anyway. We are going to stick
with the following recommendation: even if you are doing a clean install of Windows 98,
ignore FAT32 until after you have run Setup. Then convert to FAT32 if you want to, by
following the instructions in Chapter 15.

Network Identification and Configuration

If you are doing a clean install on a machine that is connected to a local area network, you should gather the information you will need to identify and configure your
machine for the network. Right-click on Network Neighborhood and choose Properties.
Go through each of the tabs of the dialog box and copy down all the information and
selected options.

The information from the Identification page will be entered during setup. The
options on the other two pages can be set after you finish installing Windows 98.
Open Network in the Control Panel, and refer to Chapter 11 for assistance.

Step by Step

As operating systems go, Windows 98 is very clever. For many configurations, you can just boot up, put the CD in the drive, and start running Setup. The system will install without a hiccup.

If such an approach strikes you as foolhardy in the extreme, we agree. The investment of a little advance work can save you many hours of frustration and grief if your computer happens to be one of the few on which things go awry.

While we have included nearly every step of the setup procedure in the following sections, we have skipped a few that require no comment. We're confident you can enter your name when requested, with no help from us.

Starting the Installation

After you've done the prep work in the previous sections of this appendix, reboot your system to Windows 95. Insert the Windows 98 CD in your CD-ROM drive. If Windows 95 is set up to automatically run a CD when it is inserted, you will see the screen shown in Figure A.1. Otherwise, open My Computer and double-click your CD-ROM drive to get to the same screen. Either way, click Yes and you will be on your way.

FIGURE A.1:   You're on your way!

NOTE If you are doing a clean install of Windows 98, start your computer with the boot disk you created earlier. Switch to your CD-ROM drive by typing d: and pressing Enter, where d is the letter of the drive. Then type setup.exe and press Enter. Alternatively, switch to the appropriate drive on your network connection, or to the directory or hard drive where you copied the Win98 folder from the CD. When Setup starts, it will run Scandisk to check your hard drives. When Scandisk finishes, press x to exit.

You'll see the Welcome screen shown in Figure A.2. The left side of the screen, including the estimated time required to complete the installation, will remain throughout the setup process to show your progress. Total time estimates vary from 30 to 60 minutes or more depending on how much you install and the speed of your system. Expect to spend somewhat more time than the estimate.

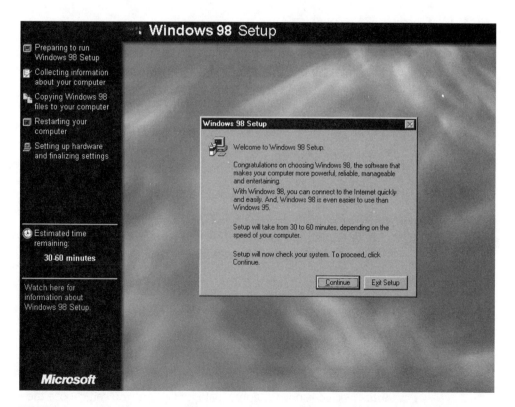

FIGURE A.2: This setup screen will keep you informed about the progress of your installation.

Read the information presented in the dialog box, then click Continue. Windows 98 will perform a quick survey of your system, prepare the Setup Wizard, and ask you to read and consent to the license agreement. Click Next to move on.

TIP **If you are doing a clean install, your mouse may not be functional at this time. Use the Tab key to move the highlight between dialog box choices, and Enter to OK the dialog.**

When doing a clean install, you'll be asked at this point to choose a directory for installation—the default is \Windows on your C: drive, but you can choose another location or a different name for the directory.

Setup will then perform a more thorough check of your system, including looking for installed components of Windows and making sure you have enough hard drive space to complete the installation.

Save System Files

The next dialog asks if you want the install program to save your Windows 95 system files. These files make it possible to quickly uninstall Windows 98, should you run into trouble. So it's a good idea to select Yes.

You can then skip down to the section on choosing an Internet channel set. You won't see the Setup Options dialog box because Windows 98 will set up the same options and components as you have in Windows 95. Remember that after installation you can use the Add/Remove Programs function in the Control Panel to easily add or remove any components.

NOTE **If you're doing a clean install, you won't be offered the save system files option because you're not overwriting anything.**

Setup Options

The next choice you have to make, for a clean install only, is about how much of the OS you want to install. You can select:

Typical   The major components (as defined by the setup program) are installed.

Portable   Includes options appropriate for laptops. You can choose the components you want to install or let the system install the major components (as in the Typical install).

Compact   Selects a minimum configuration—for situations where space is tight.

Custom   Lets you make selections at every step. Don't be put off by the designation of this choice as for "experts." Even a reasonably competent beginner can handle this installation.

Selecting Components

If you selected Custom install, you choose the components you want. For a Typical, Compact, or Portable installation, you can choose the components you want or let Windows 98 choose what to install based on the type of installation selected.

The main categories of components are listed in the window. Click Details to see the total items that make up the category. Check the ones you want installed. A click of the mouse will also remove check marks in front of items you don't want.

Identify Your Computer

This dialog asks you to give your computer a name that will identify it on your local area network. You are also asked to enter the name of your workgroup and a description of your computer. This is the information you gathered from the Identification tab of the Network dialog box before you eliminated Windows 95.

Choose an Internet Channel Set

Channels are designed to offer easy access to selected parts of the Internet. Windows 98 Setup comes with default channel sets based on country and language. Choose the set that you want installed. Chapter 7 describes how to use and change channels, so your selection here is only a starting point.

Making a Startup Disk

The setup program asks if you want to create a startup disk so you can boot your computer in case of trouble. The answer is definitely, positively YES!

The Startup Disk contains several programs that will enable you to boot your system and edit important files in case something gets horribly mangled. It also contains the invaluable Uninstal.exe, which enables you to get rid of all of Windows 98 and start over in case things are severe enough to require re-installation.

NOTE   Like the seat belts in your car or the smoke detector in your home, you'll only need a startup disk if thing go very badly, indeed. If you do need it, however, nothing else will do.

After the startup disk is made, there's a long pause while Setup copies files. Go get a cup of tea.

The Finishing Touches

After all the copying, the Setup Wizard needs to restart your computer and finish up. Your system might not be able to restart by itself. Wait five minutes or so, and if nothing appears to be happening, hit the Reset button. This won't harm your installation and is not a sign of installation failure.

After the restart, Windows 98 still has a few chores. It will detect and set up plug and play devices and possibly other hardware whose settings couldn't be taken over from Windows 95. This may involve restarting again.

If you did a clean install, Setup will ask you to set your time zone. Use the right and left arrow keys on the keyboard to move east and west. This is important for network connections and so that daylight time is properly scheduled. Then Setup will run through a series of other tasks, including setting up the Control Panel and putting your programs on the Start menu. The last one, updating system settings, may take quite a while. Finally, there will be another restart, and you will see the Welcome to Windows screen, which offers online registration and an introduction to Windows 98 features.

Installing Additional Hardware

If a piece of your hardware wasn't detected during the install, use the Add New Hardware function in the Control Panel to tell Windows 98 about it. See Chapter 11 if you need help with this. You may have to restart yet again after installing your hardware.

Deleting Unnecessary Files

After Windows 98 is installed and you feel safe and secure with the new system, you can free up the hard drive space occupied when you chose to Save System Files early in the installation. Go to Add/Remove Programs in the Control Panel. On the Install/Uninstall page, choose the "Delete Windows 98 uninstall information" option, and click OK.

Belt *and* Suspenders

For users who have already experienced problems with upgrading, or who just expect problems because they are well-acquainted with Murphy's Law, we present the following method for doing a clean install. It is even more thorough and even more conservative than the methods we have already discussed.

You will need 450-500MB of free space on your hard drive for this method. Note that in the following instructions the term "folder" and capitalized folder names are used when you are working in Windows. "Directory," with all lowercase names, is used when working at the DOS prompt.

1. Do all of the things discussed in the Preliminaries section of this appendix.
2. Run an up-to-date virus scanning program. Then disable it so it won't interfere with the installation process.
3. Copy the entire Win98 folder from the CD-ROM to a folder on your hard drive. Call the folder something like **Win98src**, for Windows 98 source.
4. Restart your machine using the Windows 95 boot disk you created.
5. Rename the existing windows directory to something like **oldwin**. For example, if Windows is installed in a directory called C:\Windows, type **ren c:\windows oldwin**, and press Enter.
6. Change to your source directory. For example, type **cd c:\win98src** and press Enter.
7. Type **setup** and press Enter.
8. When Setup asks you to choose a directory to install Windows 98, give the directory name of your previous Windows installation (before you changed it).
9. Work through the setup procedure as detailed in the Step by Step section.
10. When you're done, any DOS or Windows 3.1 programs you have can be easily migrated by copying their parts of the Start Menu folder in the Oldwin folder to the new Start Menu folder. If the programs keep .ini files in the Windows folder, these will need to be copied as well.
11. Try running these programs. A Windows 3.1 program may complain it can't find a .dll file. Copy the file from the Oldwin folder or its System sub-folder to the same location in the new Windows folder.
12. Re-install only those Windows 95 programs you really need.
13. When you've gotten everything back to where you expect it to be and you're sure you don't need any of the Oldwin folder, delete it.

This may be a good option for some people, and makes a *ton* of sense in a corporate environment, where all the source for supported programs is readily available on the network. But it is probably not the most common path and should be used primarily for installations where there have already been failures or the user expects to re-install everything anyway. In which case, it's the preferred method.

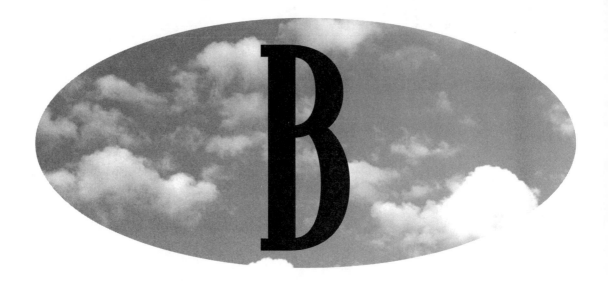

INSTALLING FOR WINDOWS 3.1 USERS

The recommended-by-Microsoft approach is to install Windows 98 right over the top of your existing Windows 3.1. Advantages to this approach include:

- You'll keep all your programs and their settings.
- If you have problems, you can use the uninstall program to auto-matically remove Windows 98 and get your original DOS and Windows 3.1 back intact.

You won't be able to boot into your previous version of DOS, but you will have the DOS mode of Windows 98, which works just as well, if not better.

TIP

A "clean install" on a freshly formatted hard drive is more trouble—you have to reinstall all your programs—but no traces of previous versions of Windows will hang around to cause difficulty. If this is what you want to do, first save your data files in a safe place. Then make a boot disk as described in the Emergency Rescue Disk section below. Be sure it gives you access to your CD-ROM drive so you can install from there. Finally, refer to the Step by Step section of Appendix A for instructions on doing a clean install.

NOTE

If you haven't used Windows 3.1 but have been true to your DOS all this time and now want to add the benefits of Windows 98 to your computing life, the installation is fairly straightforward. You'll need to make sure you have the full version of Windows 98 (not the one designed to be installed on a system with some version of Windows already present). You'll still need to review the checklist later in this chapter and do all of the tasks that apply to your setup.

Minimum Hardware

Microsoft has upped the hardware ante with Windows 98 just as they did with Windows 95. This time, you must have:

- A 486DX2-66 or better microprocessor
- 16 MB RAM
- 200 MB of free hard drive space

NOTE

We have had mixed experiences with installing Windows 98 on machines that just meet the minimum processor requirement. Sometimes the installation succeeds, but not always. A 486-75 seems to be the minimum for reliable installation.

Some of that space is used to save your Windows 3.1 system files so you can uninstall Windows 98. You can reclaim that space once you feel safe and secure with Windows 98.

The installation will fail on a lesser processor, a machine with less than 16 MB of RAM, or if you have insufficient hard drive space.

Before You Install

The Windows 98 installation program works very well, though sometimes it gets dumber than necessary. And since there's no way to tell in advance how smart Windows 98 is going to be about your particular system, we recommend a fail-safe approach to installation. Do yourself a favor and read all the items in this section carefully. Some may not apply to you, but most will.

Do Some Housecleaning

Now's the perfect time to ponder which programs on your system are really needed and to clean up some of the clutter and detritus that build up on your hard drive. Windows 98 is going to use much more hard disk space than the combination of DOS and Windows you now have, so this is an even better reason to clean house.

The first step is to take a look at installed programs you haven't used in the last year or two. Time to get rid of them. If they're DOS programs, just delete them. If they're Windows programs, you have to delete them and find all the files they've stuck in your Windows directories without telling you. Your best bet here is to get one of the ingenious programs designed to remove all traces of ill-behaved Windows applications.

TIP   **If you have any doubts about removing a program from your hard drive, just save any data files off to a floppy. You can always reinstall the program from the original disks if you suddenly need it.**

Defragment Your Hard Drive

Once you have all the extraneous files cleaned off your hard drive, you should do a complete disk defragmentation. This will consolidate your existing files on the disk, creating the maximum possible room for Windows 98 to do its thing.

> **TIP**
>
> **If you have a permanent swap file in your current Windows configuration, change it to a temporary one before you defragment. Otherwise, Windows 98 will detect and use the same swap file—a waste of resources, because Windows 98 can make its own fast and dynamic swap file on a regular or compressed disk. In other words, it can grow and shrink according to the demands of your programs. This is much more efficient and convenient.**

Any defragmentation program will do. We use SpeedDisk in Norton Utilities, but DEFRAG, provided in MS-DOS 6.x, is perfectly adequate for the job. If you're using Stacker or another third-party disk compression utility, make sure you also run their disk defragmentation utility. If you're using SpeedDisk from Version 7 or later of the Norton Utilities, you won't need to run the Stac defrag utility separately, since Norton understands Stacker.

Make an Emergency Rescue Disk

If you have a utility package like Norton Utilities, it includes a program to create a "rescue" or "emergency" disk that contains an image of your BIOS, boot sector, and hard drive partition table, as well as enough files to boot from and recover in case of serious problems. By all means, do this before beginning your upgrade process. The best time to do it is right after you've finished the defragmentation step.

If you don't have a way to automatically make such a disk, here's how to do it yourself:

1. Format a new disk in the floppy drive you can boot from (the A: drive) and use the SYS command from DOS or File Manager's Make System Disk command to make the floppy bootable.

2. Copy to the floppy all the DOS files you need to boot and to get at all the drives in your system plus whatever tools you need to revive the system after a problem (including compression software if you use it). Include:
   - SCANDISK.EXE or CHKDSK.EXE
   - MEM.EXE (to check memory usage)
   - MSD.EXE (to check the system's view of itself)
   - ATTRIB.EXE (to gain access to hidden, read-only, or system files, if needed)
   - EDIT.COM (or your favorite text editor)
   - FDISK.EXE, FORMAT.COM, SYS.COM (for the worst-case scenario, where you have to repartition and reformat your drive)
   - Copies of your current AUTOEXEC.BAT and CONFIG.SYS files
   - Any other special drivers you need, especially for your CD-ROM drive

After you've made the disk, make sure it works by booting with it in the floppy drive. Make sure you have access to the CD drive.

Clean Out AUTOEXEC.BAT and CONFIG.SYS

In the process of installation, Windows 98 will go over your AUTOEXEC.BAT and CONFIG.SYS files and remove drivers and settings that aren't needed. It places a REM at the beginning of every line loading something that Windows 98 knows. But however clever the install routine is, it still can miss some items and end up trying to execute commands that cause difficulties. You're much better off doing a preemptive strike of your own.

Here's how to make it simple:

- Disable any third-party memory managers like QEMM. Type **REM** at the beginning of every line that loads a memory manager. Replace these lines with DEVICE= lines to load HIMEM.SYS and EMM386.EXE. Don't forget to include the full path to these files.
- Disable any virus protection programs that run at start up. Check your BIOS to see if you have boot sector virus protection and disable that, too. Windows 98 is going to make changes to your boot sector. Virus protection will cause the installation to fail.
- REM out any fancy footwork in your AUTOEXEC.BAT such as calls, branches, or conditional executions.
- Disable hardware drivers except those for hardware you need to boot up and start Windows 3.1. If you're installing from a CD, leave the drivers for your CD-ROM drive; otherwise disable them. If you have a SCSI hard drive, leave those drivers, too. Other candidates for REMing out include drivers for your:
  - sound card
  - scanner
  - mouse (both versions of Windows provide their own)
  - tape back up

NOTE The idea is to let Windows 98 recognize and supply its own drivers for as much of the hardware as possible. If it happens that Windows 98 doesn't have a driver for a piece of hardware, you can always reinstate your 16-bit drivers until such time as a 32-bit driver is available.

WARNING A good memory manager, such as QEMM or NetRoom, can use areas of memory that would not normally be available. It does this by tricking DOS and Windows into believing that certain addresses are not being used when they are. Such features help circumvent the problem of inadequate available room to load everything you need into DOS's limited memory space. It's unnecessary in Windows 98, however, and can interfere with Windows 98's ability to correctly sense what hardware is on your machine.

Do a Backup

We've all heard how important it is to do backups, and we've all ignored those warnings (at times). That doesn't change our obligation to warn you yet again!

The importance of first backing up your system cannot be stressed enough. While the installation program of Windows 98 is remarkably good, and the number of systems that fail is small, you should never, never change your operating system without doing a backup. Going from any version of DOS to Windows 98 is about as significant a change as can be imagined.

Choosing a Backup Program

If you haven't invested in a third-party program, the backup program included with MS-DOS versions 6 and above is excellent. It's based on the Norton Backup program and is safe, easy to use, and reasonably fast. If you have another backup program you prefer, and are more comfortable with, by all means use it.

What to Back Up

Back up at least the root directory of your boot drive (usually C:) and your DOS and Windows directories, along with any files you simply could not live without or easily re-create. What this includes is really a personal decision, but obviously, if you're a business, the answer is different than if you use your computer primarily to run DOOM.

Take your time and review all the directories and even subdirectories on your hard drive. If you have any doubts about whether you should back up a particular file or group of files, it's best to err on the side of caution. What you don't need to back up are program files, because you can, in the worst case, re-install them from the original disks.

Starting the Installation

Once you've done all the preparatory work described, put the Windows 98 CD in the CD-ROM drive and start Windows 3.1. Open File Manager and double-click the icon for your CD-ROM drive (Figure B.1). In the right pane, double-click Setup.exe to start the installation.

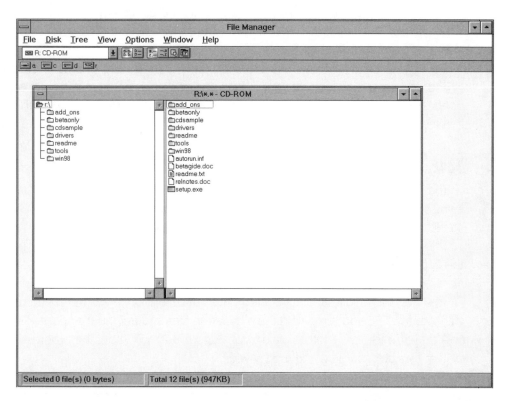

FIGURE B.1:   Use File Manager to view the files on the Windows 98 CD-ROM.

Welcome Screen

The first screen "welcomes" you to Windows 98 (as if it were a hotel) and gives an estimate of the time it will take to install. On most machines the estimate will be 30 to 60 minutes. Expect it to take somewhat longer than predicted. Click the Continue button.

Next, a setup window will open announcing that the Setup Wizard is starting. Look at the list of installation steps on the left side of your screen. The step being performed will be highlighted.

Setup will then ask you to read and consent to the license agreement. You must click "I accept the Agreement" before you can click Next to move on.

Select the Directory

In the next dialog box, you're asked to specify the directory for the installation of Windows 98. The default is C:\WINDOWS. Unless you have a good reason to install elsewhere, accept the default.

If you select *Other directory*, you'll be prompted for the directory name and location.

The next procedure looks at your system to first determine what Windows components are installed and then to see if you have enough hard drive space to install Windows 98.

Save System Files

The Save System Files dialog box gives you a chance at an additional bit of security. If you select Yes, the Setup Wizard will save enough of your existing Windows 3.1 files so that (should worse come to worst), you can uninstall Windows 98.

This is highly unlikely to be necessary, but as you can tell from the earlier parts of this appendix, "Better Safe Than Sorry" is our motto. So, the strong recommendation is to say Yes.

This step will require additional hard drive space, but once you're up and running with Windows 98 you can delete the old system files and free up the space.

After you click Yes, another dialog box (Figure B.2) will show the progress of the system files being located and then saved.

NOTE   If you have more than one hard drive, you'll be prompted for the preferred location for the system files. You can pick any drive where you have enough open space.

Setup Options

The Setup Wizard presents you with four possible setup options, as shown in Figure B.3. For the majority of people, Typical is the best option. It requires the least input from you and anything you later decide you want to install is easily available.

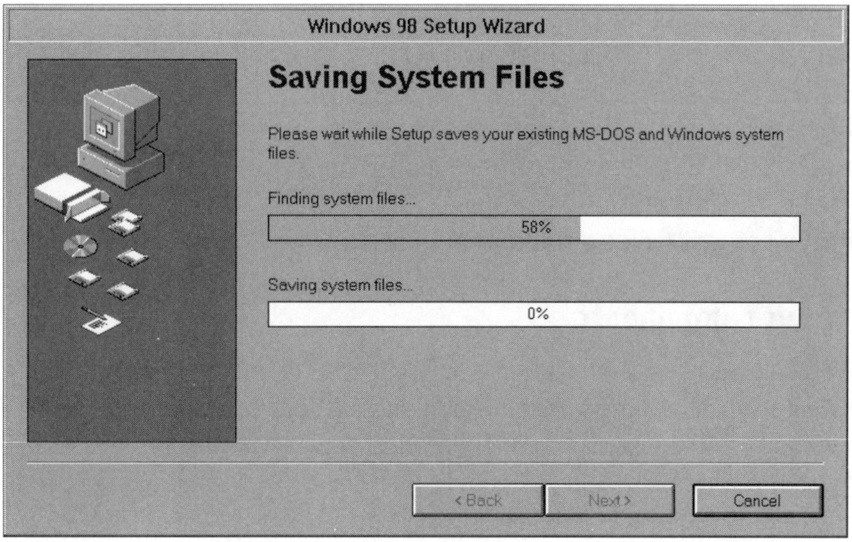

FIGURE B.2: Saving the Windows 3.1 system files

If you're an experienced Windows user and a bit of a control freak (or just plain curious), Custom is also a perfectly good option. You have to provide more information and make more choices as you go, so installation is a little slower, but in exchange you get the opportunity to customize right from the start.

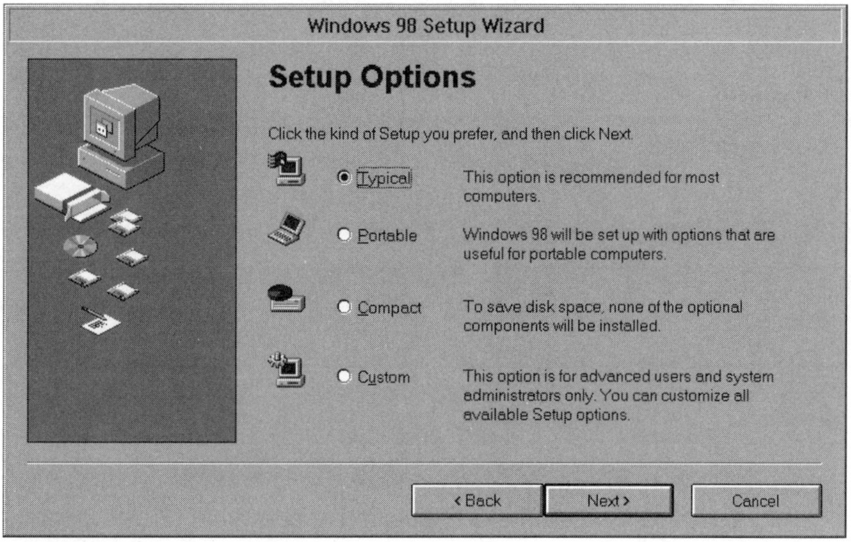

FIGURE B.3: Choosing a setup option

The portable option is useful for laptop computers but not necessary. The regular installation can detect PC Cards and built-in pointers without being told that a portable computer is involved.

Compact is recommended only when hard drive space is limited and cannot be enlarged. You'll get the basic functionality, but most accessories and many system tools will not be installed.

After you choose the option you want, click Next.

Windows Components

If you selected Custom install, you will be asked to choose the components you want. For a Typical, Compact, or Portable installation, you will see a dialog asking whether you want to view the components and decide which to install. Select Yes and you'll see the window shown in Figure B.4. If you say No, Setup will choose what to install based on the type of installation you selected.

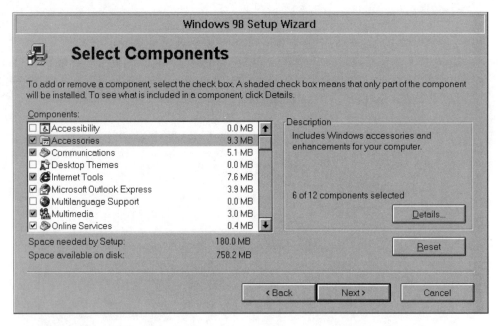

FIGURE B.4:   Windows components

To decide what to install, view each option in turn. For example, as shown in the figure, when you highlight Accessories a description appears to the right. Directly under the description you'll see how many of the components have already been selected (by the Setup Wizard) to be installed. For Accessories, it's six of the twelve available.

Click the Details button for a list of the twelve Accessories. As you highlight each item, a description appears to the right. Items with check marks next to them will be installed. Remove the check marks next to items you *don't* want installed.

When you've made your choices—bearing in mind that any you miss can be installed later—click the Next button.

Settings

The next dialog box, Identification, asks for the name of your computer, the workgroup name, and a description of the computer. If you're on a network, provide the correct information. If you're not connected, leave the default information and click Next.

In the Computer Settings dialog box, you'll see a list of the keyboard and language settings that will be installed. If any are incorrect, highlight the setting and click the Change button.

The Internet channels that Windows 98 starts with as the default listing are tailored to specific countries. In the Internet Channels window, choose the country whose channel set you'd like to see.

Emergency Startup Disk

The next step is to create an Emergency Startup Disk. In case of a complete freeze, you can use this disk to start your computer. You'll need a single high-density floppy disk. It doesn't have to be new, but anything already on the disk will be deleted in the process of making the Emergency Startup Disk. Click Next.

Put the floppy disk in the drive when the setup program requests it.

When the process of creating the disk is completed, you'll be notified to remove the floppy disk and then click OK.

Copying Files

The process of copying files is the longest stage of the installation. It'll go faster if you have a high-speed CD-ROM drive; slower if you don't. But expect a half-hour or so before you have to do anything more.

Identifying Hardware

After all the copying, the Setup Wizard needs to restart your computer and finish up. Your system might not be able to restart by itself. Wait five minutes or so and if nothing appears to be happening, hit the Reset button. This won't harm your installation and is not a sign of installation failure.

Windows 98 then builds a driver database and attempts to identify all the hardware attached to the computer. That includes the video card, monitor, sound card, modem, and printer. In general, plug-and-play technology does a very good job of figuring everything out. If it doesn't, you can later manually install a modem, printer, or other device.

TIP   **You'll be asked at some point for a Windows password. If you're not on a network, don't provide one. Just press Enter. You can always add a password later, if necessary. To stop being asked for a password after installation, right-click the Network Neighborhood icon on the desktop and select Properties. On the Configuration page, under Primary Network Logon, select Windows Logon. Click OK. When you reboot, the password window will not appear.**

Welcome to Windows 98

After a restart or two, Windows 98 will begin and you'll see a "Welcome to Windows 98" dialog box. Click a subject to register the product or for a lesson in how Windows 98 works. Or just click Begin to work through everything "Welcome to Windows 98" has to offer.

Index

Note to the Reader: Throughout this index **boldface** page numbers indicate primary discussions of a topic. *Italicized* page numbers indicate illustrations.

B

D

N

O

P

W

Master Your
WINDOWS® 98
Destiny

WITH THESE BESTSELLING SYBEX TITLES

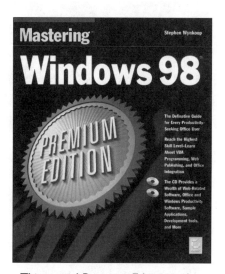

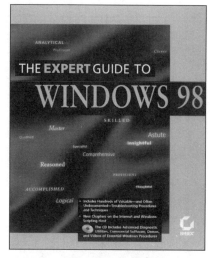

The best-selling *Mastering Windows 95* just got better in its latest edition. It not only covers Microsoft's new 32-bit operating system from beginning to end, but also includes new additions and enhancements. The new Explorer, installation, built-in applications, networking, optimization—it's all here in this absolutely essential guide to the newest version of the Windows operating system.

ISBN: 0-7821-1961-1
1,184pp; 7½" x 9"; Softcover; $34.99

This special Premium Edition is the complete solution for Windows users. It covers all of the essential topics, including an overview of the operating system, installation concerns, settings, and the file management system. Secrets of scripting, the Registry and other powerful features are explained. Also included are more than 400 pages of advanced customization and internet coverage for power users, as well as two CDs.

ISBN: 0-7821-2186-1
1,584pp; 7½" x 9"; Hardcover; $59.99

Based on Mark Minasi's seminar, this book is the Windows 98 troubleshooting bible for MIS professionals, consultants and power users. It's the most accessible guide to networking, installing, and supporting Windows 98. The companion CD includes animations of the book's procedures, and several commercial Windows antivirus, diagnostic, and troubleshooting utilities.

ISBN: 0-7821-1974-3
1,008pp; 7½" x 9"; Softcover; $49.99

SYBEX®
www.sybex.com

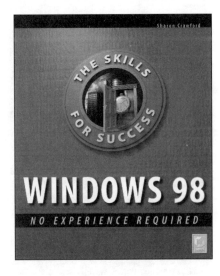
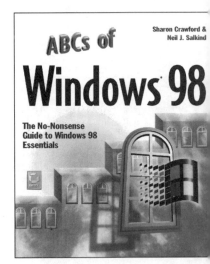

START USING NEW
WINDOWS® 98
FEATURES IMMEDIATELY

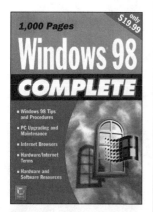

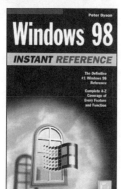

Internet

Files, Folders, and the Desktop